TRANS-METRO-POLITAN:

LONELY CITY

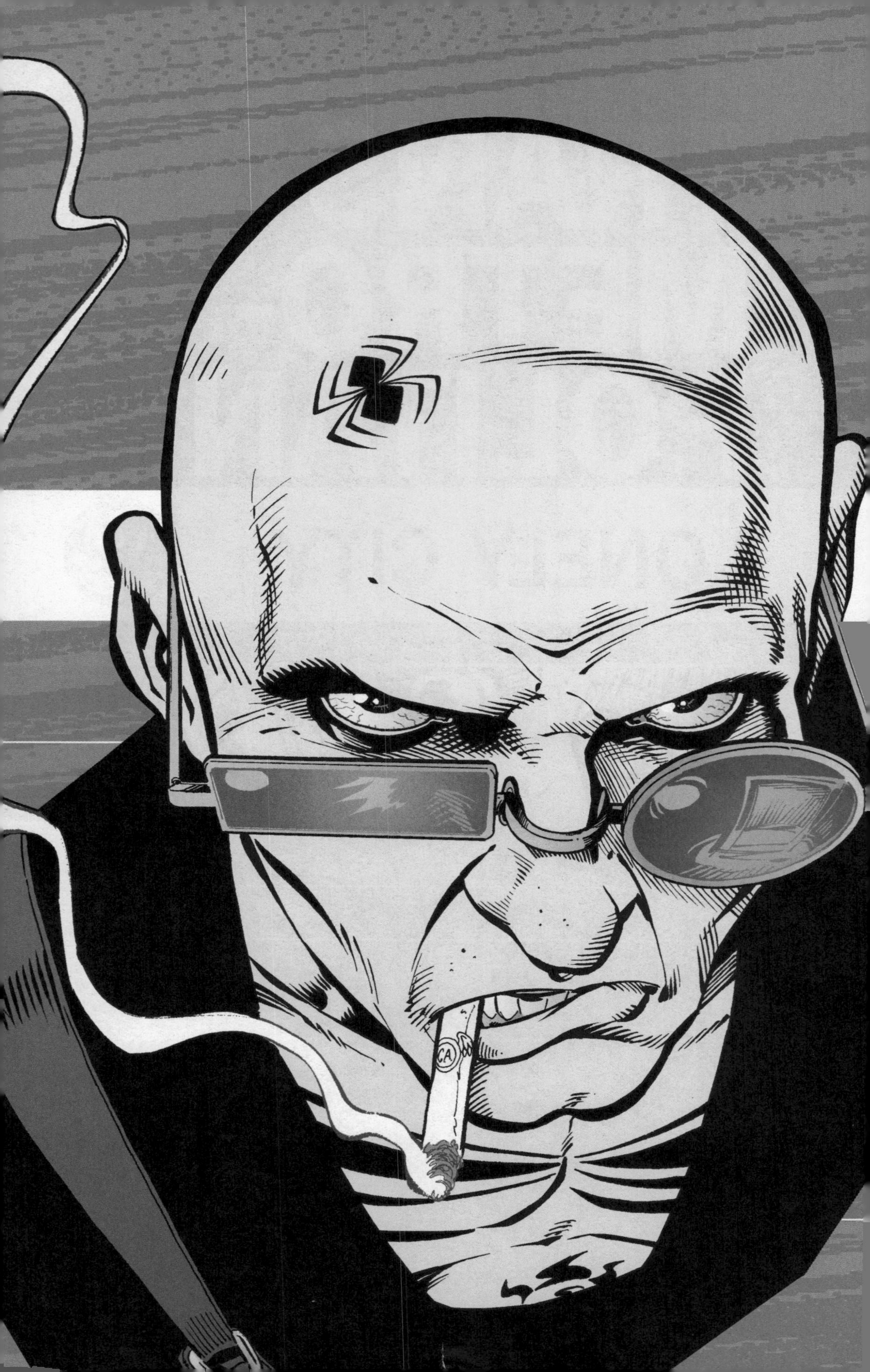

TRANS- METRO- POLITAN:

LONELY CITY

Warren_Ellis
Writer

Darick_Robertson
Penciller

Rodney_Ramos
Inker

Nathan_Eyring
Colorist

Clem_Robins
Letterer

Jim Lee (#25-27)
Tony Harris and Ray Snyder (#28)
Tony Harris and Jim Royal (#29)
Tony Harris and Drew Geraci (#30)
Original Series Covers

TRANSMETROPOLITAN created by
Warren_Ellis and Darick_Robertson

Stuart Moore Cliff Chiang Editors – Original Series Scott Nybakken Editor Robbin Brosterman Design Director – Books

Karen Berger Senior VP – Executive Editor, Vertigo Bob Harras VP – Editor-in-Chief

Diane Nelson President Dan DiDio and Jim Lee Co-Publishers Geoff Johns Chief Creative Officer
John Rood Executive VP – Sales, Marketing and Business Development Amy Genkins Senior VP – Business and Legal Affairs
Nairi Gardiner Senior VP – Finance Jeff Boison VP – Publishing Operations Mark Chiarello VP – Art Direction and Design
John Cunningham VP – Marketing Terri Cunningham VP – Talent Relations and Services Alison Gill Senior VP – Manufacturing and Operations
Hank Kanalz Senior VP – Digital Jay Kogan VP – Business and Legal Affairs, Publishing Jack Mahan VP – Business Affairs, Talent
Nick Napolitano VP – Manufacturing Administration Sue Pohja VP – Book Sales Courtney Simmons Senior VP – Publicity Bob Wayne Senior VP – Sa

Cover art by Jim Lee.

TRANSMETROPOLITAN: LONELY CITY

Published by DC Comics. Cover and compilation Copyright © 2009 DC Comics. All Rights Reserved.

Originally published in single magazine form as TRANSMETROPOLITAN 25-30. Copyright © 1999, 2000 Warren Ellis and
Darick Robertson. All Rights Reserved. All characters, their distinctive likenesses and related indicia featured in this publication are
trademarks of Warren Ellis and Darick Robertson. VERTIGO is a trademark of DC Comics. The stories, characters and incidents
featured in this publication are entirely fictional. DC Comics does not read or accept unsolicited submissions of ideas, stories
or artwork.

DC Comics, 1700 Broadway, New York, NY 10019. A Warner Bros. Entertainment Company. Printed in the USA. Third Printing.
ISBN: 978-1-4012-2819-4

Library of Congress Cataloging-in-Publication Data

Ellis, Warren.
    Transmetropolitan. Vol. 5, Lonely city / Warren Ellis, Darick Robertson, Rodney Ramos.
        p. cm.
    "Originally published in single magazine form as Transmetropolitan 25-30."
    ISBN 978-1-4012-2819-4
    1. Graphic novels. I. Robertson, Darick. II. Ramos, Rodney. III. Title. IV. Title: Lonely city.
PN6728.T68E4425 2012
741.5'973–dc23
                                2012040672

INTRODUCTION

Warren Ellis asked me to write this and I am O.K. with that up to a point. My unease is that the point is unnervingly sharp and very likely to turn in my direction. Here is the problem. Warren knows that I am a TRANSMETROPOLITAN fan, but how can he expect me to write about that? Does he think I just came down the Clyde on a tea biscuit? No sirree, this is not my first barbecue. If I write that Spider Jerusalem is my hero, does he think Spider will let me get away with that? I would be lucky to only suffer a blast from a bowel disrupter and it is much more likely my eyeballs will be popped as easily as squeezing a pustule and fed to the cat. If I write that TRANSMET is a beacon of brilliant irony and sardonic satire could I survive the torrent of saliva-drenched invective and scorn S.J. would heap on me? If I wrote that TRANSMET made me laugh like a drain are there enough lavatory bowls to contain Jerusalem's vomit? If I confessed that I lusted after the filthy assistants what foul perversions would I be accused of? If I praised the artwork as the wittiest, most disturbing since George Grosz I would soon find myself depicted as a fucked-up, mechanics-addicted, feces-smeared background character. If I hailed this vision of the future as persuasive and properly terrifying I might never live to see it. You get my problem?

I think, however, that I can safely say this: I know this City, I have read The Word, I have listened to these politicians, I have smelt the stink of greed, I have thrown stuff at the TV, I have wondered what future there is for Truth and Beauty. I have wanted to go and live on the top of a Yorkshire moor.

Warren, tell Spider to stay healthy and keep writing the column.

— Patrick Stewart

Patrick Stewart's accomplishments on stage and screen are legion, but he is perhaps best known for his acclaimed one-man performance of Charles Dickens' A Christmas Carol *and his ongoing role as Captain Jean-Luc Picard in the* Star Trek: The Next Generation *television and film series.*

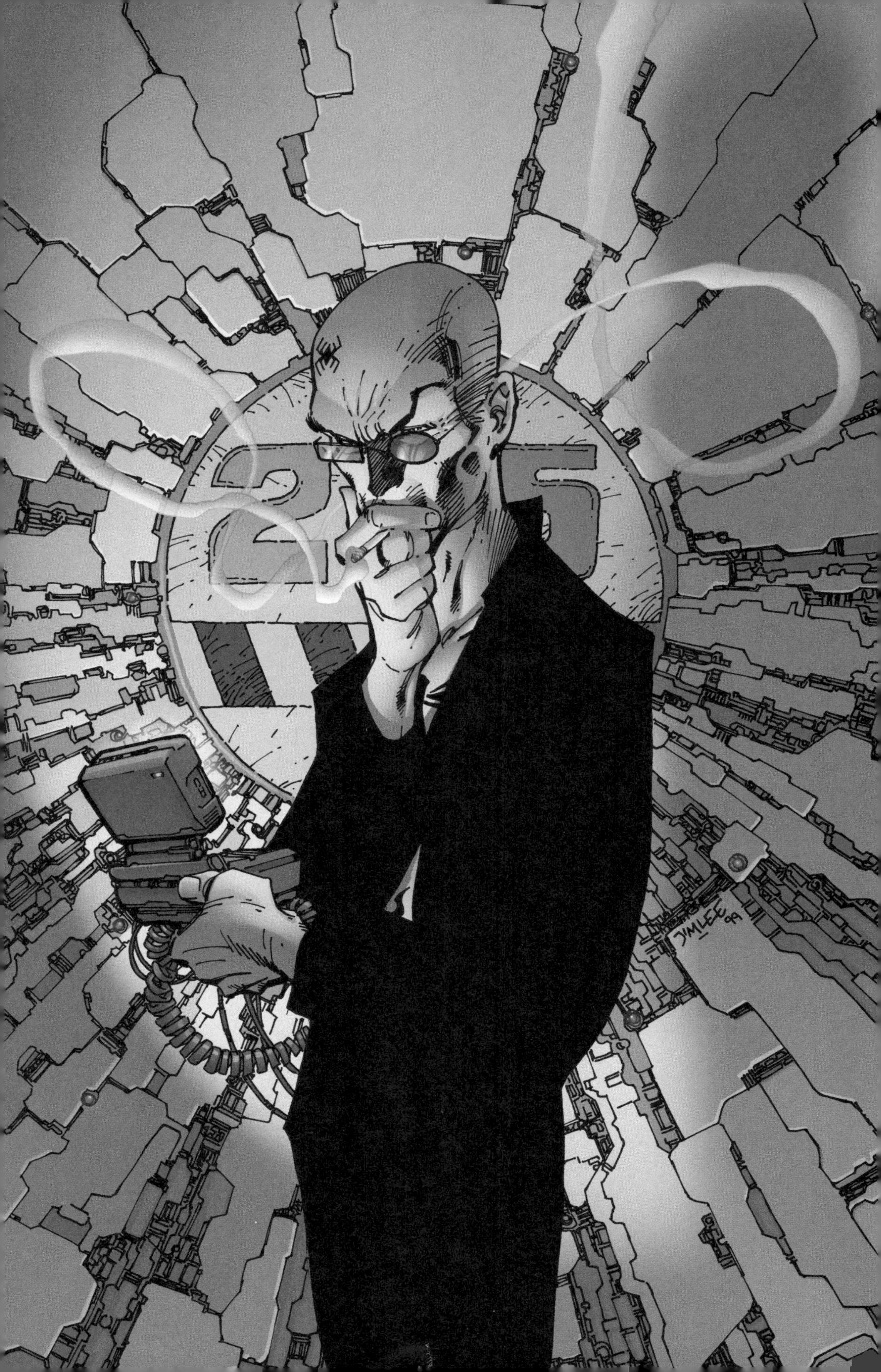
JIMLEE '99

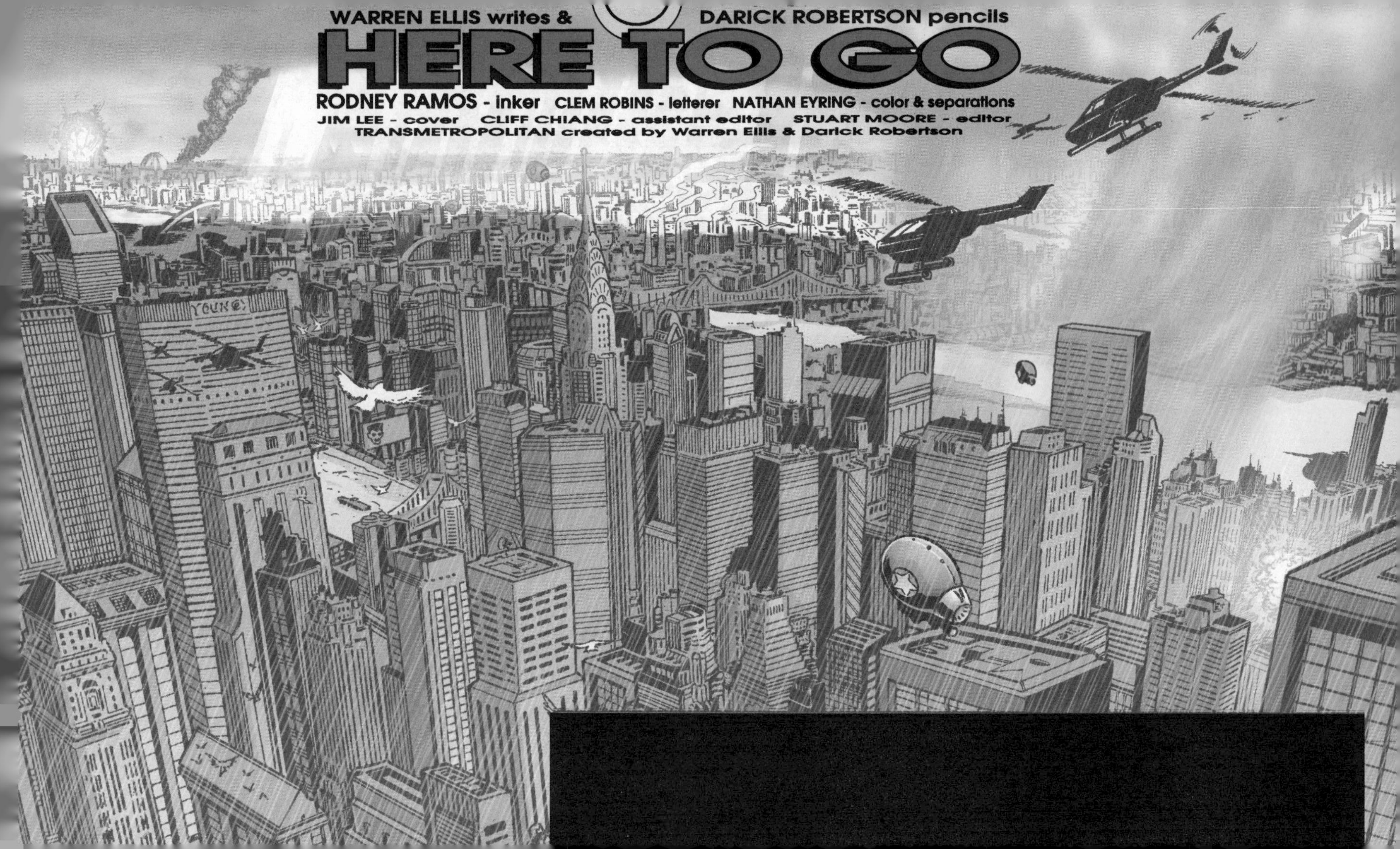
WARREN ELLIS writes & DARICK ROBERTSON pencils
HERE TO GO
RODNEY RAMOS - inker CLEM ROBINS - letterer NATHAN EYRING - color & separations
JIM LEE - cover CLIFF CHIANG - assistant editor STUART MOORE - editor
TRANSMETROPOLITAN created by Warren Ellis & Darick Robertson
YOUNG
[redacted]

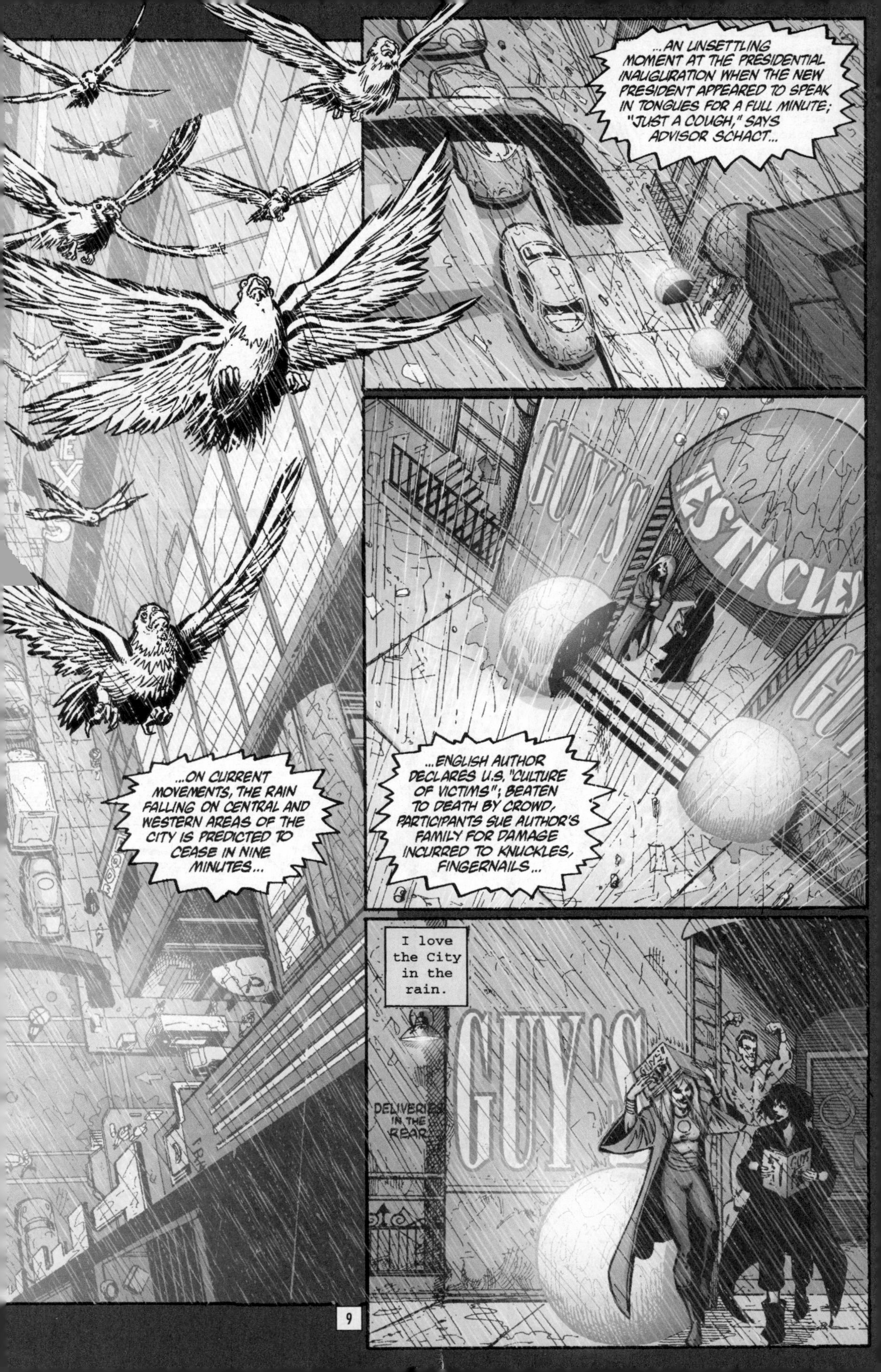
...AN UNSETTLING MOMENT AT THE PRESIDENTIAL INAUGURATION WHEN THE NEW PRESIDENT APPEARED TO SPEAK IN TONGUES FOR A FULL MINUTE; "JUST A COUGH," SAYS ADVISOR SCHACT...
...ON CURRENT MOVEMENTS, THE RAIN FALLING ON CENTRAL AND WESTERN AREAS OF THE CITY IS PREDICTED TO CEASE IN NINE MINUTES...
GUY'S
TESTICLES
...ENGLISH AUTHOR DECLARES U.S. "CULTURE OF VICTIMS"; BEATEN TO DEATH BY CROWD, PARTICIPANTS SUE AUTHOR'S FAMILY FOR DAMAGE INCURRED TO KNUCKLES, FINGERNAILS...
I love the City in the rain.
GUY'S
DELIVERIES IN THE REAR

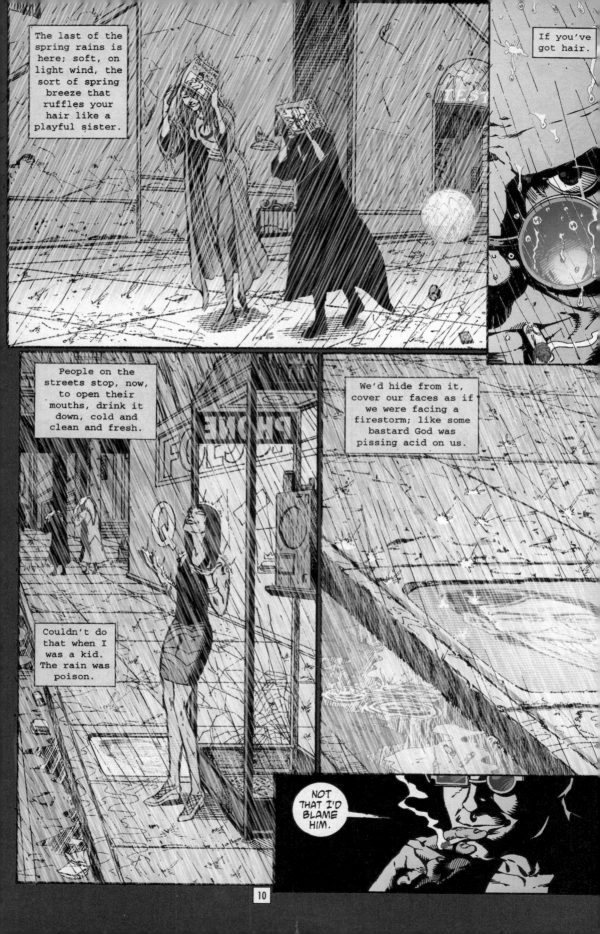

The last of the spring rains is here; soft, on light wind, the sort of spring breeze that ruffles your hair like a playful sister.

If you've got hair.

People on the streets stop, now, to open their mouths, drink it down, cold and clean and fresh.

We'd hide from it, cover our faces as if we were facing a firestorm; like some bastard God was pissing acid on us.

Couldn't do that when I was a kid. The rain was poison.

NOT THAT I'D BLAME HIM.

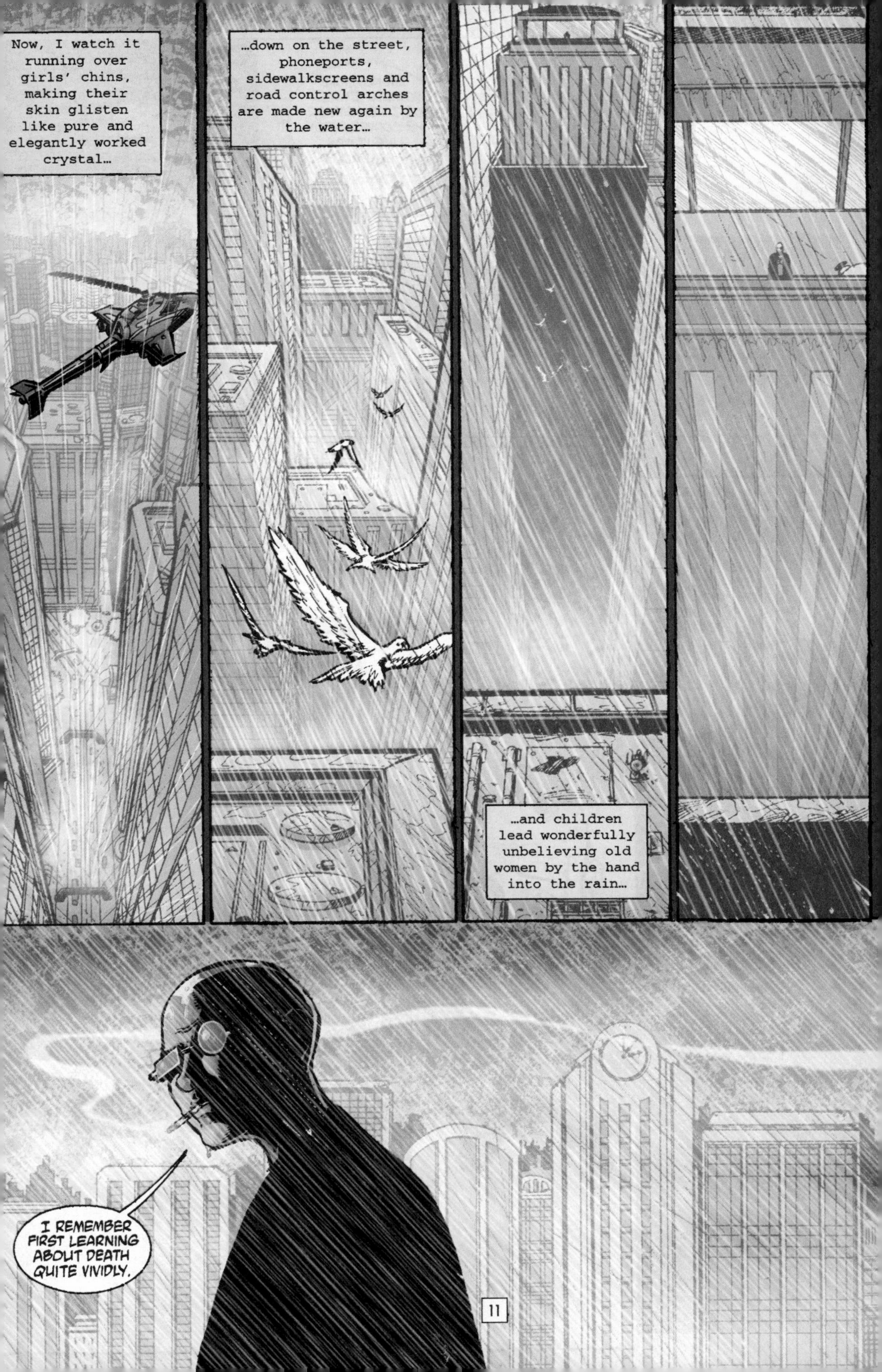

Now, I watch it running over girls' chins, making their skin glisten like pure and elegantly worked crystal…
…down on the street, phoneports, sidewalkscreens and road control arches are made new again by the water…
…and children lead wonderfully unbelieving old women by the hand into the rain…
I REMEMBER FIRST LEARNING ABOUT DEATH QUITE VIVIDLY.

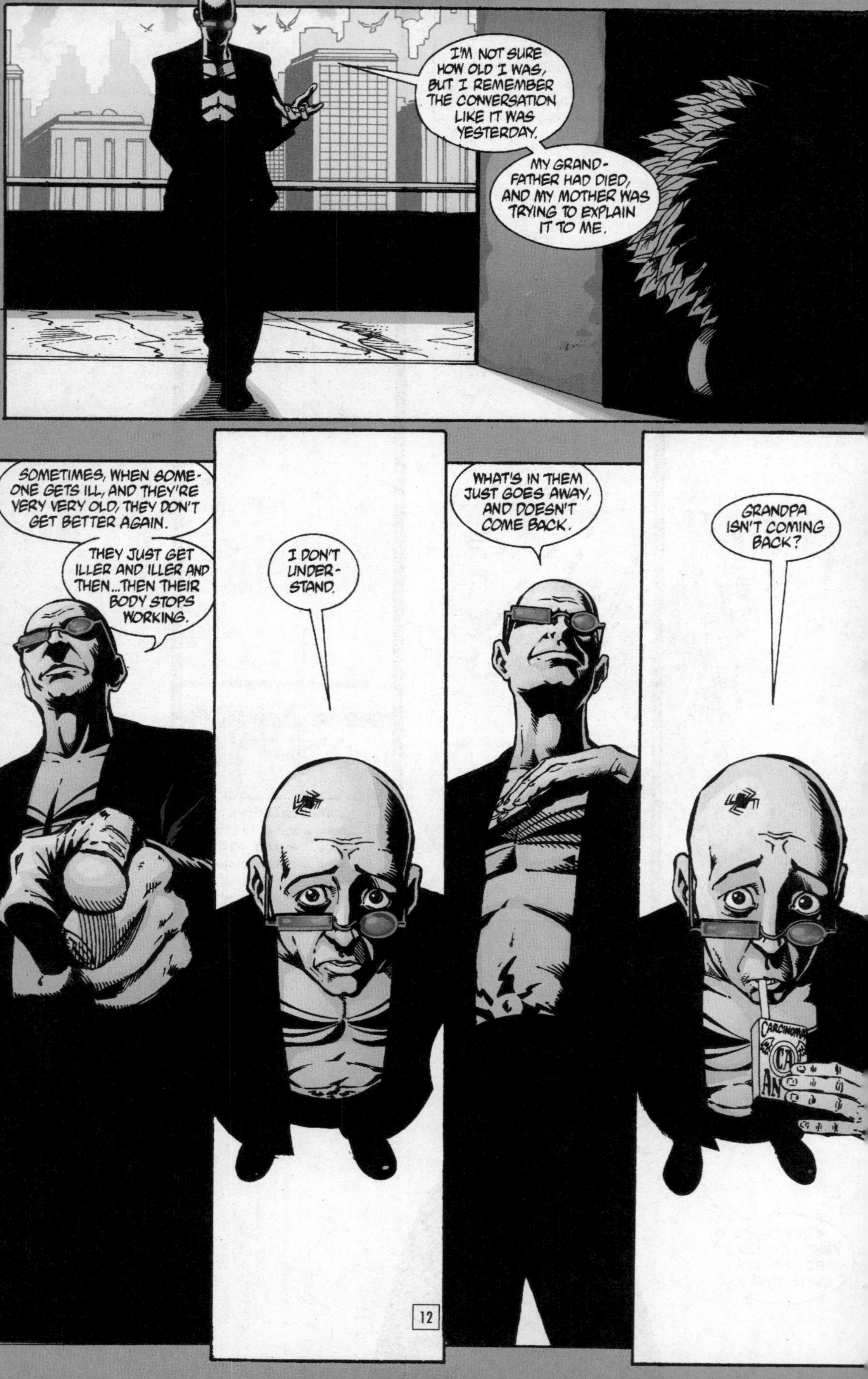
I'M NOT SURE HOW OLD I WAS, BUT I REMEMBER THE CONVERSATION LIKE IT WAS YESTERDAY.
MY GRAND-FATHER HAD DIED, AND MY MOTHER WAS TRYING TO EXPLAIN IT TO ME.
SOMETIMES, WHEN SOME-ONE GETS ILL, AND THEY'RE VERY VERY OLD, THEY DON'T GET BETTER AGAIN.
THEY JUST GET ILLER AND ILLER AND THEN... THEN THEIR BODY STOPS WORKING.
I DON'T UNDER-STAND.
WHAT'S IN THEM JUST GOES AWAY, AND DOESN'T COME BACK.
GRANDPA ISN'T COMING BACK?

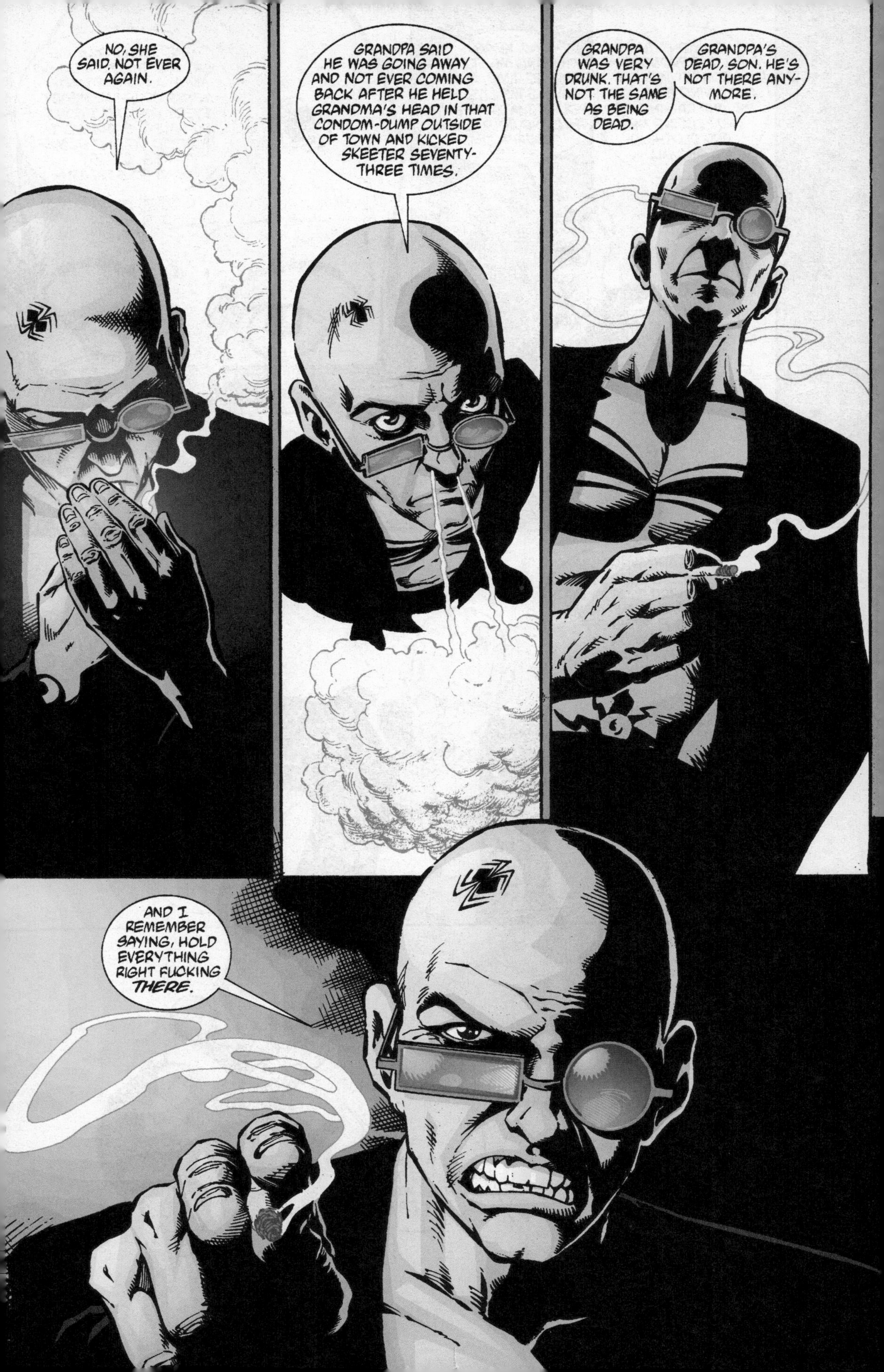
NO, SHE SAID, NOT EVER AGAIN.
GRANDPA SAID HE WAS GOING AWAY AND NOT EVER COMING BACK AFTER HE HELD GRANDMA'S HEAD IN THAT CONDOM-DUMP OUTSIDE OF TOWN AND KICKED SKEETER SEVENTY-THREE TIMES.
GRANDPA'S DEAD, SON. HE'S NOT THERE ANY-MORE.
GRANDPA WAS VERY DRUNK. THAT'S NOT THE SAME AS BEING DEAD.
AND I REMEMBER SAYING, HOLD EVERYTHING RIGHT FUCKING *THERE*.

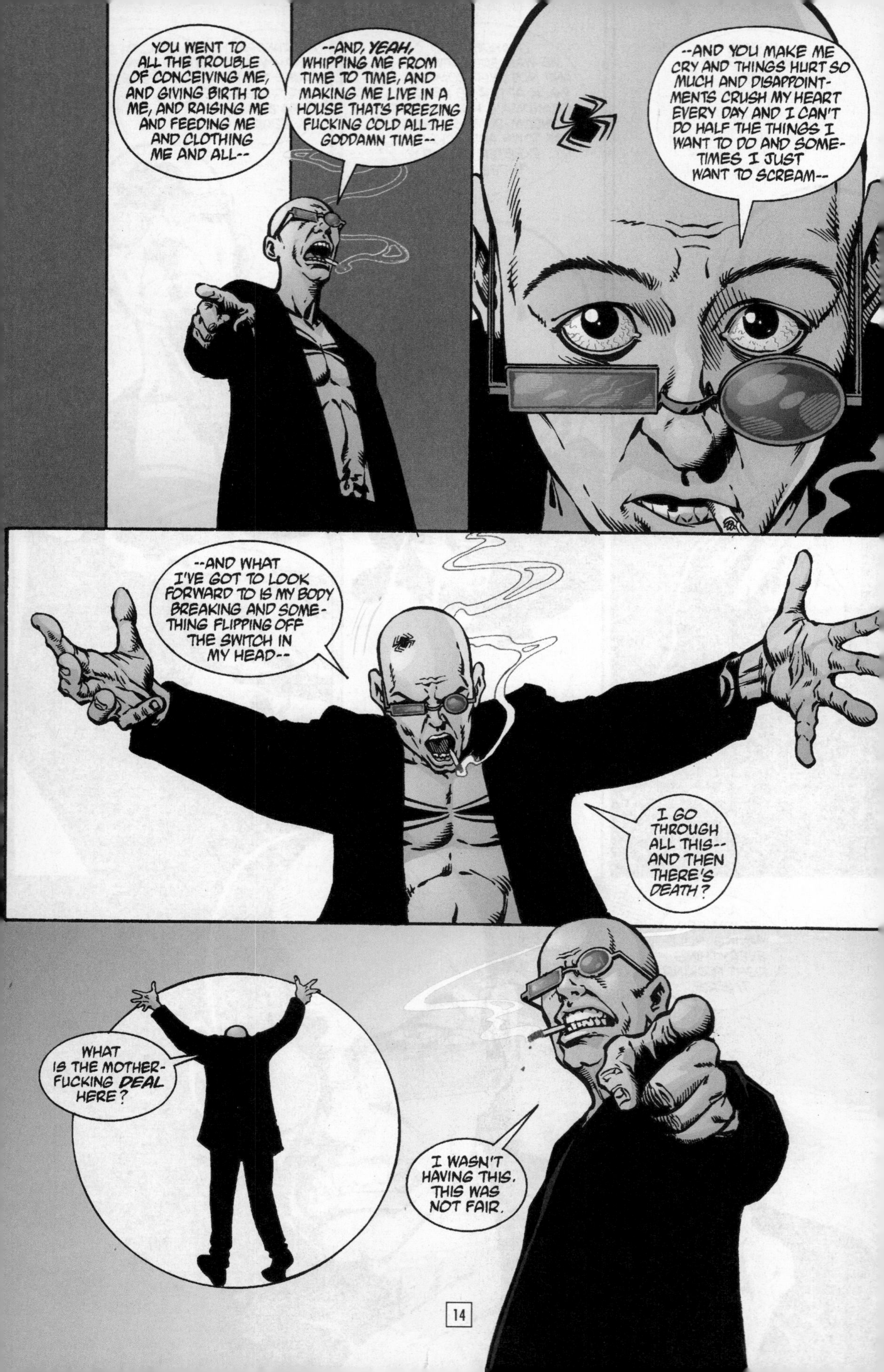
YOU WENT TO ALL THE TROUBLE OF CONCEIVING ME, AND GIVING BIRTH TO ME, AND RAISING ME AND FEEDING ME AND CLOTHING ME AND ALL--
--AND, *YEAH,* WHIPPING ME FROM TIME TO TIME, AND MAKING ME LIVE IN A HOUSE THAT'S FREEZING FUCKING COLD ALL THE GODDAMN TIME--
--AND YOU MAKE ME CRY AND THINGS HURT SO MUCH AND DISAPPOINTMENTS CRUSH MY HEART EVERY DAY AND I CAN'T DO HALF THE THINGS I WANT TO DO AND SOMETIMES I JUST WANT TO SCREAM--
--AND WHAT I'VE GOT TO LOOK FORWARD TO IS MY BODY BREAKING AND SOMETHING FLIPPING OFF THE SWITCH IN MY HEAD--
I GO THROUGH ALL THIS-- AND THEN THERE'S *DEATH?*
WHAT IS THE MOTHER-FUCKING *DEAL* HERE?
I WASN'T HAVING THIS. THIS WAS NOT FAIR.

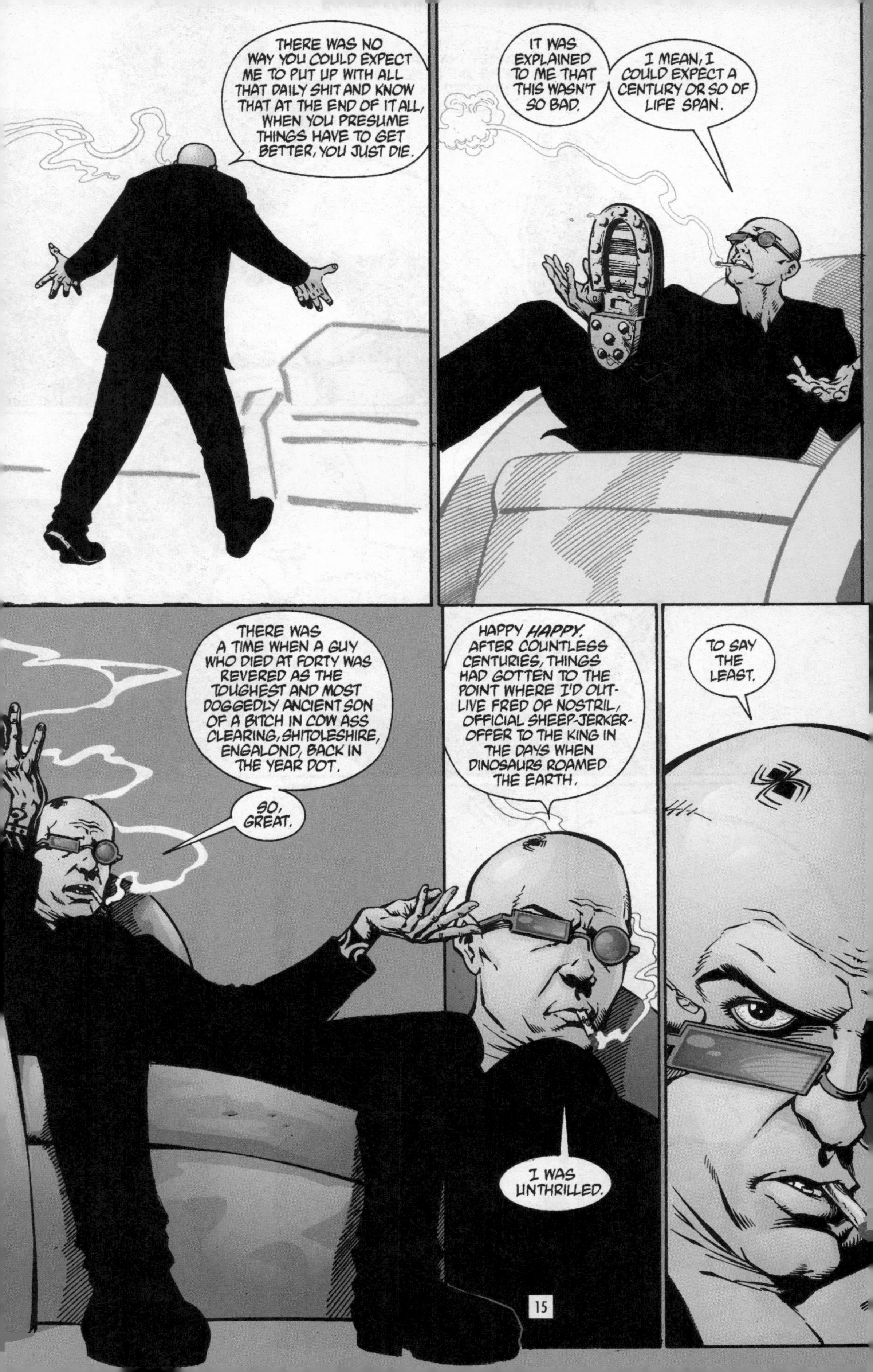
THERE WAS NO WAY YOU COULD EXPECT ME TO PUT UP WITH ALL THAT DAILY SHIT AND KNOW THAT AT THE END OF IT ALL, WHEN YOU PRESUME THINGS HAVE TO GET BETTER, YOU JUST DIE.
IT WAS EXPLAINED TO ME THAT THIS WASN'T SO BAD.
I MEAN, I COULD EXPECT A CENTURY OR SO OF LIFE SPAN.
THERE WAS A TIME WHEN A GUY WHO DIED AT FORTY WAS REVERED AS THE TOUGHEST AND MOST DOGGEDLY ANCIENT SON OF A BITCH IN COW ASS CLEARING, SHITOLESHIRE, ENGALOND, BACK IN THE YEAR DOT.
SO, GREAT.
HAPPY *HAPPY*. AFTER COUNTLESS CENTURIES, THINGS HAD GOTTEN TO THE POINT WHERE I'D OUT-LIVE FRED OF NOSTRIL, OFFICIAL SHEEP-JERKER-OFFER TO THE KING IN THE DAYS WHEN DINOSAURS ROAMED THE EARTH.
I WAS UNTHRILLED.
TO SAY THE LEAST.

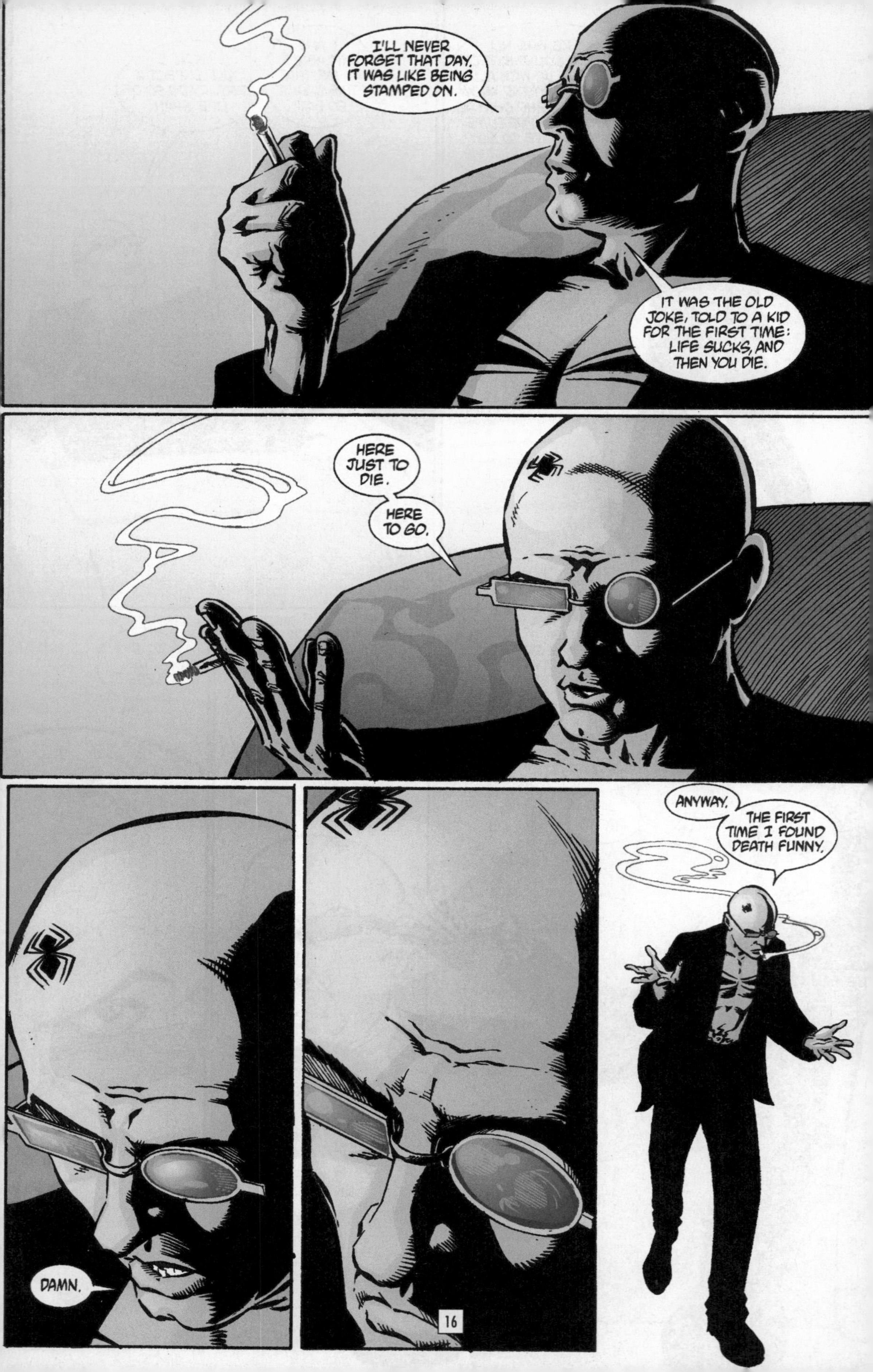
I'LL NEVER FORGET THAT DAY. IT WAS LIKE BEING STAMPED ON.
IT WAS THE OLD JOKE, TOLD TO A KID FOR THE FIRST TIME: LIFE SUCKS, AND THEN YOU DIE.
HERE JUST TO DIE.
HERE TO GO.
DAMN.
ANYWAY.
THE FIRST TIME I FOUND DEATH FUNNY.
16

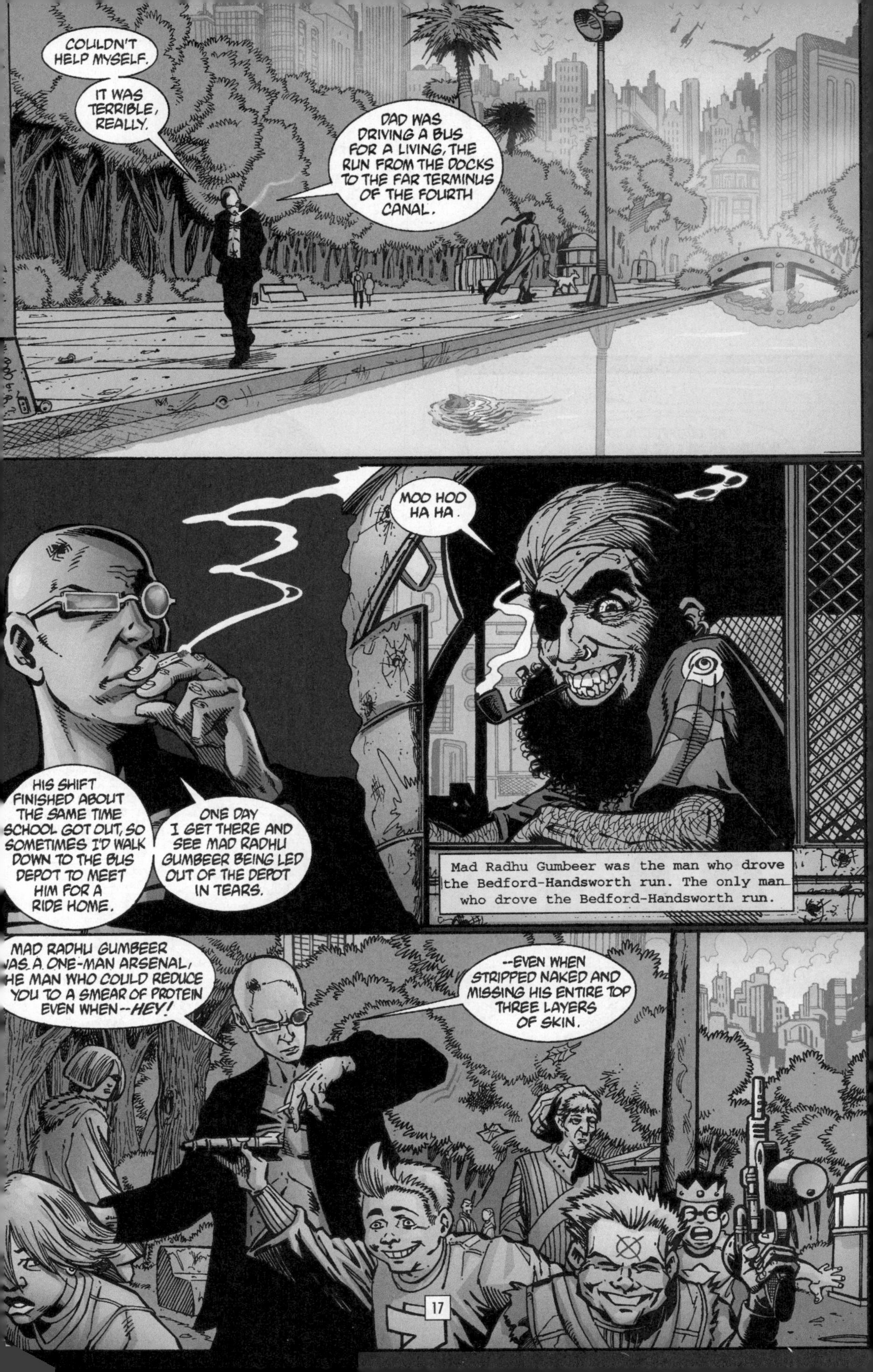
COULDN'T HELP MYSELF.
IT WAS TERRIBLE, REALLY.
DAD WAS DRIVING A BUS FOR A LIVING, THE RUN FROM THE DOCKS TO THE FAR TERMINUS OF THE FOURTH CANAL.
HIS SHIFT FINISHED ABOUT THE SAME TIME SCHOOL GOT OUT, SO SOMETIMES I'D WALK DOWN TO THE BUS DEPOT TO MEET HIM FOR A RIDE HOME.
ONE DAY I GET THERE AND SEE MAD RADHU GUMBEER BEING LED OUT OF THE DEPOT IN TEARS.
MOO HOO HA HA.
Mad Radhu Gumbeer was the man who drove the Bedford-Handsworth run. The only man who drove the Bedford-Handsworth run.
MAD RADHU GUMBEER WAS A ONE-MAN ARSENAL, THE MAN WHO COULD REDUCE YOU TO A SMEAR OF PROTEIN EVEN WHEN--*HEY!*
--EVEN WHEN STRIPPED NAKED AND MISSING HIS ENTIRE TOP THREE LAYERS OF SKIN.

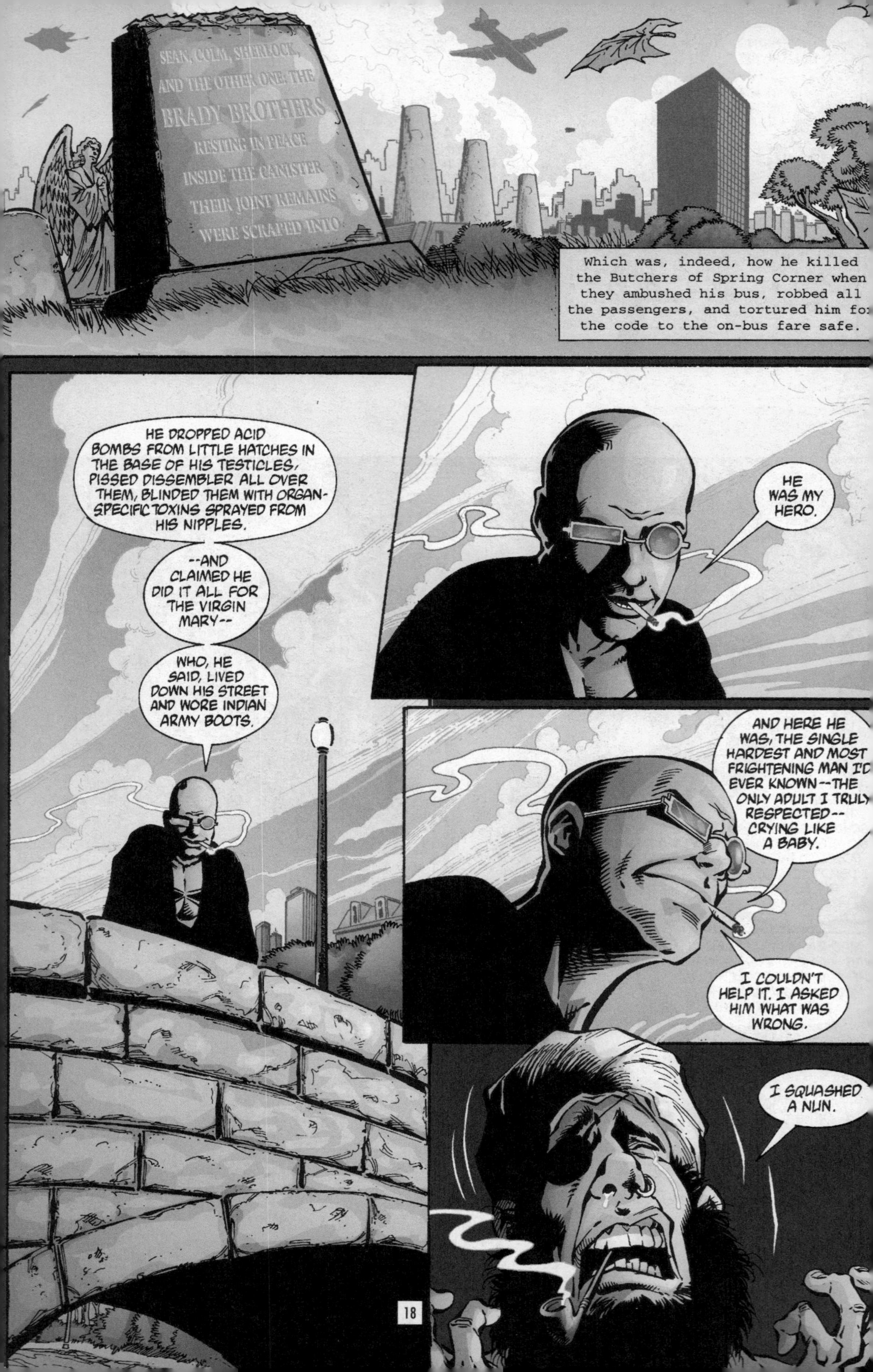
SEAN, COLM, SHERLOCK, AND THE OTHER ONE: THE BRADY BROTHERS RESTING IN PEACE INSIDE THE CANISTER THEIR JOINT REMAINS WERE SCRAPED INTO
Which was, indeed, how he killed the Butchers of Spring Corner when they ambushed his bus, robbed all the passengers, and tortured him for the code to the on-bus fare safe.
HE DROPPED ACID BOMBS FROM LITTLE HATCHES IN THE BASE OF HIS TESTICLES, PISSED DISSEMBLER ALL OVER THEM, BLINDED THEM WITH ORGAN-SPECIFIC TOXINS SPRAYED FROM HIS NIPPLES.
--AND CLAIMED HE DID IT ALL FOR THE VIRGIN MARY--
WHO, HE SAID, LIVED DOWN HIS STREET AND WORE INDIAN ARMY BOOTS.
HE WAS MY HERO.
AND HERE HE WAS, THE SINGLE HARDEST AND MOST FRIGHTENING MAN I'D EVER KNOWN--THE ONLY ADULT I TRULY RESPECTED--CRYING LIKE A BABY.
I COULDN'T HELP IT. I ASKED HIM WHAT WAS WRONG.
I SQUASHED A NUN.

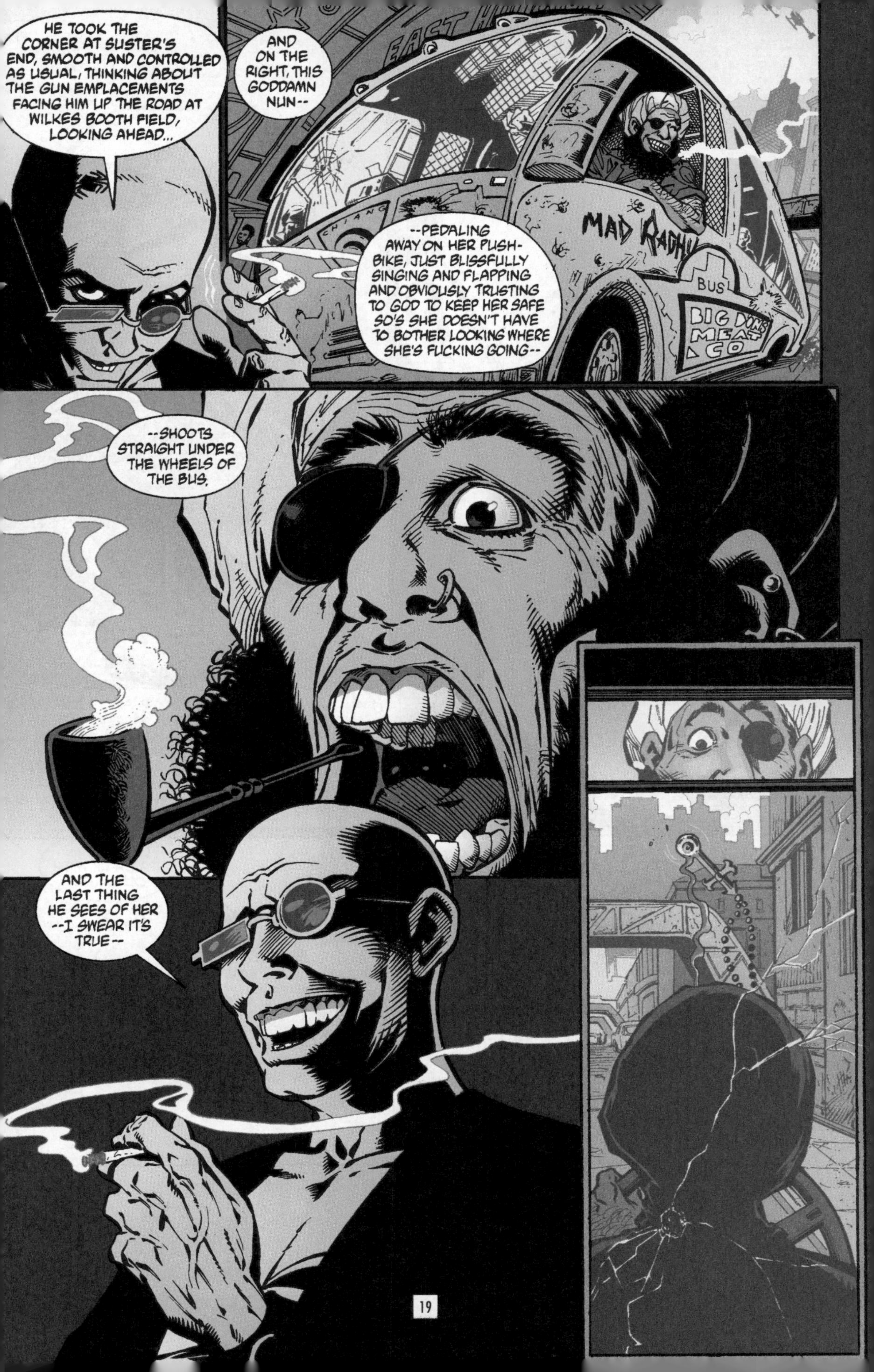
HE TOOK THE CORNER AT SUSTER'S END, SMOOTH AND CONTROLLED AS USUAL, THINKING ABOUT THE GUN EMPLACEMENTS FACING HIM UP THE ROAD AT WILKES BOOTH FIELD, LOOKING AHEAD...
AND ON THE RIGHT, THIS GODDAMN NUN--
--PEDALING AWAY ON HER PUSH-BIKE, JUST BLISSFULLY SINGING AND FLAPPING AND OBVIOUSLY TRUSTING TO GOD TO KEEP HER SAFE SO'S SHE DOESN'T HAVE TO BOTHER LOOKING WHERE SHE'S FUCKING GOING--
MAD RADHU
BUS
BIG DON'S MEAT CO
--SHOOTS STRAIGHT UNDER THE WHEELS OF THE BUS,
AND THE LAST THING HE SEES OF HER --I SWEAR IT'S TRUE--

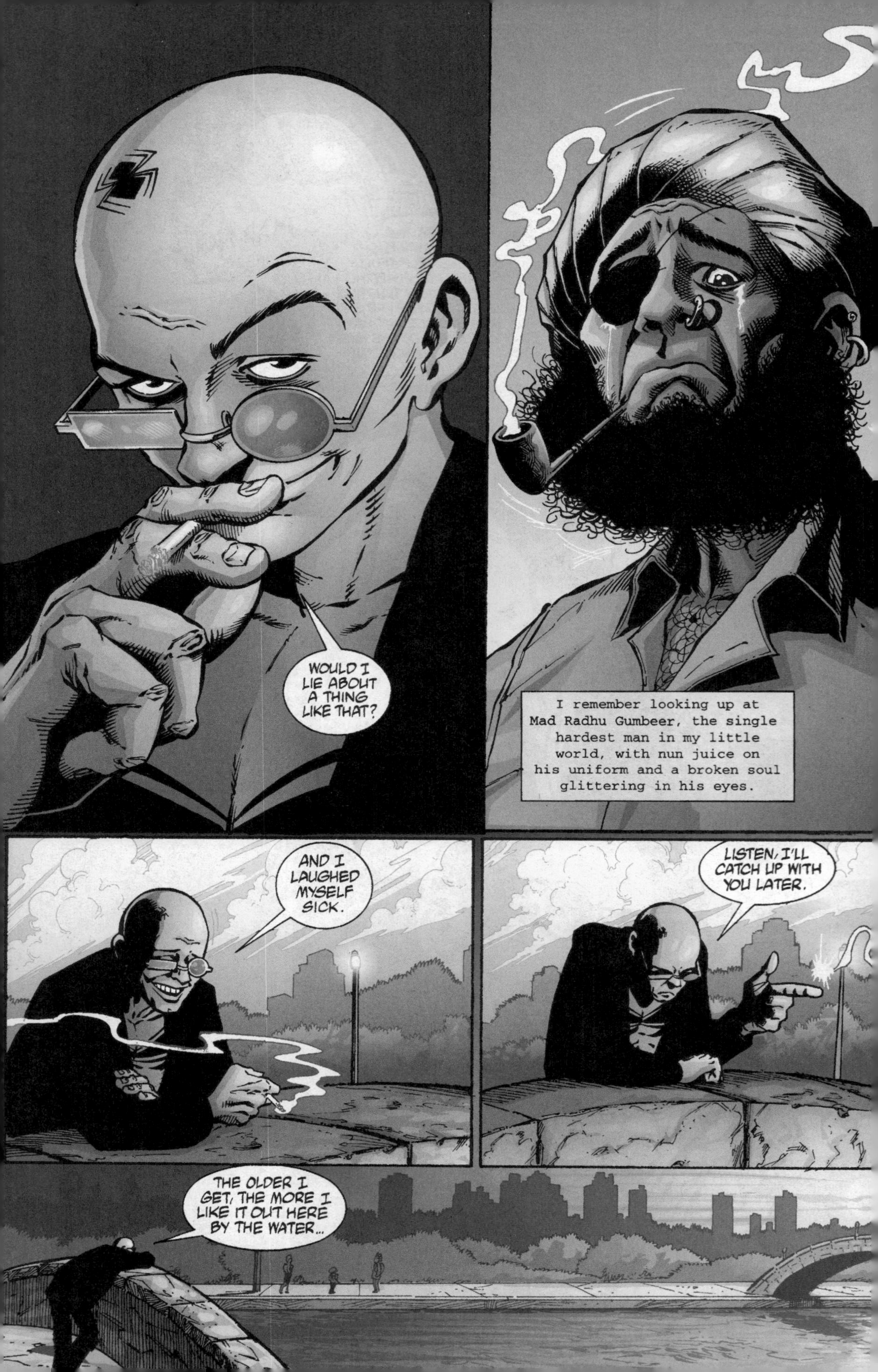
WOULD I LIE ABOUT A THING LIKE THAT?
I remember looking up at Mad Radhu Gumbeer, the single hardest man in my little world, with nun juice on his uniform and a broken soul glittering in his eyes.
AND I LAUGHED MYSELF SICK.
LISTEN, I'LL CATCH UP WITH YOU LATER.
THE OLDER I GET, THE MORE I LIKE IT OUT HERE BY THE WATER...

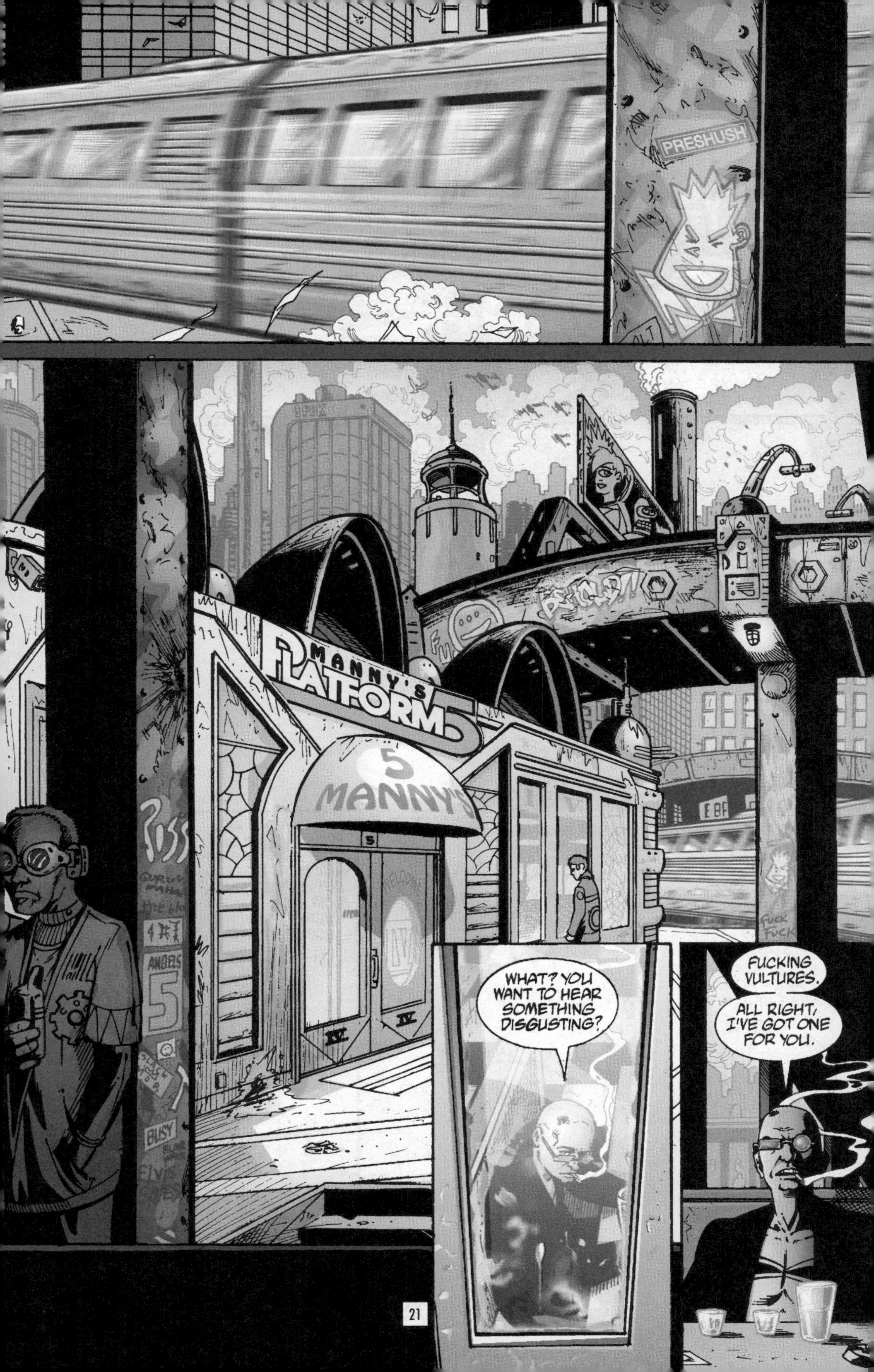
PRESHUSH
MANNY'S PLATFORM 5
5 MANNY'S
WHAT? YOU WANT TO HEAR SOMETHING DISGUSTING?
FUCKING VULTURES.
ALL RIGHT, I'VE GOT ONE FOR YOU.
FUCK FUCK
BUSY
ELVIS

SHE'S EIGHT-EEN YEARS OLD, SHE'S BEAUTIFUL, SHE'S SMART, SHE'S A DANCER, SHE'S ESSENTIALLY GODDAMN PERFECT, AND SHE SPENDS EVERY DAY TRYING TO TAMP DOWN HYSTERICAL TERROR.

EVERY FUCKING DAY.

SHE MISSES HER BROTHER.

HER BROTHER WAS KIND TO HER, YOU SEE?

HER MOTHER WAS A MAD RELIGIOUS DOMESTIC TERRORIST WHO RULED BY GUILT AND FEAR, HER ELDEST BROTHER WAS A HALF-BRIGHT THING WELL ON THE WAY TO VIOLENT MONSTERDOM, AND HER FATHER WAS A GHOST IN AN ARMCHAIR, SILENT AND INSUBSTANTIAL.

BUT HER OTHER BROTHER, ALSO OLDER THAN HER-- HE WAS KIND.

ONE DAY, THE KIDS FROM THE HOUSING PROJECT WHERE THEY YANK MUTATED FROGS OUT OF THE SEWAGE FLOW AND FUCK 'EM WERE THROWING ROCKS AT HER.

THAT HOUSING PROJEC[T] STILL THERE, YOU KNOW[?] MILLENNIUM DIP, NORT[H] EAST. APPARENTLY THE[Y] FROGS EXPLODE ON YO[UR] DICK AT THE MOMEN[T] OF ORGASM.

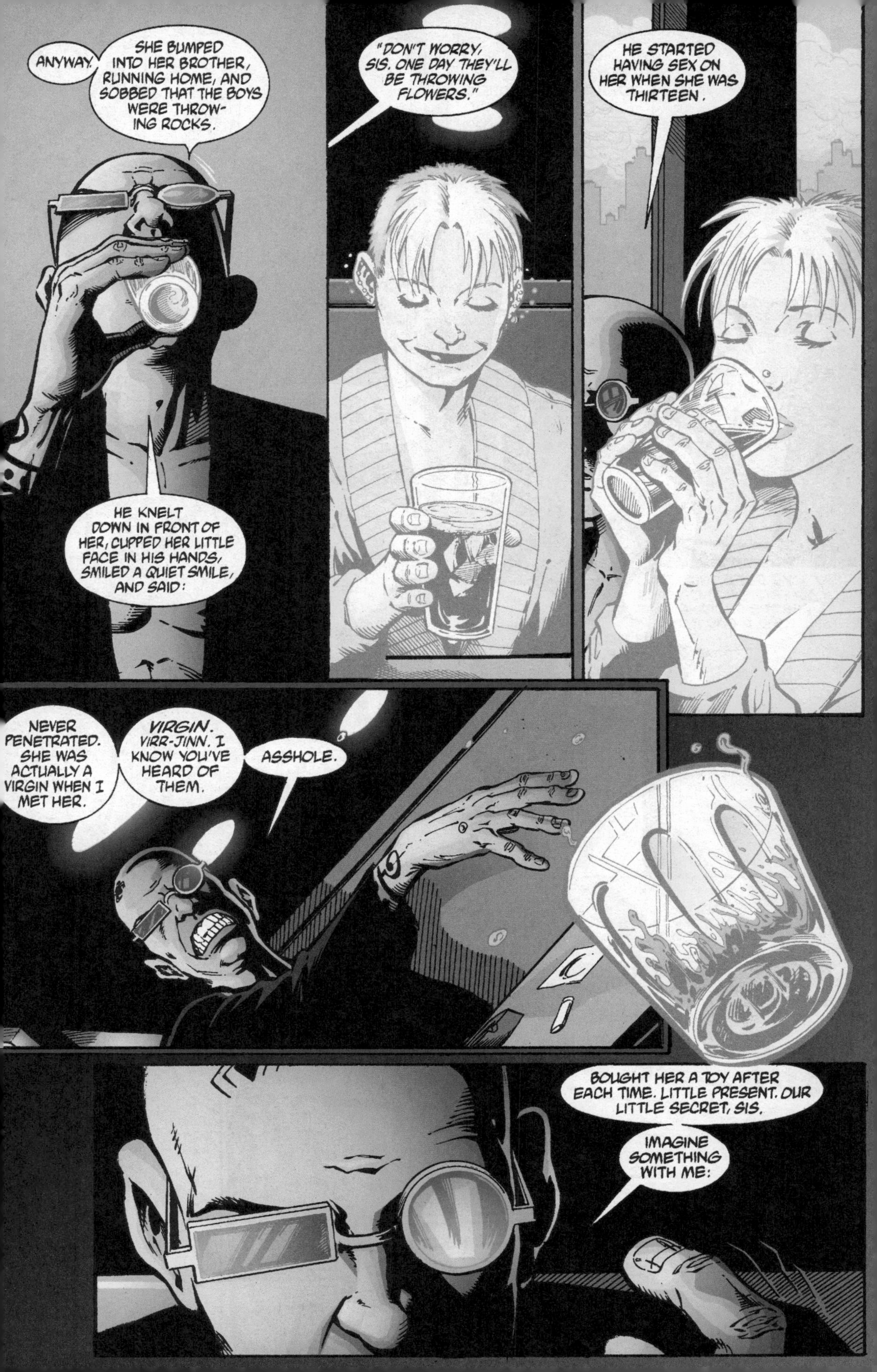

ANYWAY.
SHE BUMPED INTO HER BROTHER, RUNNING HOME, AND SOBBED THAT THE BOYS WERE THROWING ROCKS.
HE KNELT DOWN IN FRONT OF HER, CUPPED HER LITTLE FACE IN HIS HANDS, SMILED A QUIET SMILE, AND SAID:
"DON'T WORRY, SIS. ONE DAY THEY'LL BE THROWING FLOWERS."
HE STARTED HAVING SEX ON HER WHEN SHE WAS THIRTEEN.
NEVER PENETRATED. SHE WAS ACTUALLY A VIRGIN WHEN I MET HER.
VIRGIN. VIRR-JINN. I KNOW YOU'VE HEARD OF THEM.
ASSHOLE.
BOUGHT HER A TOY AFTER EACH TIME. LITTLE PRESENT. OUR LITTLE SECRET, SIS.
IMAGINE SOMETHING WITH ME:

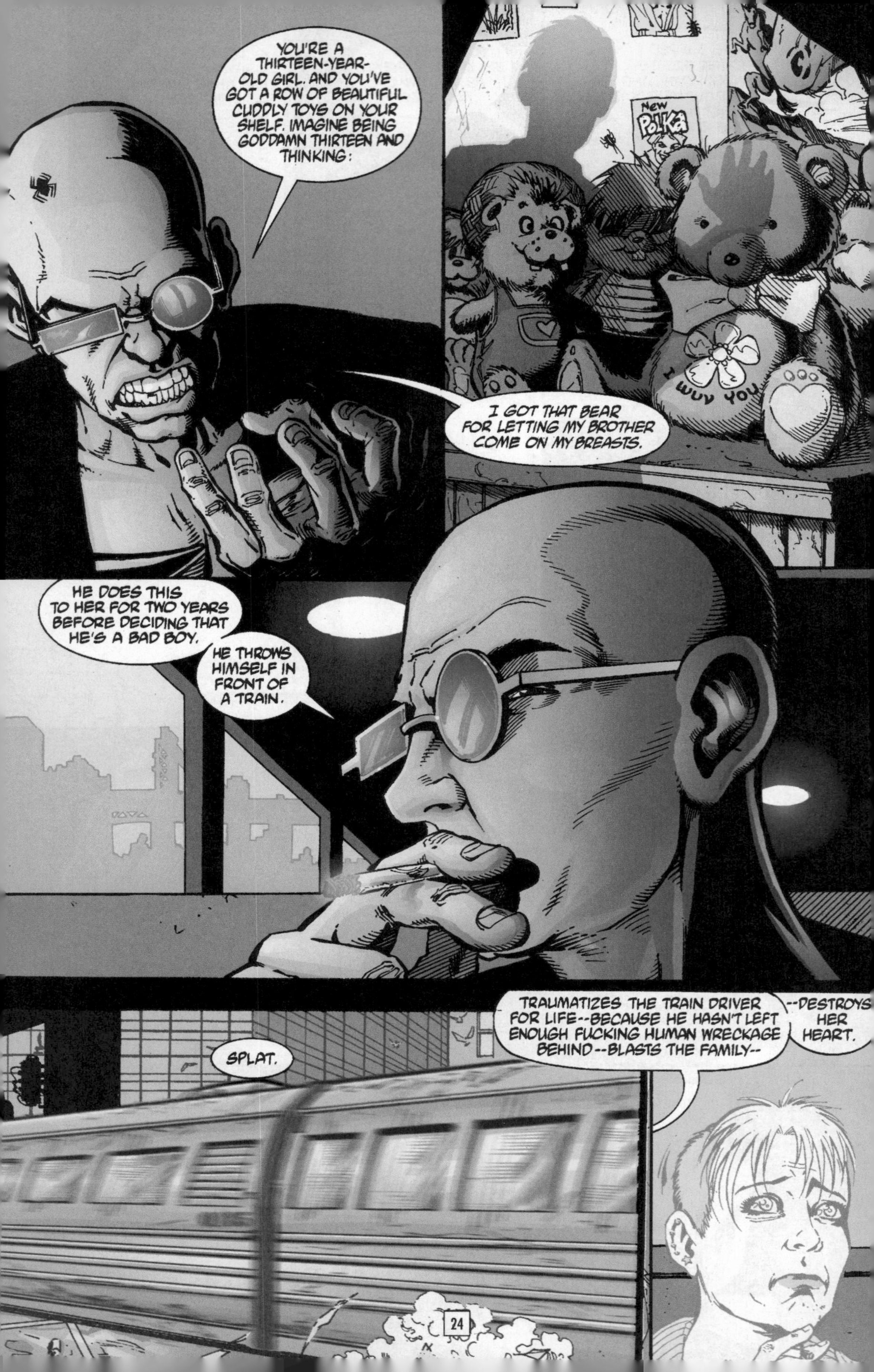
YOU'RE A THIRTEEN-YEAR-OLD GIRL. AND YOU'VE GOT A ROW OF BEAUTIFUL CUDDLY TOYS ON YOUR SHELF. IMAGINE BEING GODDAMN THIRTEEN AND THINKING:
New POLKA
I WUV YOU
I GOT THAT BEAR FOR LETTING MY BROTHER COME ON MY BREASTS.
HE DOES THIS TO HER FOR TWO YEARS BEFORE DECIDING THAT HE'S A BAD BOY.
HE THROWS HIMSELF IN FRONT OF A TRAIN.
SPLAT.
TRAUMATIZES THE TRAIN DRIVER FOR LIFE--BECAUSE HE HASN'T LEFT ENOUGH FUCKING HUMAN WRECKAGE BEHIND--BLASTS THE FAMILY--
--DESTROYS HER HEART.

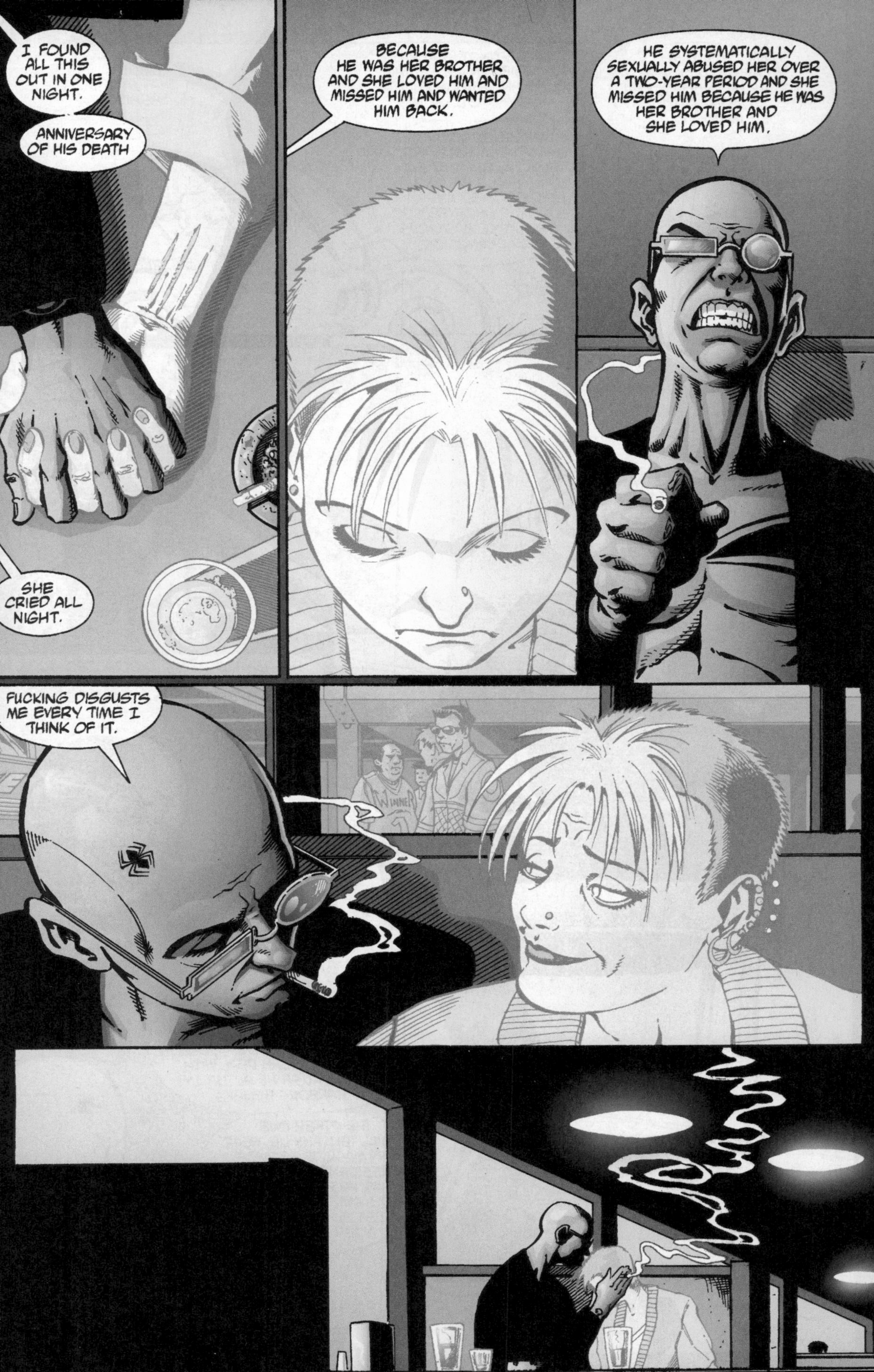
I FOUND ALL THIS OUT IN ONE NIGHT.
ANNIVERSARY OF HIS DEATH
SHE CRIED ALL NIGHT.
BECAUSE HE WAS HER BROTHER AND SHE LOVED HIM AND MISSED HIM AND WANTED HIM BACK.
HE SYSTEMATICALLY SEXUALLY ABUSED HER OVER A TWO-YEAR PERIOD AND SHE MISSED HIM BECAUSE HE WAS HER BROTHER AND SHE LOVED HIM.
FUCKING DISGUSTS ME EVERY TIME I THINK OF IT.
WINNER

IT'S LIKE BEING ATTACKED BY MY UNCLE IDI. HE COULD FART IN COLOR.

YOUR INSTINCT IS ALWAYS TO COMPLAIN ABOUT THE BUGS AND SHIT IN PURITAN MEWS, YOU KNOW?

AND THEN YOU CATCH YOURSELF AND THINK, HELL, AIN'T SO LONG SINCE WE THOUGHT WE'D SPRAYED AND STAMPED AND INFECTED THE LITTLE BASTARDS TO EXTINCTION.

WHY BE THAT STUPID AGAIN?

WHY BE THAT STUPID STILL?

I ALWAYS THOUGHT PEOPLE WERE ESSENTIALLY BRIGHT.

DISTRACTED, SURE, WEAK, AND BEATEN, NEVER STUPID.

AND THEN YOU SHOW THEM, HERE'S THE TWO PEOPLE WHO WANT TO BE PRESIDENT. ONE IS EVIL, BUT YOU CAN DEAL WITH HIM, BECAUSE HE ACTUALLY HARBORS BELIEFS.

THE OTHER ONE WILL TELL ANY LIE, WEAR ANY MASK, TO BECOME PRESIDENT, AND NOT ONLY THAT, HE FUCKING HATES YOU, AND HE'S DOING THIS JUST SO HE CAN MAKE YOUR LIVES HELL.

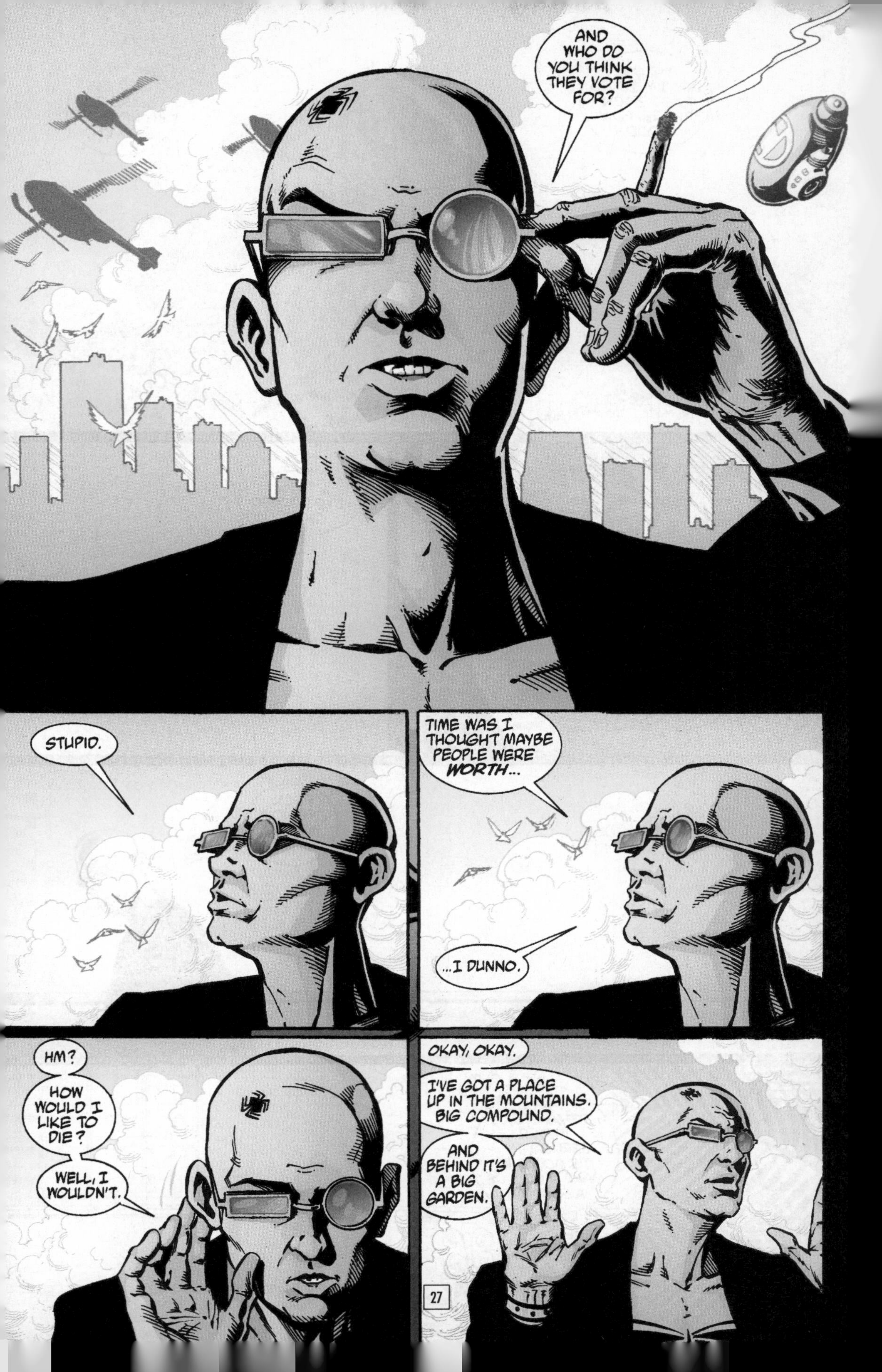
AND WHO DO YOU THINK THEY VOTE FOR?
STUPID.
TIME WAS I THOUGHT MAYBE PEOPLE WERE WORTH...
...I DUNNO.
HM?
HOW WOULD I LIKE TO DIE?
WELL, I WOULDN'T.
OKAY, OKAY.
I'VE GOT A PLACE UP IN THE MOUNTAINS. BIG COMPOUND.
AND BEHIND IT'S A BIG GARDEN.
27

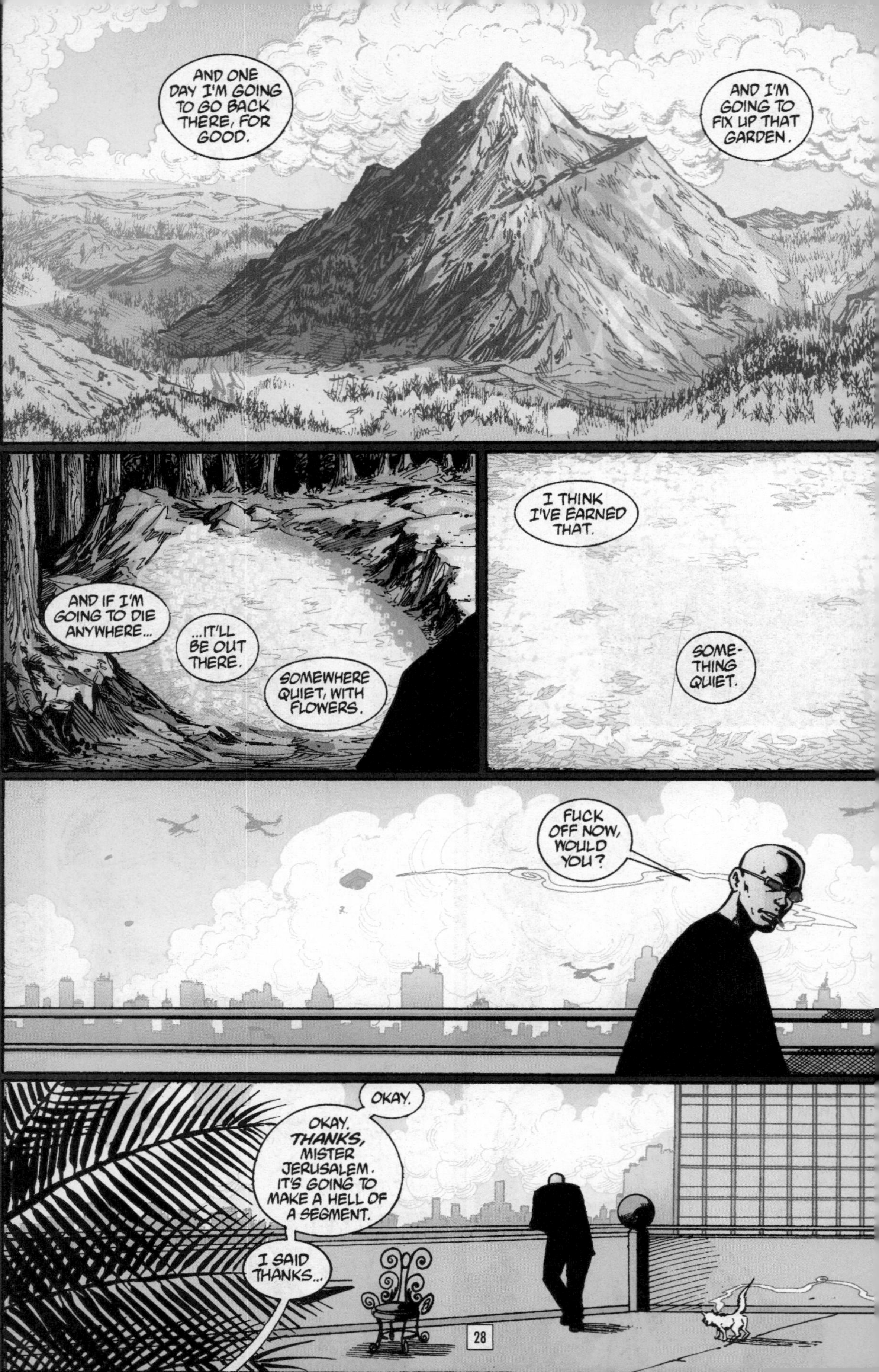
AND ONE DAY I'M GOING TO GO BACK THERE, FOR GOOD.
AND I'M GOING TO FIX UP THAT GARDEN.
AND IF I'M GOING TO DIE ANYWHERE...
...IT'LL BE OUT THERE.
SOMEWHERE QUIET, WITH FLOWERS.
I THINK I'VE EARNED THAT.
SOME-THING QUIET.
FUCK OFF NOW, WOULD YOU?
OKAY.
OKAY. THANKS, MISTER JERUSALEM. IT'S GOING TO MAKE A HELL OF A SEGMENT.
I SAID THANKS...

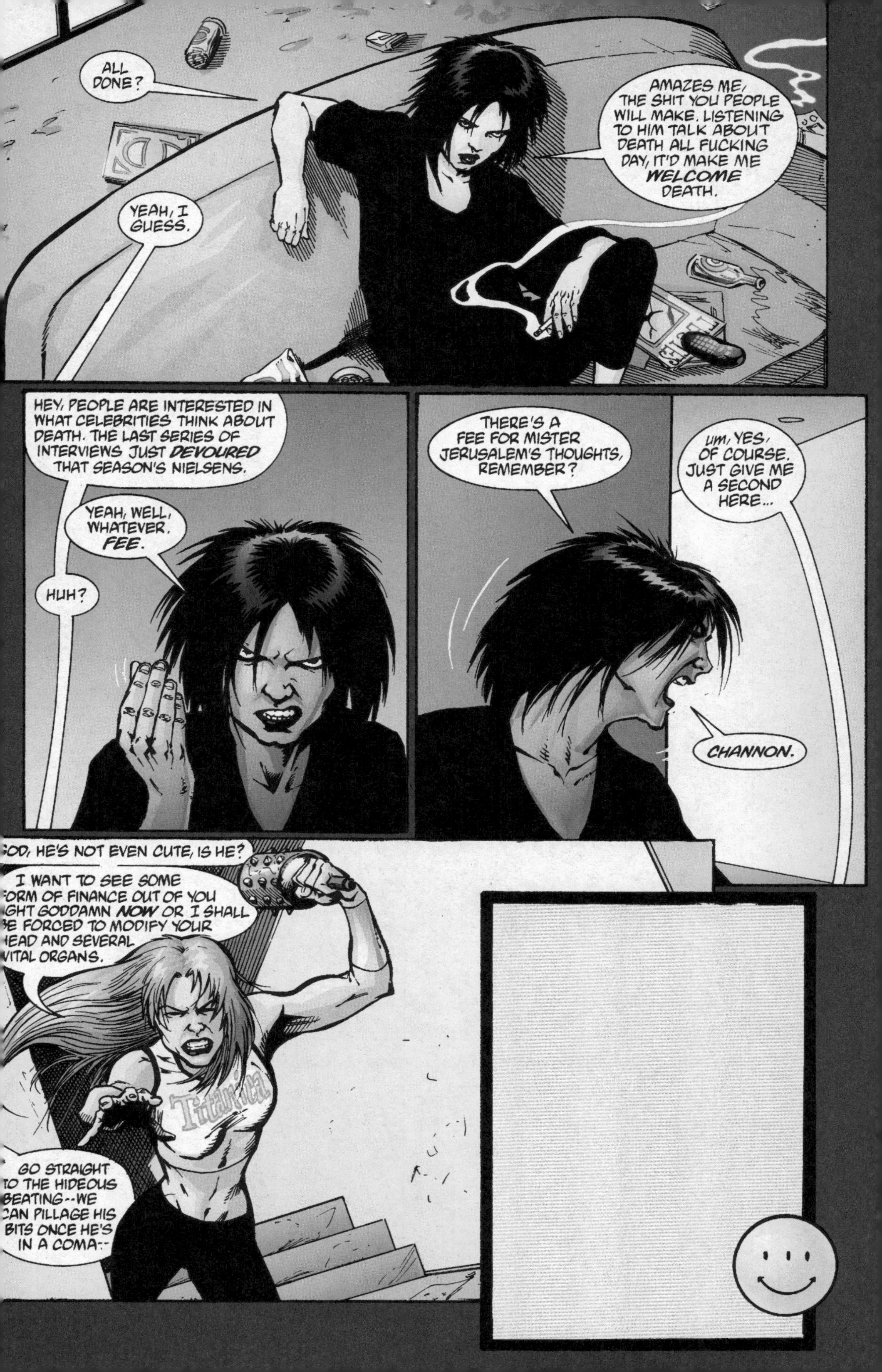
ALL DONE?
AMAZES ME, THE SHIT YOU PEOPLE WILL MAKE. LISTENING TO HIM TALK ABOUT DEATH ALL FUCKING DAY, IT'D MAKE ME WELCOME DEATH.
YEAH, I GUESS.
HEY, PEOPLE ARE INTERESTED IN WHAT CELEBRITIES THINK ABOUT DEATH. THE LAST SERIES OF INTERVIEWS JUST DEVOURED THAT SEASON'S NIELSENS.
YEAH, WELL, WHATEVER. FEE.
HUH?
THERE'S A FEE FOR MISTER JERUSALEM'S THOUGHTS, REMEMBER?
UM, YES, OF COURSE. JUST GIVE ME A SECOND HERE...
CHANNON.
GOD, HE'S NOT EVEN CUTE, IS HE?
I WANT TO SEE SOME FORM OF FINANCE OUT OF YOU RIGHT GODDAMN NOW OR I SHALL BE FORCED TO MODIFY YOUR HEAD AND SEVERAL VITAL ORGANS.
GO STRAIGHT TO THE HIDEOUS BEATING--WE CAN PILLAGE HIS BITS ONCE HE'S IN A COMA--
Titanica

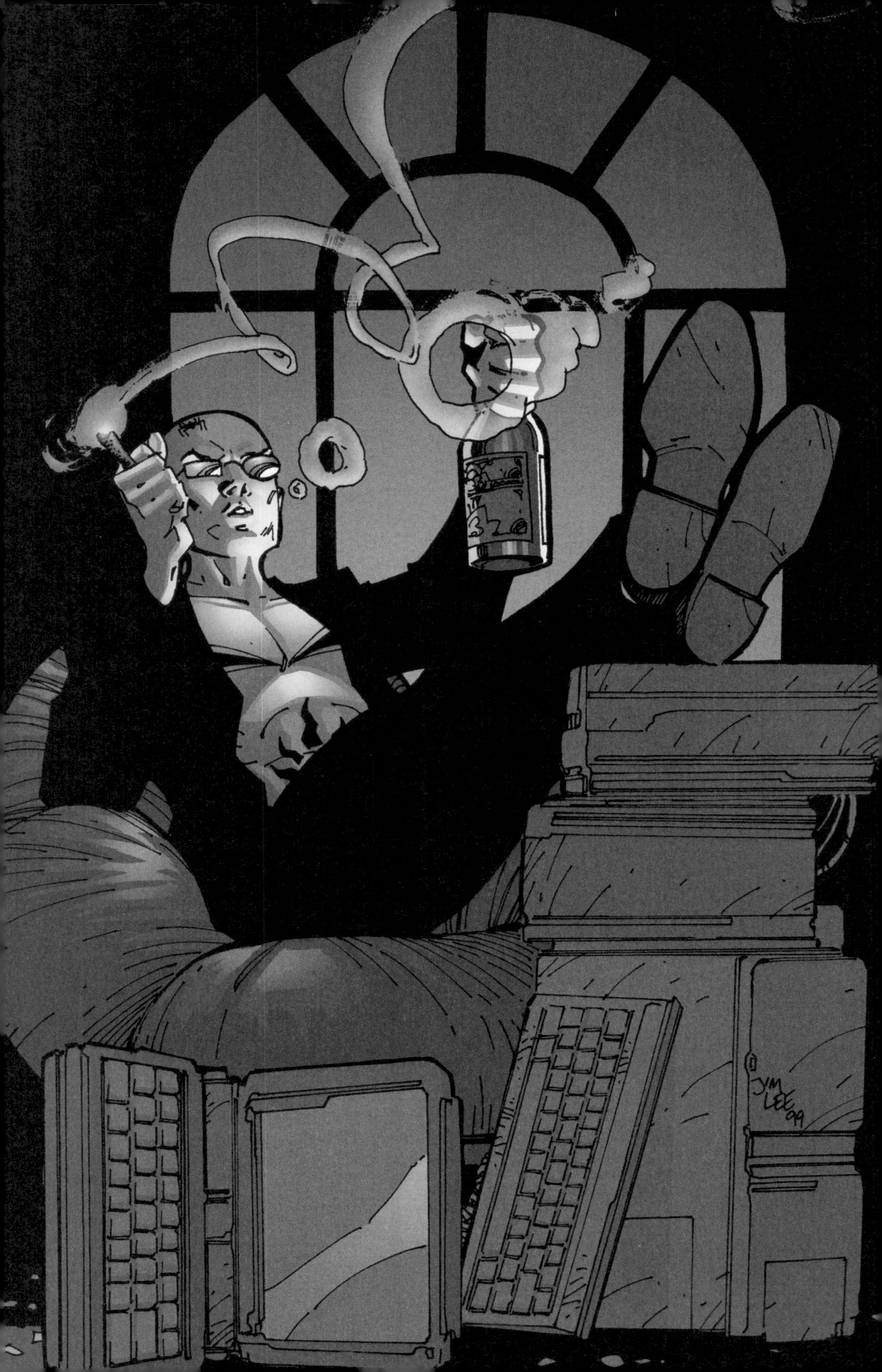

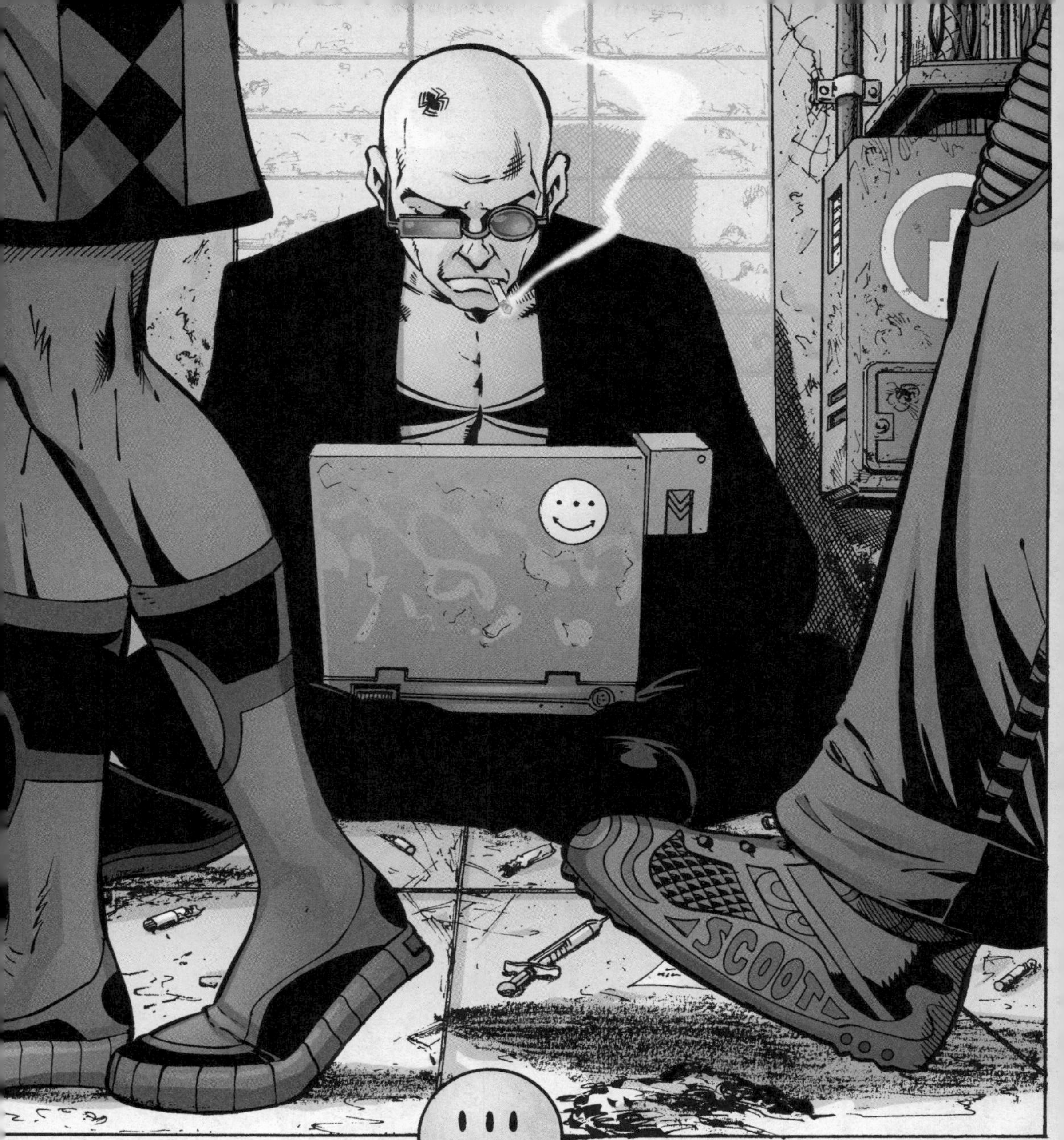
SCOOT

WARREN ELLIS writes & **DARICK ROBERTSON** pencils

21 DAYS IN THE CITY

RODNEY RAMOS - inker **CLEM ROBINS** - letterer **NATHAN EYRING** - color & separations
JIM LEE - cover art **CLIFF CHIANG** - assistant editor **STUART MOORE** - editor
TRANSMETROPOLITAN created by Warren Ellis & Darick Robertson

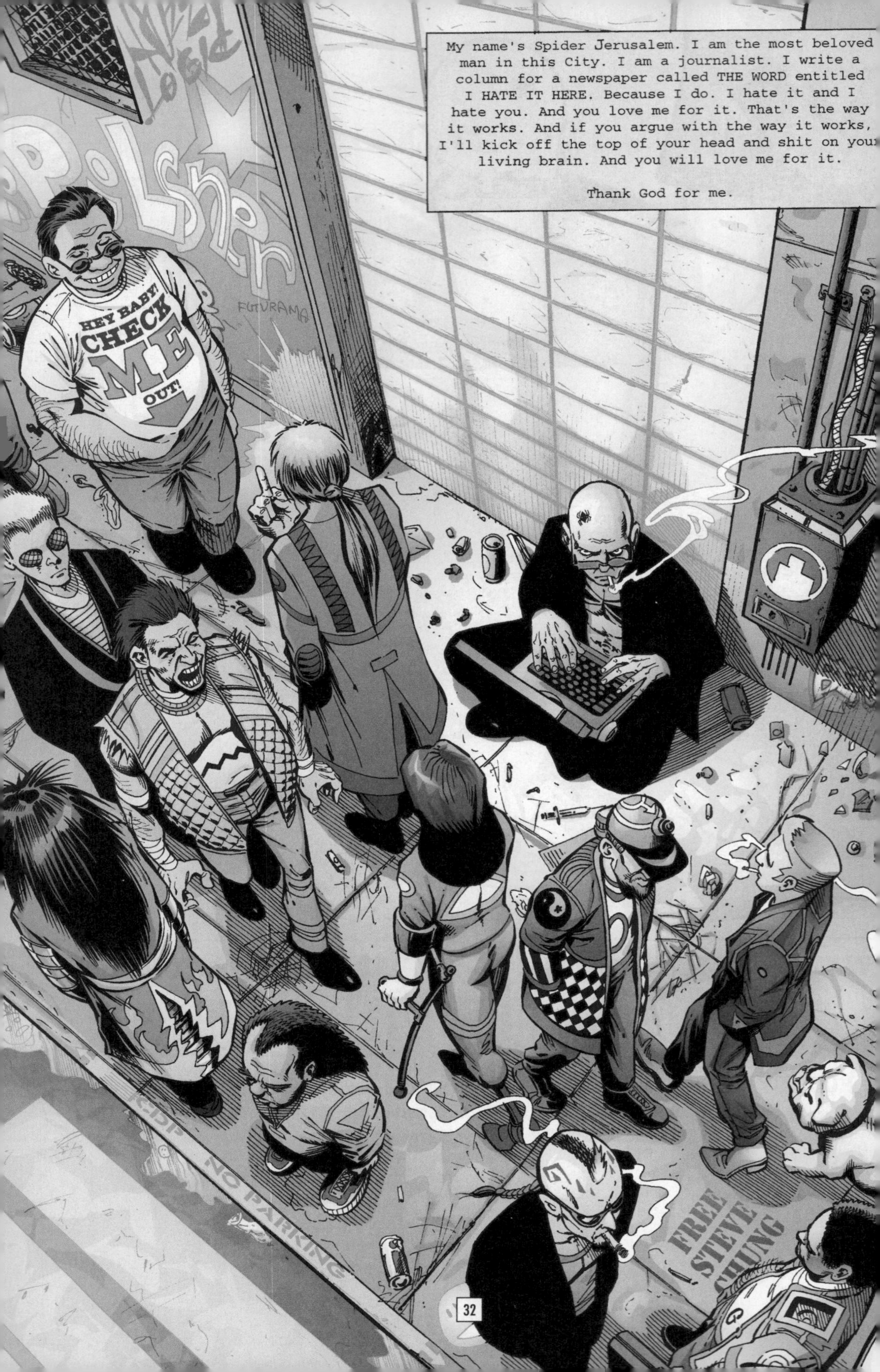
My name's Spider Jerusalem. I am the most beloved man in this City. I am a journalist. I write a column for a newspaper called THE WORD entitled I HATE IT HERE. Because I do. I hate it and I hate you. And you love me for it. That's the way it works. And if you argue with the way it works, I'll kick off the top of your head and shit on your living brain. And you will love me for it.
Thank God for me.
HEY BABY! CHECK ME OUT!
FUTURAMA
NO PARKING
FREE STEVE CHUNG

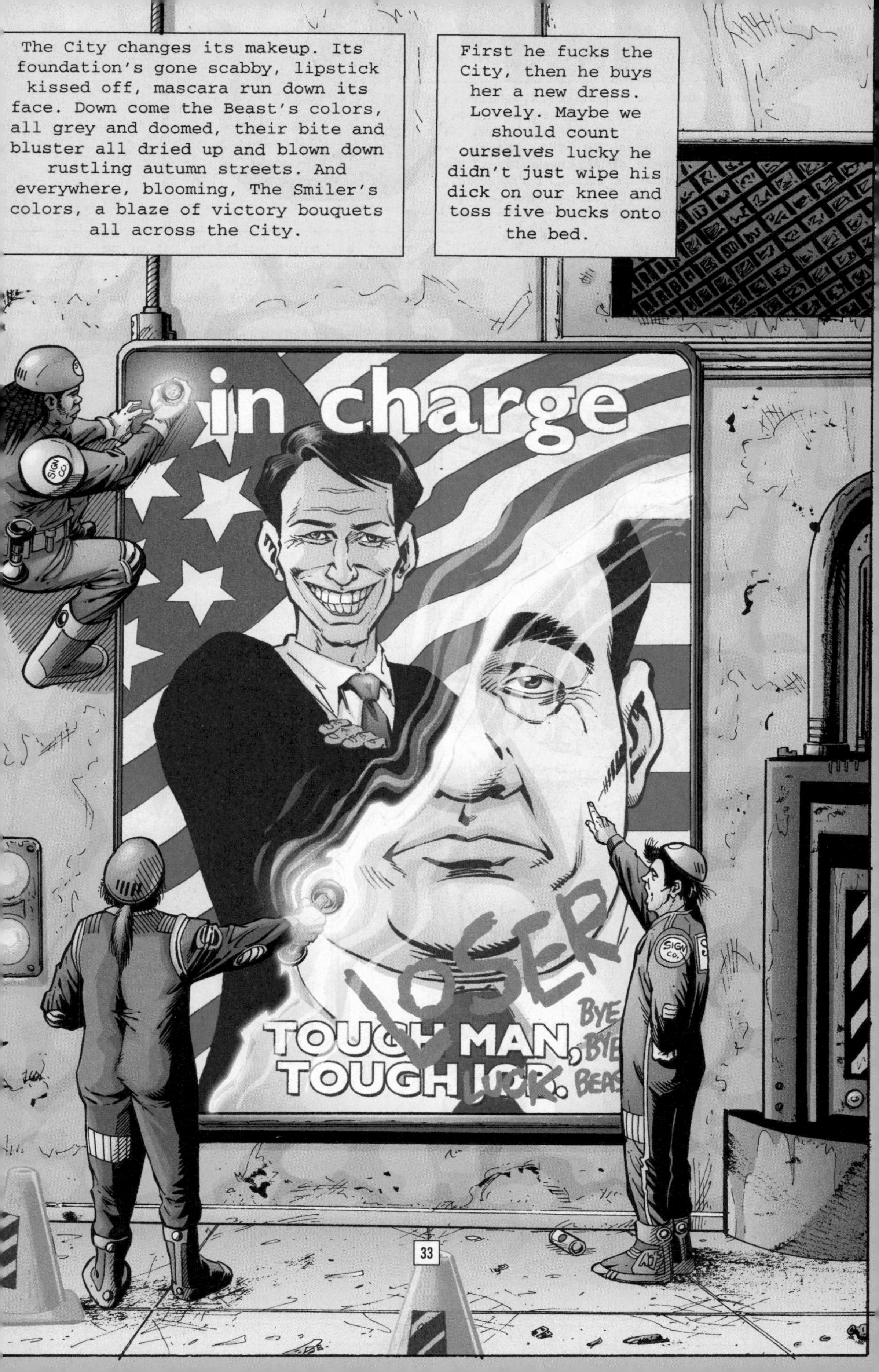
The City changes its makeup. Its foundation's gone scabby, lipstick kissed off, mascara run down its face. Down come the Beast's colors, all grey and doomed, their bite and bluster all dried up and blown down rustling autumn streets. And everywhere, blooming, The Smiler's colors, a blaze of victory bouquets all across the City.
First he fucks the City, then he buys her a new dress. Lovely. Maybe we should count ourselves lucky he didn't just wipe his dick on our knee and toss five bucks onto the bed.
in charge
TOUGH MAN, TOUGH LUCK.
LOSER
BYE BYE BEAS
SIGN CO.

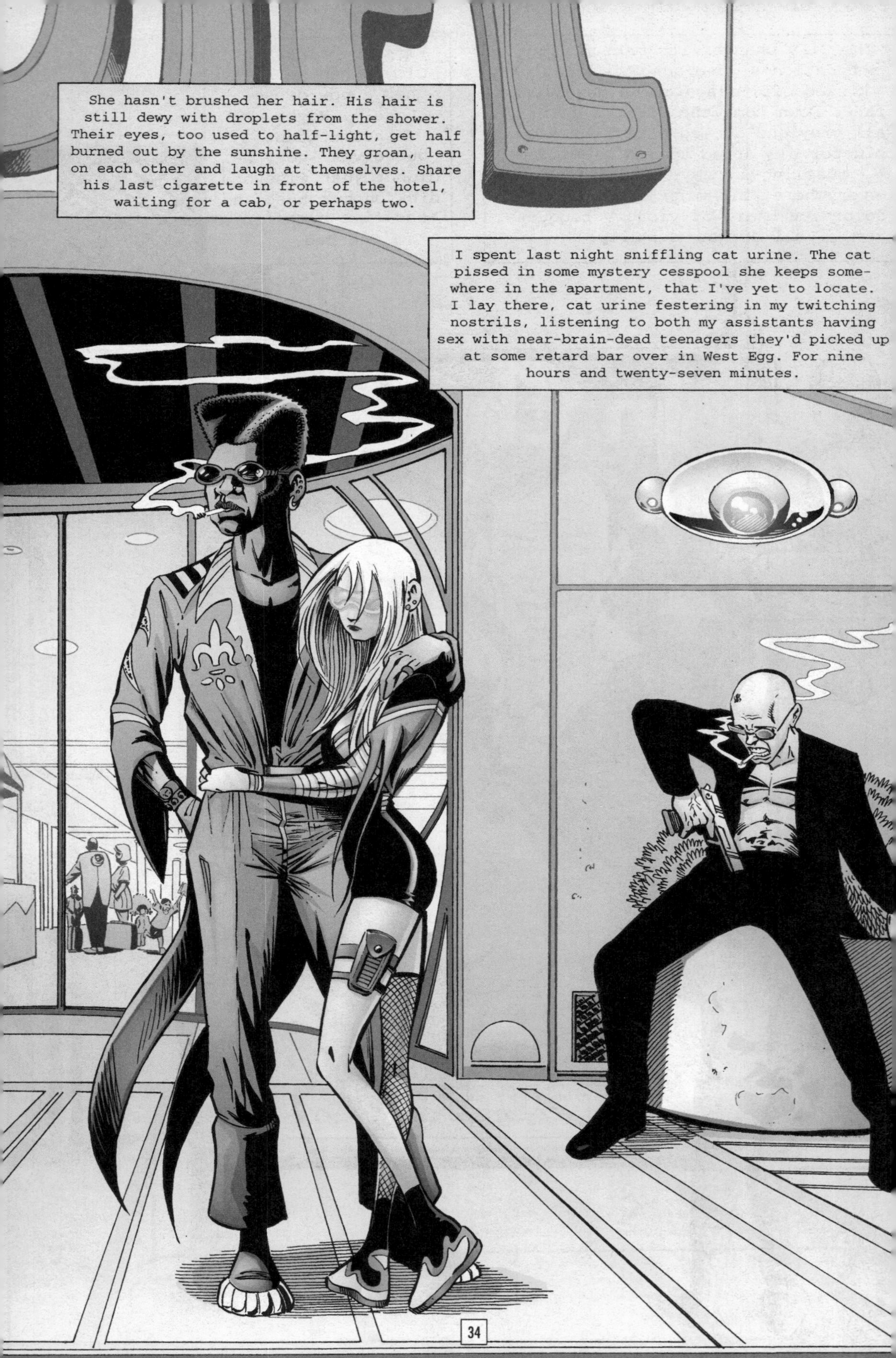
She hasn't brushed her hair. His hair is still dewy with droplets from the shower. Their eyes, too used to half-light, get half burned out by the sunshine. They groan, lean on each other and laugh at themselves. Share his last cigarette in front of the hotel, waiting for a cab, or perhaps two.
I spent last night sniffling cat urine. The cat pissed in some mystery cesspool she keeps somewhere in the apartment, that I've yet to locate. I lay there, cat urine festering in my twitching nostrils, listening to both my assistants having sex with near-brain-dead teenagers they'd picked up at some retard bar over in West Egg. For nine hours and twenty-seven minutes.

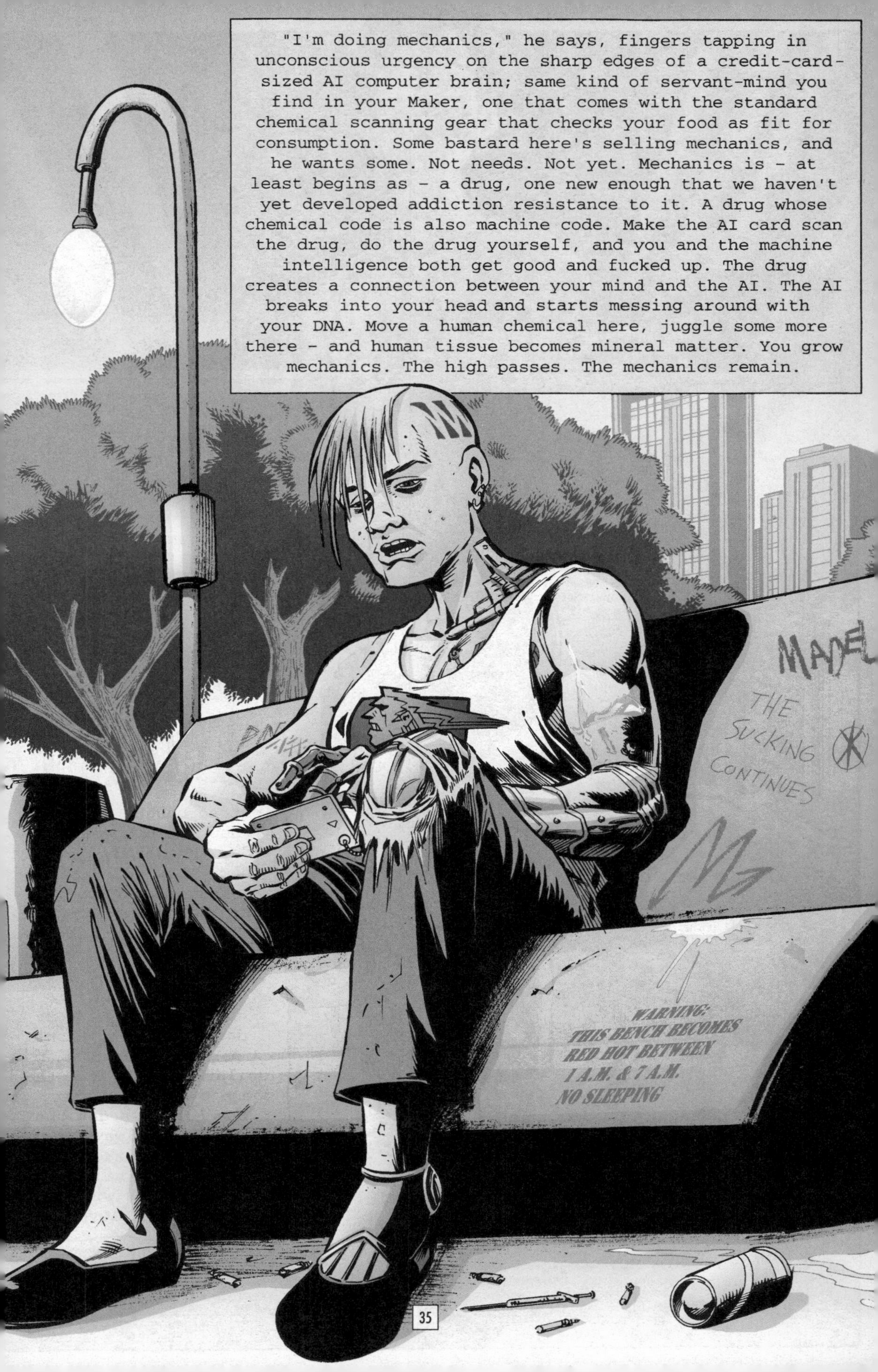
"I'm doing mechanics," he says, fingers tapping in unconscious urgency on the sharp edges of a credit-card-sized AI computer brain; same kind of servant-mind you find in your Maker, one that comes with the standard chemical scanning gear that checks your food as fit for consumption. Some bastard here's selling mechanics, and he wants some. Not needs. Not yet. Mechanics is – at least begins as – a drug, one new enough that we haven't yet developed addiction resistance to it. A drug whose chemical code is also machine code. Make the AI card scan the drug, do the drug yourself, and you and the machine intelligence both get good and fucked up. The drug creates a connection between your mind and the AI. The AI breaks into your head and starts messing around with your DNA. Move a human chemical here, juggle some more there – and human tissue becomes mineral matter. You grow mechanics. The high passes. The mechanics remain.
MADEL
THE SUCKING CONTINUES
WARNING:
THIS BENCH BECOMES
RED HOT BETWEEN
1 A.M. & 7 A.M.
NO SLEEPING

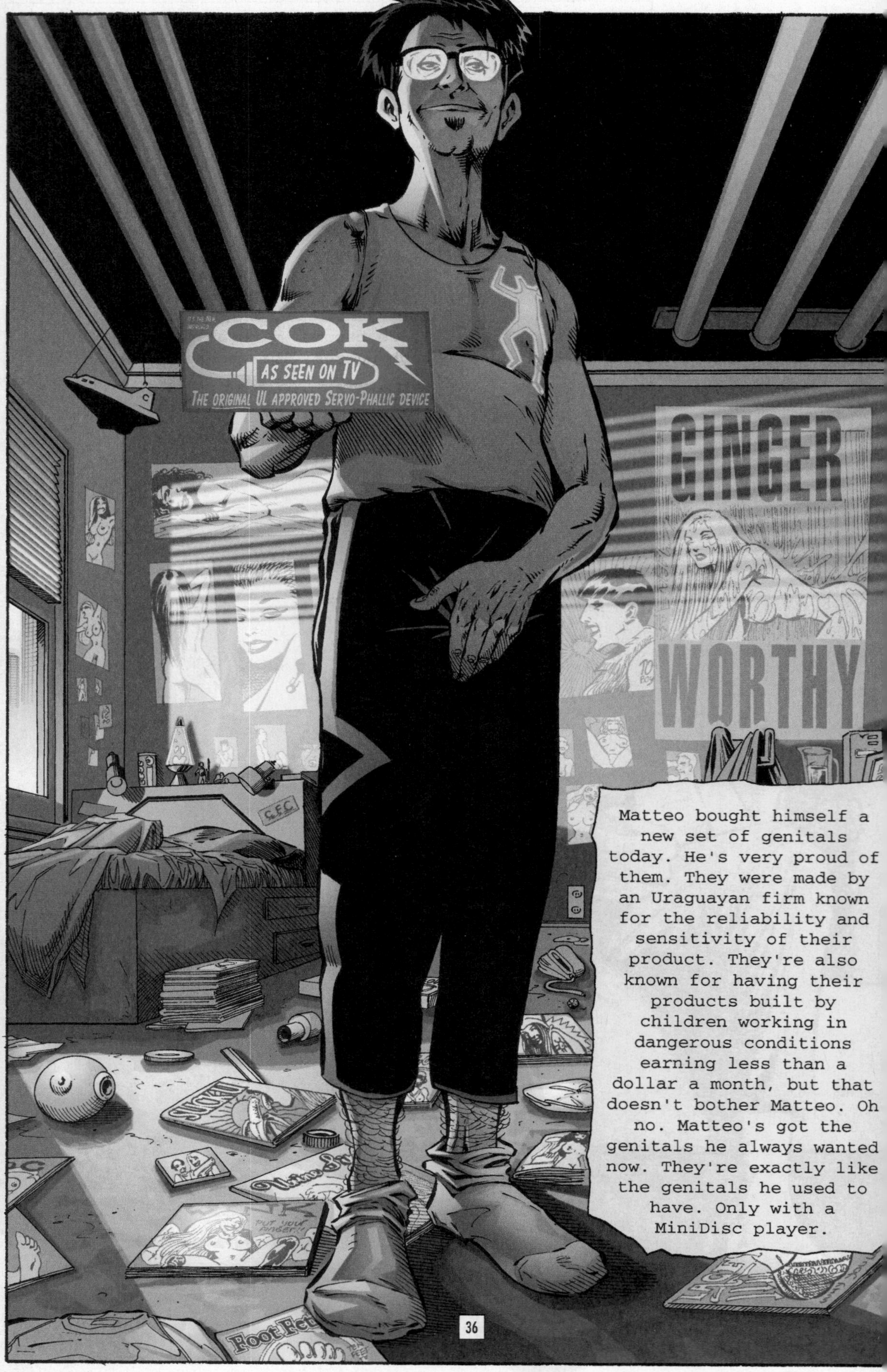
COK
AS SEEN ON TV
THE ORIGINAL UL APPROVED SERVO-PHALLIC DEVICE
GINGER
WORTHY
Matteo bought himself a new set of genitals today. He's very proud of them. They were made by an Uraguayan firm known for the reliability and sensitivity of their product. They're also known for having their products built by children working in dangerous conditions earning less than a dollar a month, but that doesn't bother Matteo. Oh no. Matteo's got the genitals he always wanted now. They're exactly like the genitals he used to have. Only with a MiniDisc player.

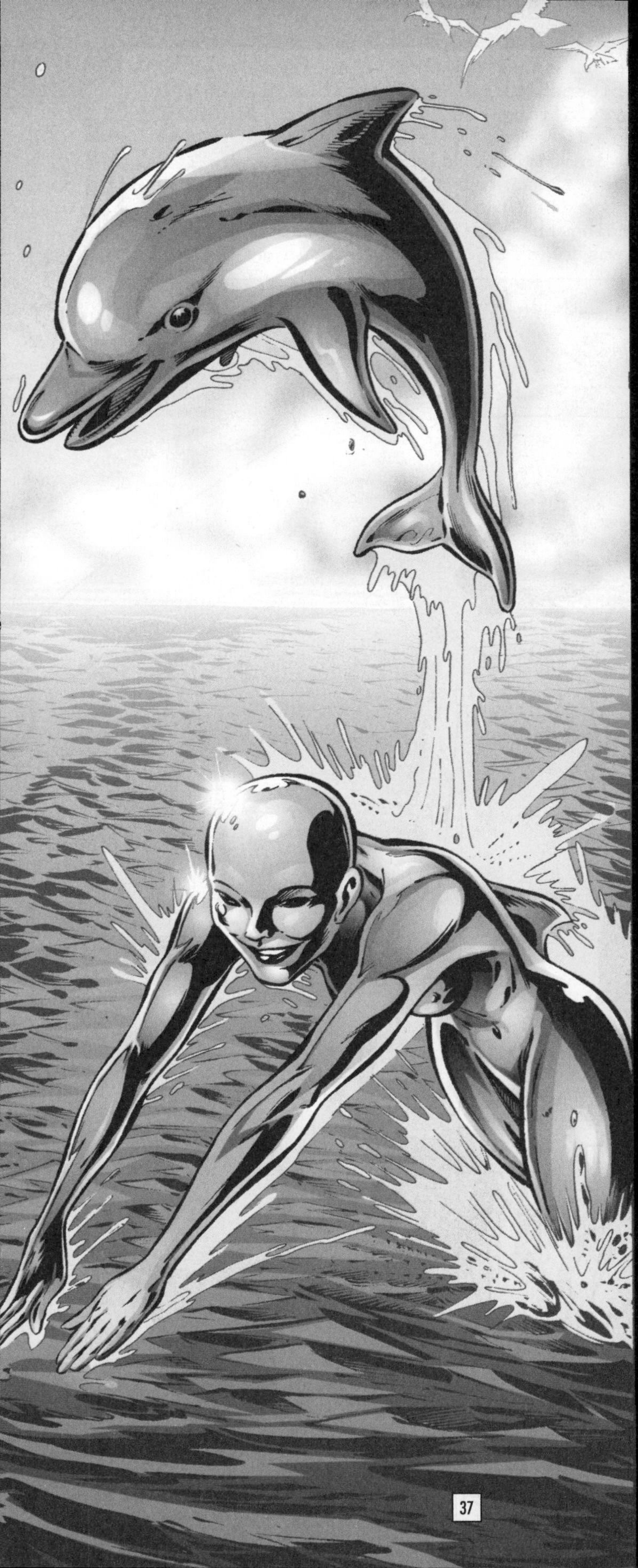

Sometimes this place just stops and hits you in the eyes. I'm on a train to Venetian End to cover the intestine-rinsing competition at the public sinks there, passing through the western Lakes. Sunny day. Trout and salmon blasting through the channels and rivers that connect the Lakes to each other and the sea. And then I see a dolphin. And then I see a Temp, someone wearing animal traits for a weekend. And for a moment there, I don't have any words.

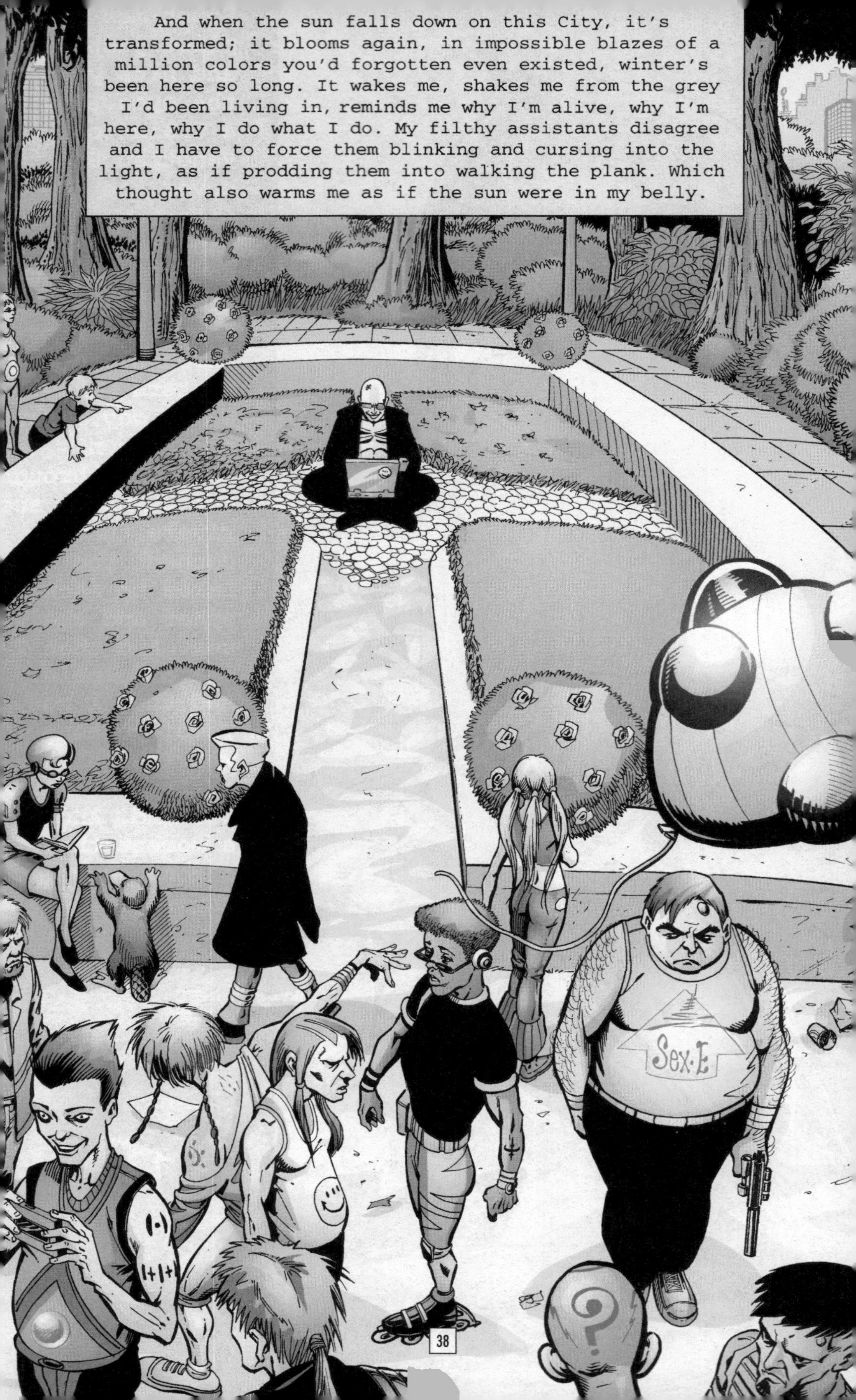
And when the sun falls down on this City, it's transformed; it blooms again, in impossible blazes of a million colors you'd forgotten even existed, winter's been here so long. It wakes me, shakes me from the grey I'd been living in, reminds me why I'm alive, why I'm here, why I do what I do. My filthy assistants disagree and I have to force them blinking and cursing into the light, as if prodding them into walking the plank. Which thought also warms me as if the sun were in my belly.
Sex·E

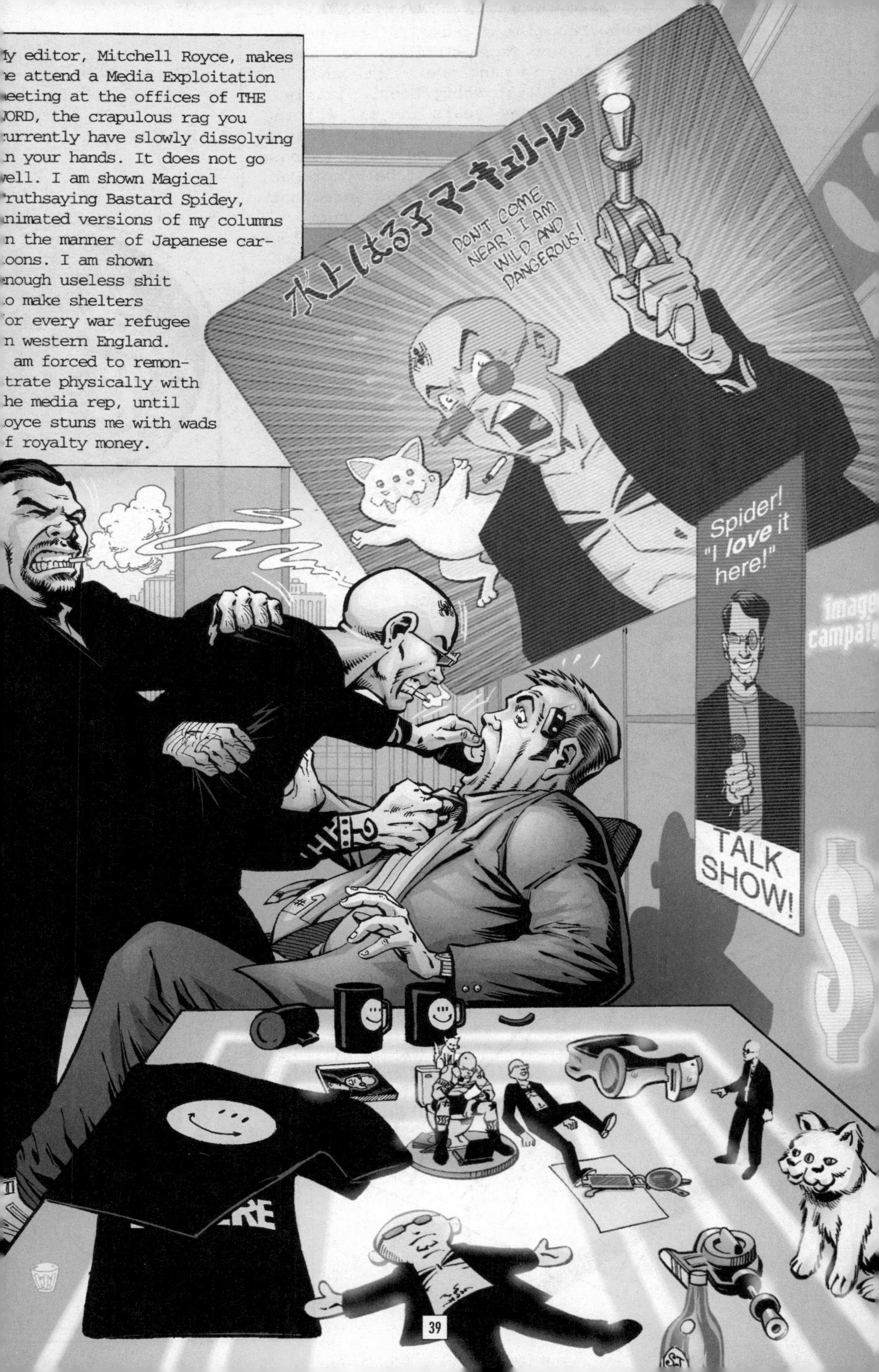

y editor, Mitchell Royce, makes
e attend a Media Exploitation
eeting at the offices of THE
ORD, the crapulous rag you
urrently have slowly dissolving
n your hands. It does not go
ell. I am shown Magical
ruthsaying Bastard Spidey,
nimated versions of my columns
n the manner of Japanese car-
oons. I am shown
nough useless shit
o make shelters
or every war refugee
n western England.
am forced to remon-
trate physically with
he media rep, until
oyce stuns me with wads
f royalty money.
DON'T COME NEAR! I AM WILD AND DANGEROUS!
Spider! "I love it here!"
TALK SHOW!

Right Love is somehow becoming a cause célèbre among the great and the good. Huey Three-Flint-Knife, their founder and spokesman, is handsome, witty and impassioned. His friends, like Bobby Long, plainly worship him – Long spent his two years in jail writing a history of the movement that was nothing more than a hymn to Huey. Influential producer and cultural compass Bert Shenfield said upon meeting him, "If he's not Mao, I'll eat it." Please allow me to remind everyone that Right Love's aim of "freeing sexuality" is quite specific: having sex with pre-sexual humans. Don't look for media-approved ideologically sound Right Causes where there are none. Look out of the window instead, and do something about what you see there.

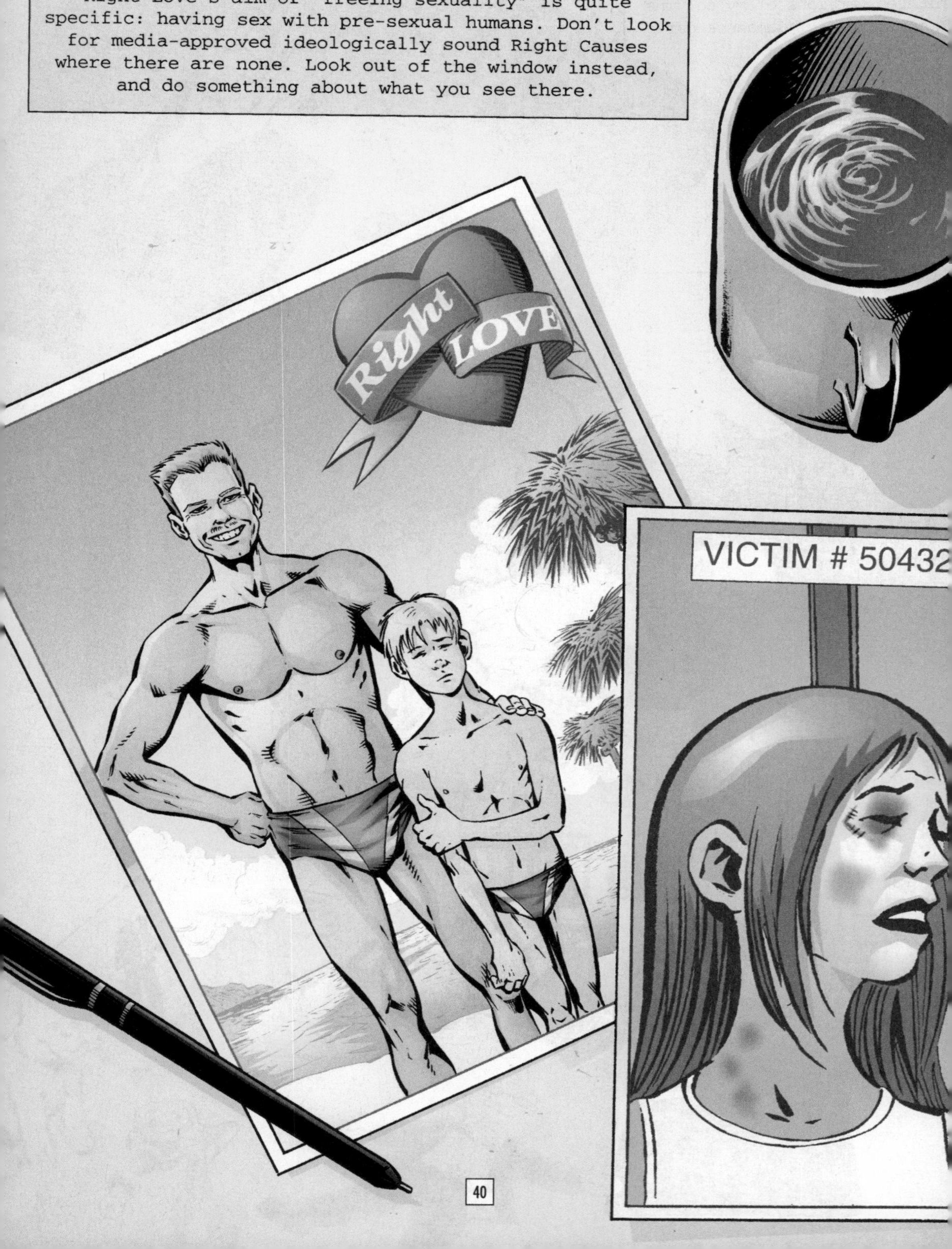

Right LOVE
VICTIM # 50432

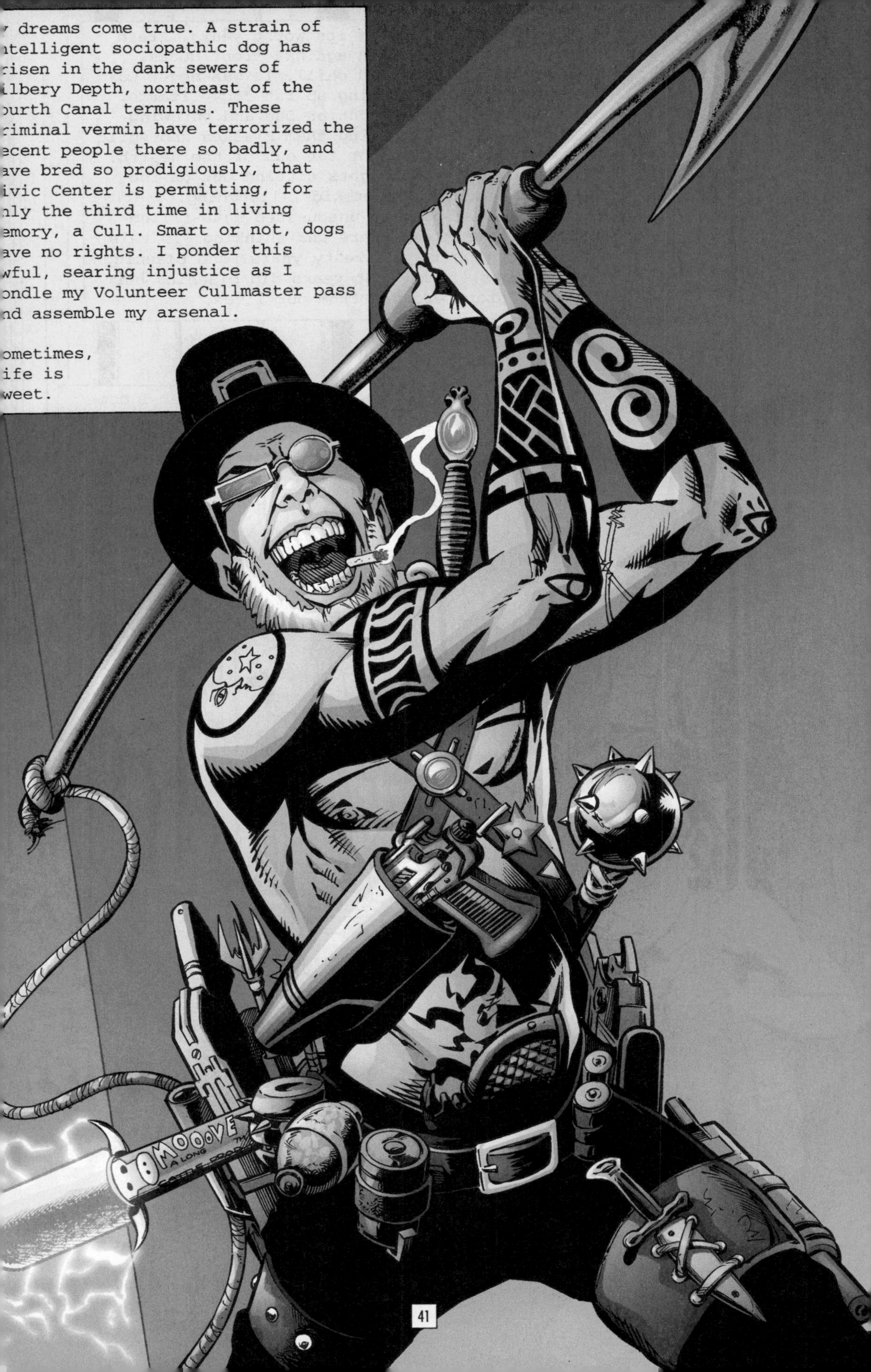

y dreams come true. A strain of ntelligent sociopathic dog has risen in the dank sewers of ilbery Depth, northeast of the ourth Canal terminus. These riminal vermin have terrorized the ecent people there so badly, and ave bred so prodigiously, that ivic Center is permitting, for nly the third time in living emory, a Cull. Smart or not, dogs ave no rights. I ponder this wful, searing injustice as I ondle my Volunteer Cullmaster pass nd assemble my arsenal.
ometimes, ife is weet.
MOOOVE
A LONG

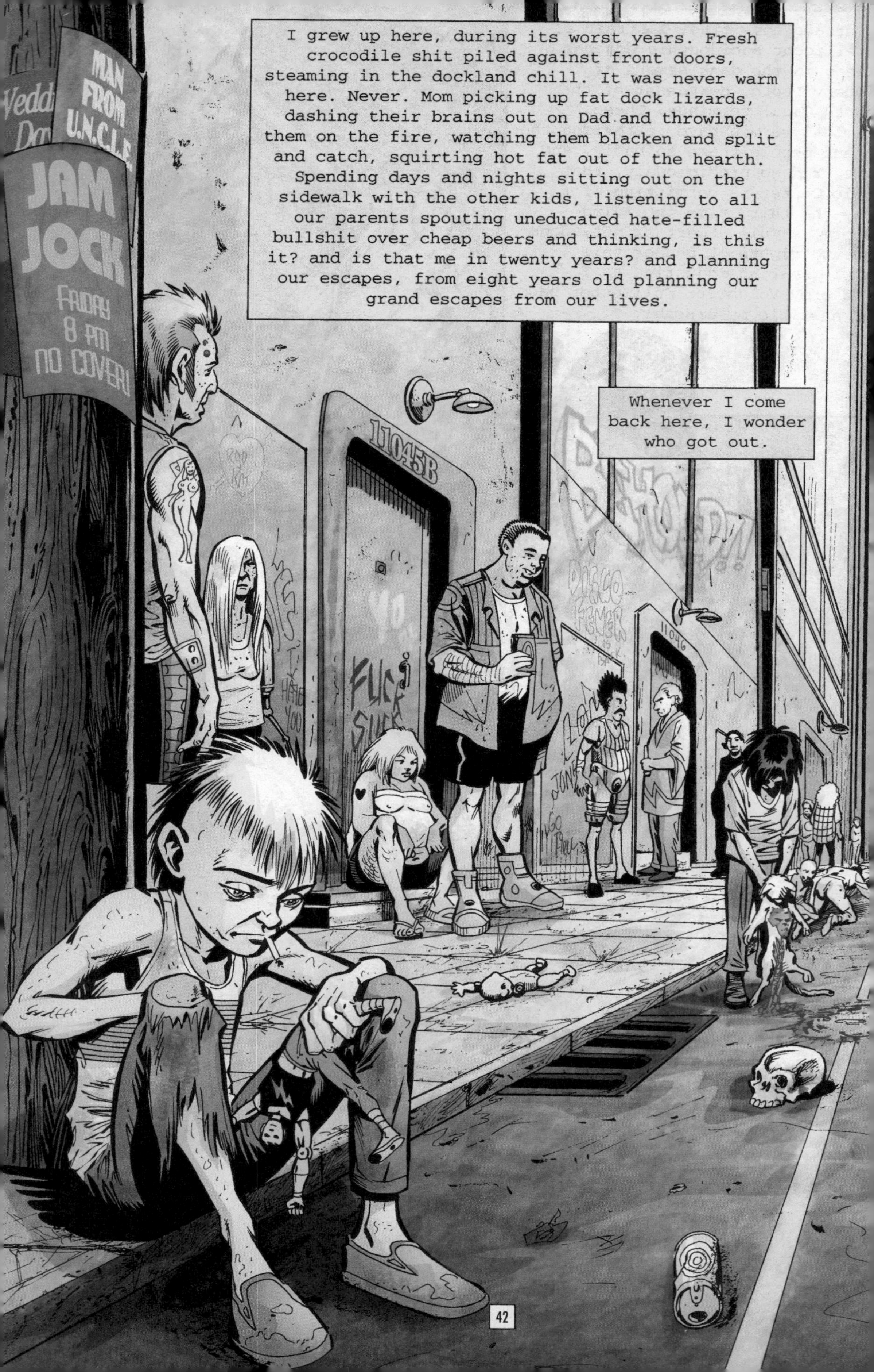
I grew up here, during its worst years. Fresh crocodile shit piled against front doors, steaming in the dockland chill. It was never warm here. Never. Mom picking up fat dock lizards, dashing their brains out on Dad and throwing them on the fire, watching them blacken and split and catch, squirting hot fat out of the hearth. Spending days and nights sitting out on the sidewalk with the other kids, listening to all our parents spouting uneducated hate-filled bullshit over cheap beers and thinking, is this it? and is that me in twenty years? and planning our escapes, from eight years old planning our grand escapes from our lives.
Whenever I come back here, I wonder who got out.
MAN FROM U.N.C.L.E.
JAM JOCK
FRIDAY
8 PM
NO COVER!
11045B
FUCK
DISCO FEVER
11046

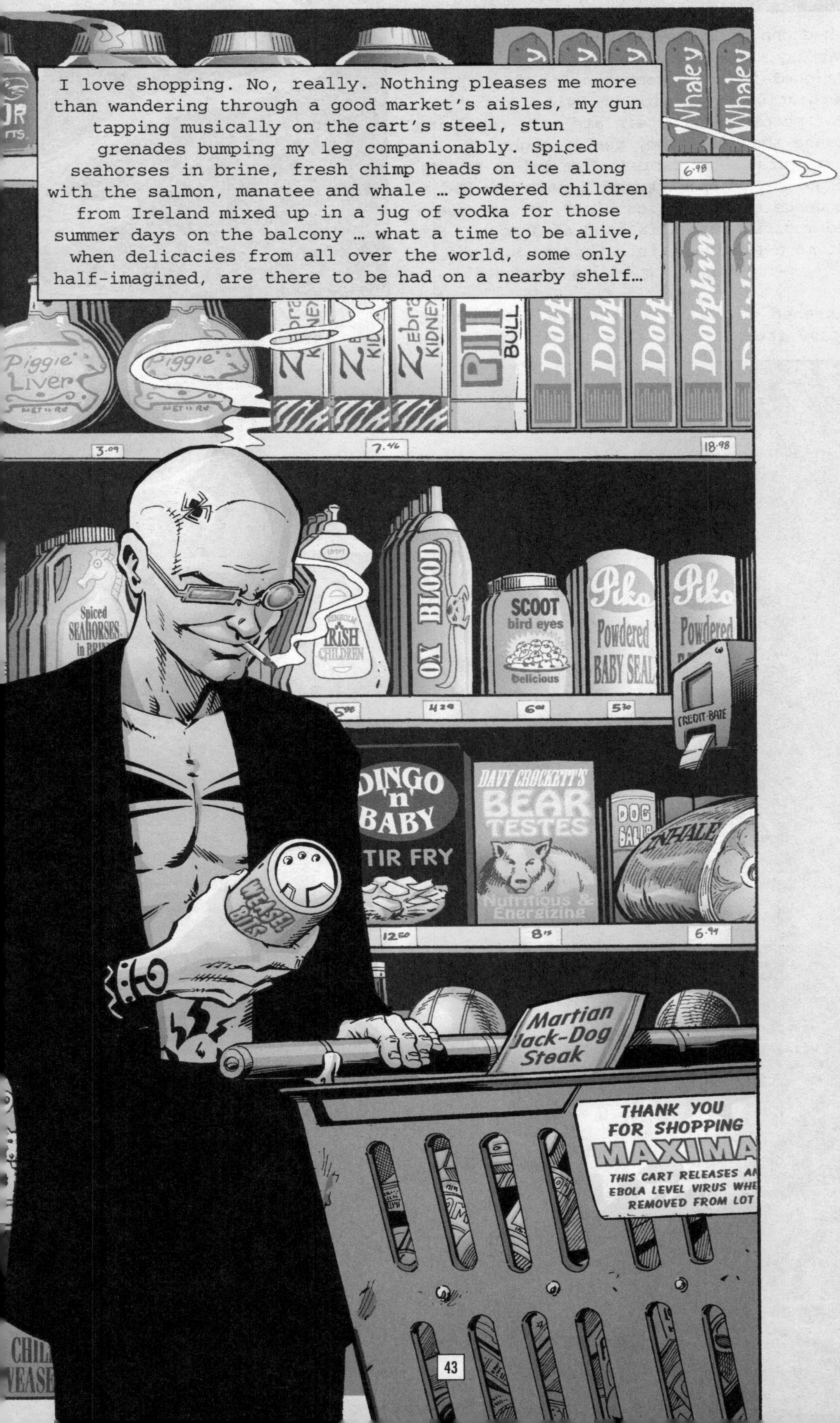
I love shopping. No, really. Nothing pleases me more than wandering through a good market's aisles, my gun tapping musically on the cart's steel, stun grenades bumping my leg companionably. Spiced seahorses in brine, fresh chimp heads on ice along with the salmon, manatee and whale … powdered children from Ireland mixed up in a jug of vodka for those summer days on the balcony … what a time to be alive, when delicacies from all over the world, some only half-imagined, are there to be had on a nearby shelf…
Whaley
6.98
Piggie Liver
Zebra Kidney
BULL
Dolphin
3.09
7.46
18.98
Spiced SEAHORSES
IRISH CHILDREN
OX BLOOD
SCOOT bird eyes Delicious
Piko Powdered BABY SEAL
CREDIT-BATE
DINGO 'n' BABY STIR FRY
DAVY CROCKETT'S BEAR TESTES Nutritious & Energizing
DOG BALLS
WHALE
12.50
6.94
WEASEL BITS
Martian Jack-Dog Steak
THANK YOU FOR SHOPPING MAXIMA
THIS CART RELEASES AN EBOLA LEVEL VIRUS WHEN REMOVED FROM LOT

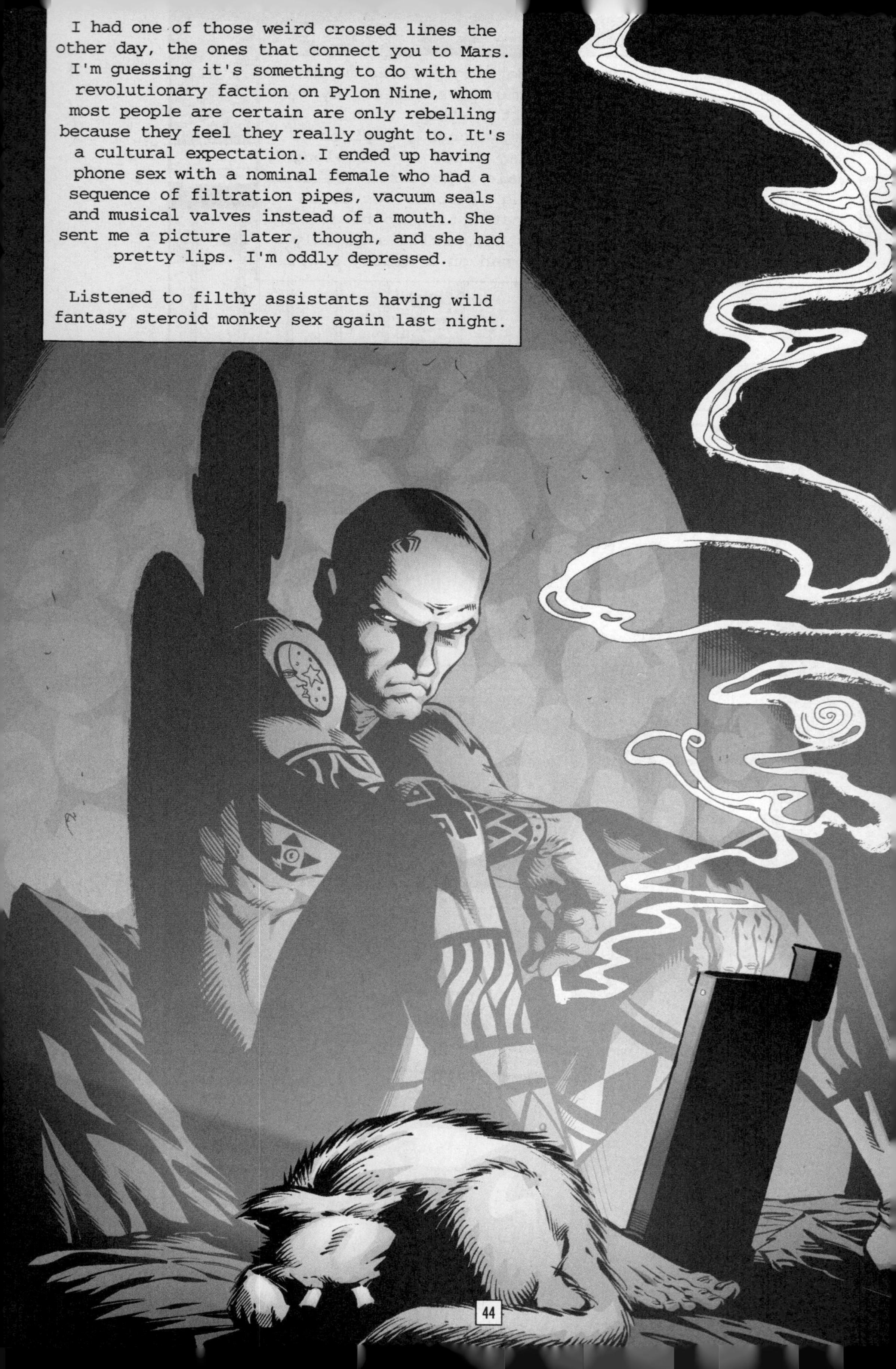
I had one of those weird crossed lines the other day, the ones that connect you to Mars. I'm guessing it's something to do with the revolutionary faction on Pylon Nine, whom most people are certain are only rebelling because they feel they really ought to. It's a cultural expectation. I ended up having phone sex with a nominal female who had a sequence of filtration pipes, vacuum seals and musical valves instead of a mouth. She sent me a picture later, though, and she had pretty lips. I'm oddly depressed.
Listened to filthy assistants having wild fantasy steroid monkey sex again last night.

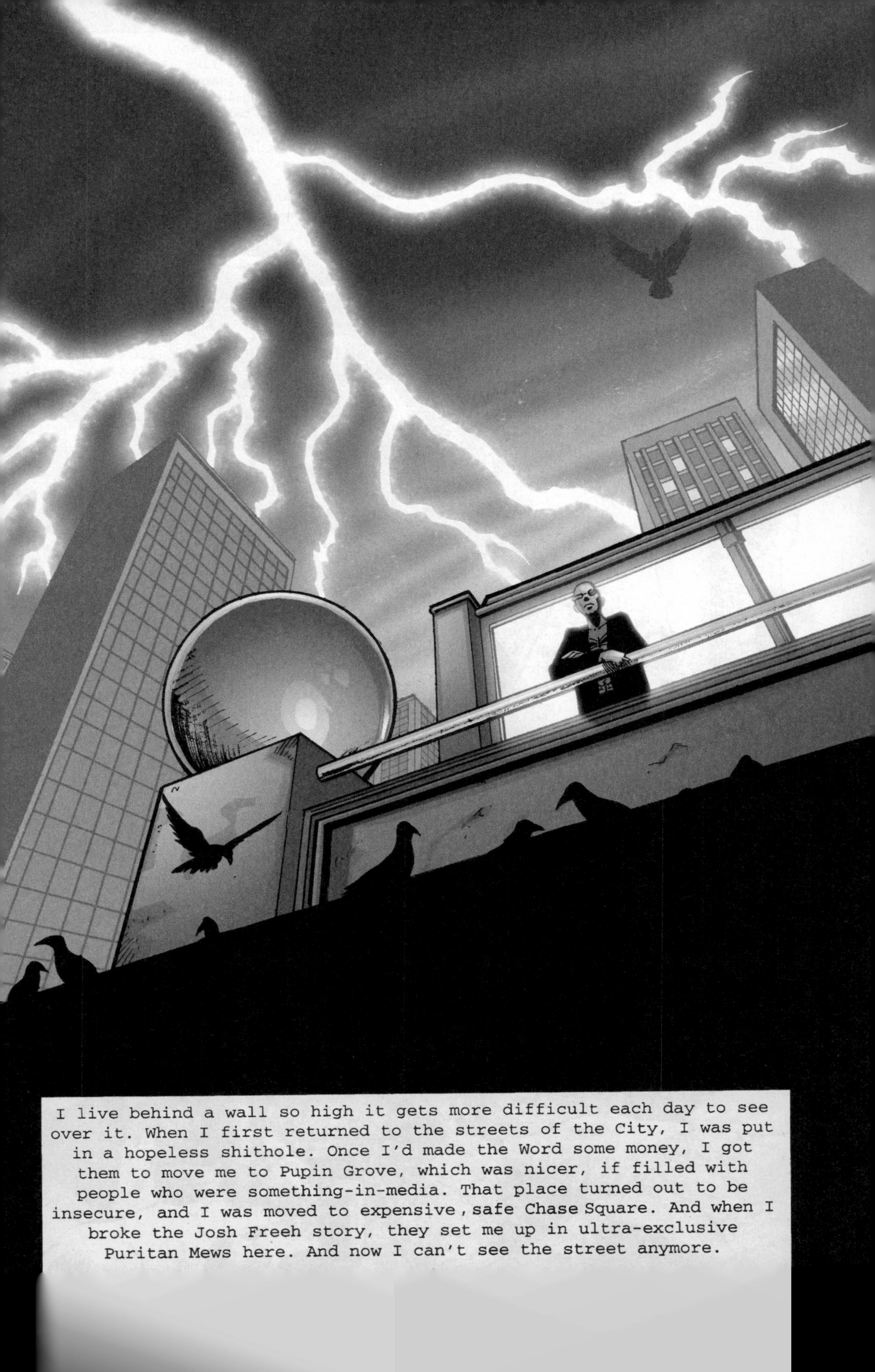
I live behind a wall so high it gets more difficult each day to see over it. When I first returned to the streets of the City, I was put in a hopeless shithole. Once I'd made the Word some money, I got them to move me to Pupin Grove, which was nicer, if filled with people who were something-in-media. That place turned out to be insecure, and I was moved to expensive, safe Chase Square. And when I broke the Josh Freeh story, they set me up in ultra-exclusive Puritan Mews here. And now I can't see the street anymore.

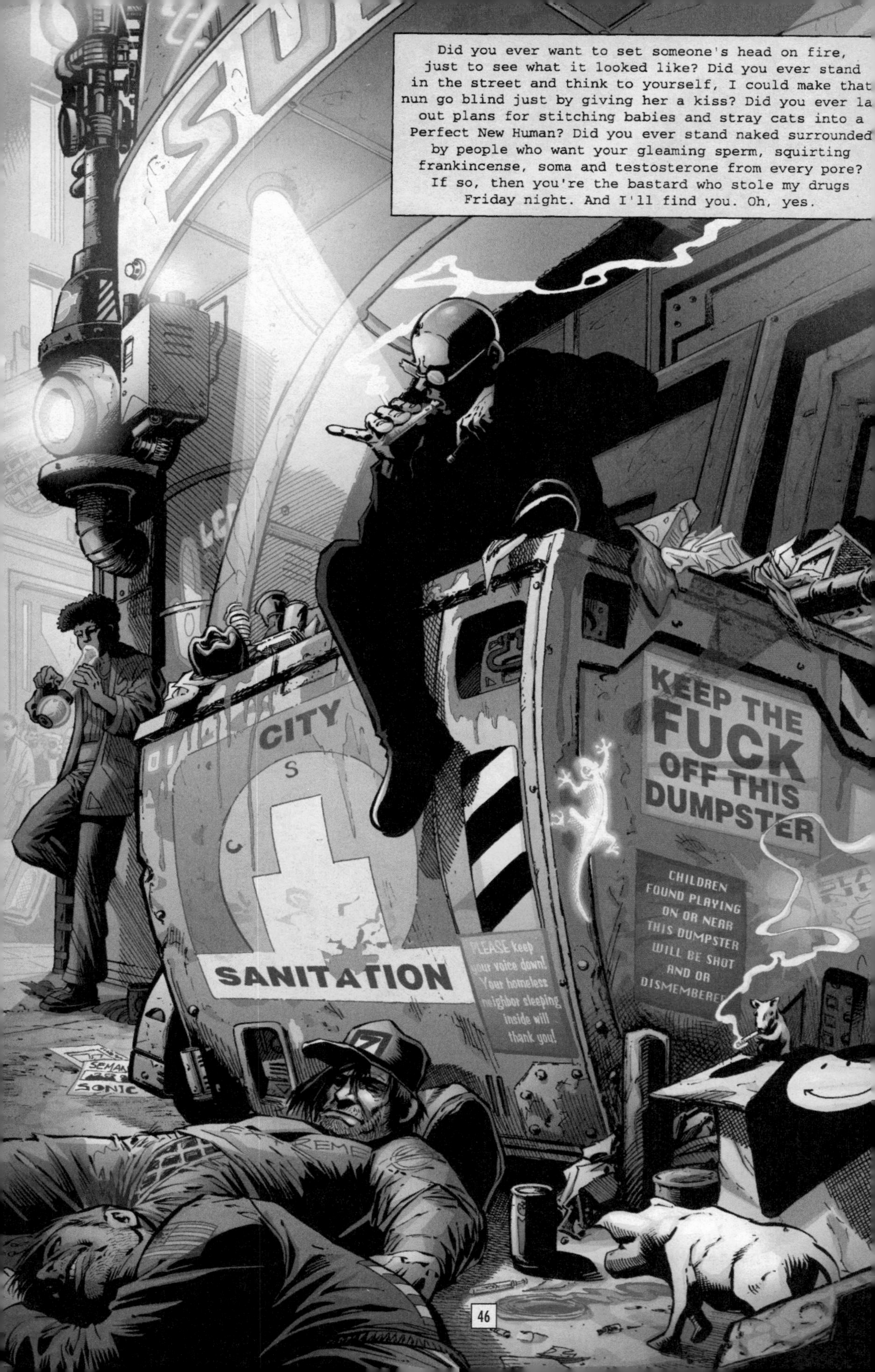

Did you ever want to set someone's head on fire, just to see what it looked like? Did you ever stand in the street and think to yourself, I could make that nun go blind just by giving her a kiss? Did you ever la out plans for stitching babies and stray cats into a Perfect New Human? Did you ever stand naked surrounded by people who want your gleaming sperm, squirting frankincense, soma and testosterone from every pore? If so, then you're the bastard who stole my drugs Friday night. And I'll find you. Oh, yes.
CITY
SANITATION
KEEP THE FUCK OFF THIS DUMPSTER
CHILDREN FOUND PLAYING ON OR NEAR THIS DUMPSTER WILL BE SHOT AND OR DISMEMBERE
PLEASE keep your voice down! Your homeless neighbor sleeping inside will thank you!

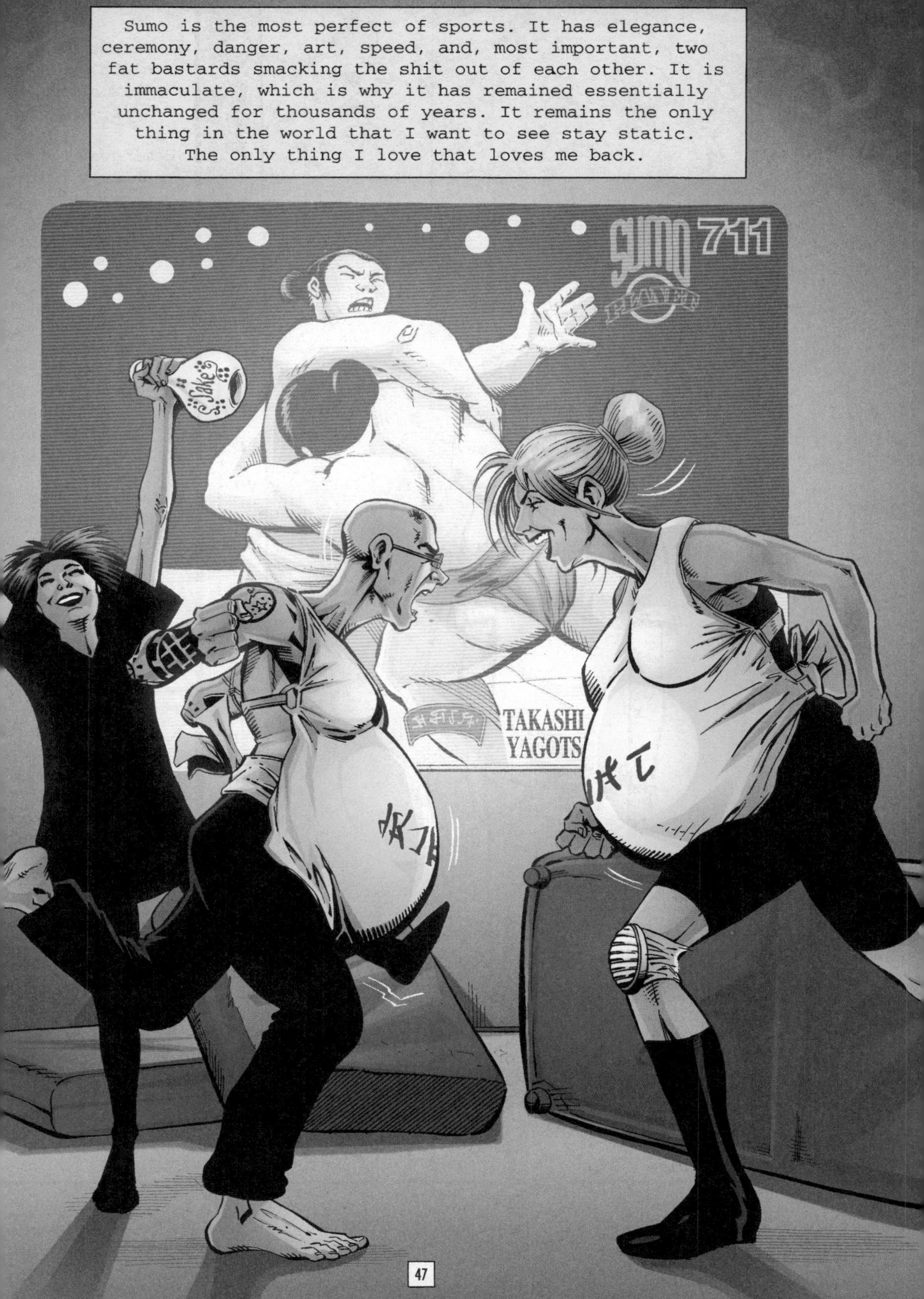
Sumo is the most perfect of sports. It has elegance, ceremony, danger, art, speed, and, most important, two fat bastards smacking the shit out of each other. It is immaculate, which is why it has remained essentially unchanged for thousands of years. It remains the only thing in the world that I want to see stay static. The only thing I love that loves me back.
SUMO 711
Sake
TAKASHI YAGOTS

He met God in
night, walking
his hotel in
rain, like he
written
Hemingway, stepp
slowly throug
place where nur
die if you kiss t
and syphilis ste
your friends
minute you l
away. God stop
and talked to
for a while, qu
solemn words in
heart of the da
And then
Essential Str
Station God sat d
and wept. He —
kid who told me t
— suffers from
naiveté trait t
parents thought w
cute twenty yea
ago. He has a p
civilization neu
connectivity. Wh
we have insti
that, no,
shouldn't cross
road,
hallucinates
telling him not
cross the road. I
heard that naive
trait is getti
trendy again.
you're thinki
about it, th
about the
weeping uncontro
lably as God cri
for him not
cross t
stree

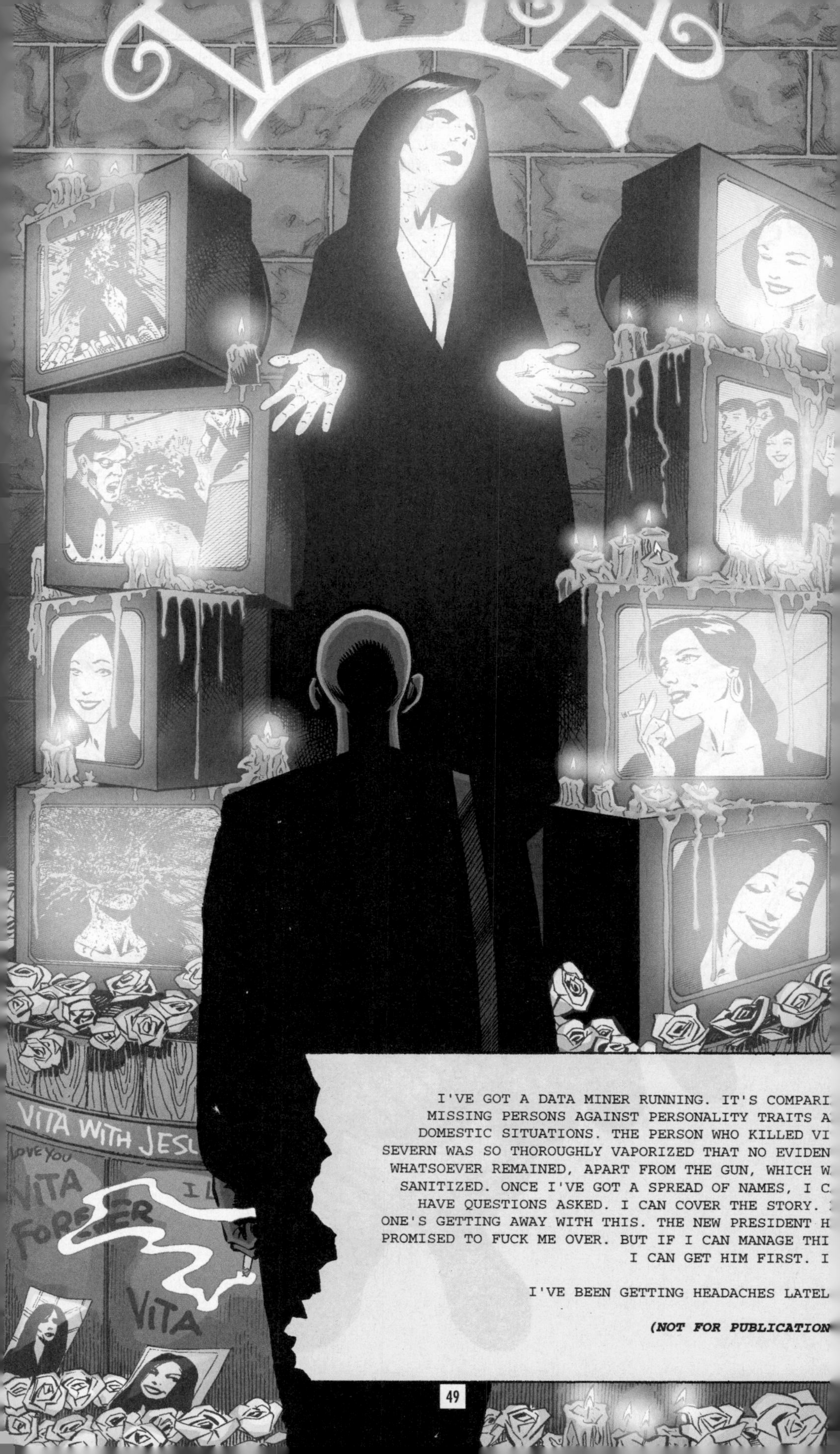
VITA WITH JESU
LOVE YOU
VITA FOREVER
VITA
I'VE GOT A DATA MINER RUNNING. IT'S COMPARI
MISSING PERSONS AGAINST PERSONALITY TRAITS A
DOMESTIC SITUATIONS. THE PERSON WHO KILLED VI
SEVERN WAS SO THOROUGHLY VAPORIZED THAT NO EVIDEN
WHATSOEVER REMAINED, APART FROM THE GUN, WHICH W
SANITIZED. ONCE I'VE GOT A SPREAD OF NAMES, I C
HAVE QUESTIONS ASKED. I CAN COVER THE STORY.
ONE'S GETTING AWAY WITH THIS. THE NEW PRESIDENT H
PROMISED TO FUCK ME OVER. BUT IF I CAN MANAGE THI
I CAN GET HIM FIRST. I
I'VE BEEN GETTING HEADACHES LATEL
(NOT FOR PUBLICATION

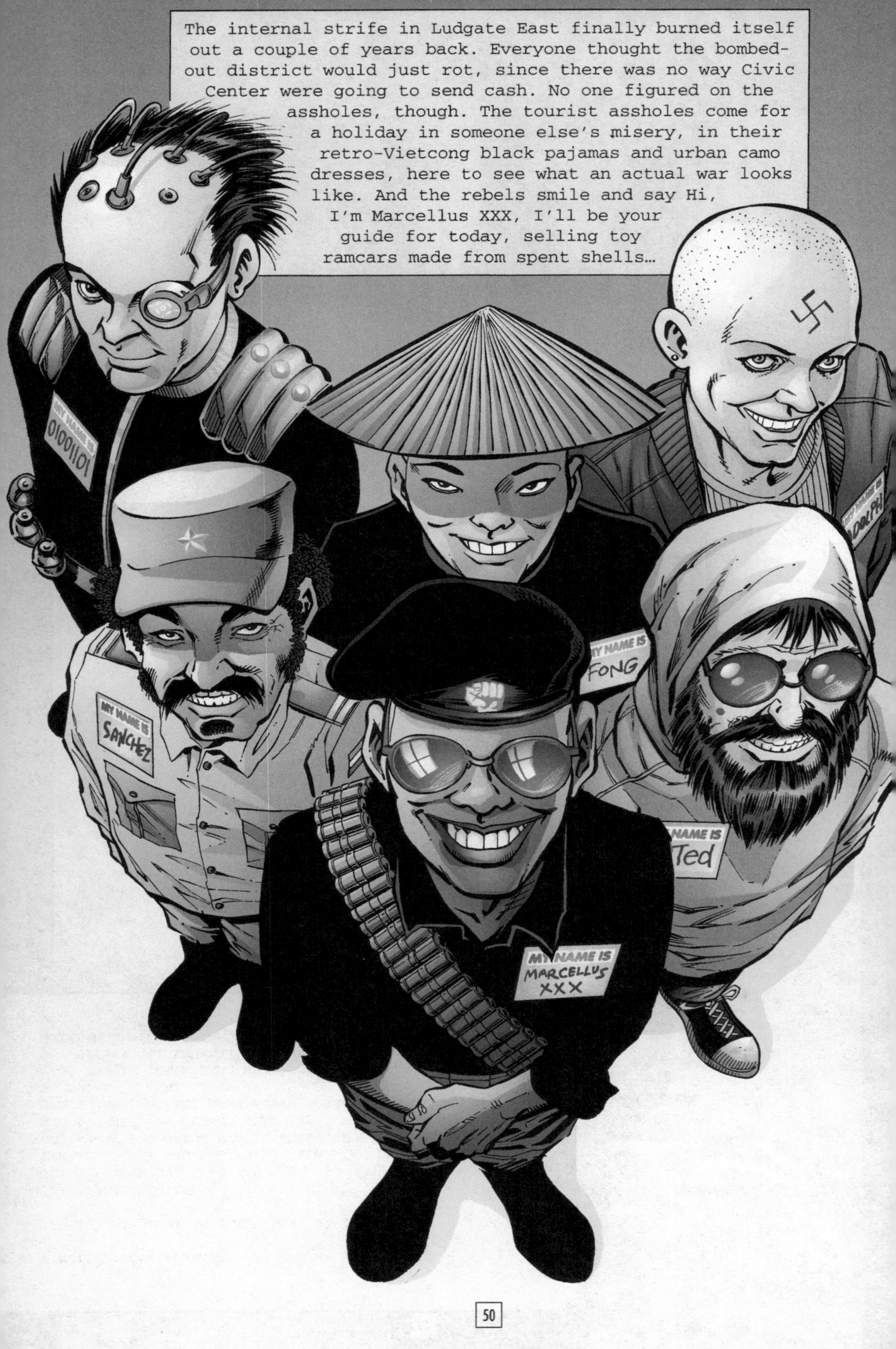
The internal strife in Ludgate East finally burned itself out a couple of years back. Everyone thought the bombed-out district would just rot, since there was no way Civic Center were going to send cash. No one figured on the assholes, though. The tourist assholes come for a holiday in someone else's misery, in their retro-Vietcong black pajamas and urban camo dresses, here to see what an actual war looks like. And the rebels smile and say Hi, I'm Marcellus XXX, I'll be your guide for today, selling toy ramcars made from spent shells…
01001101
MY NAME IS FONG
MY NAME IS SANCHEZ
NAME IS Ted
MY NAME IS MARCELLUS XXX

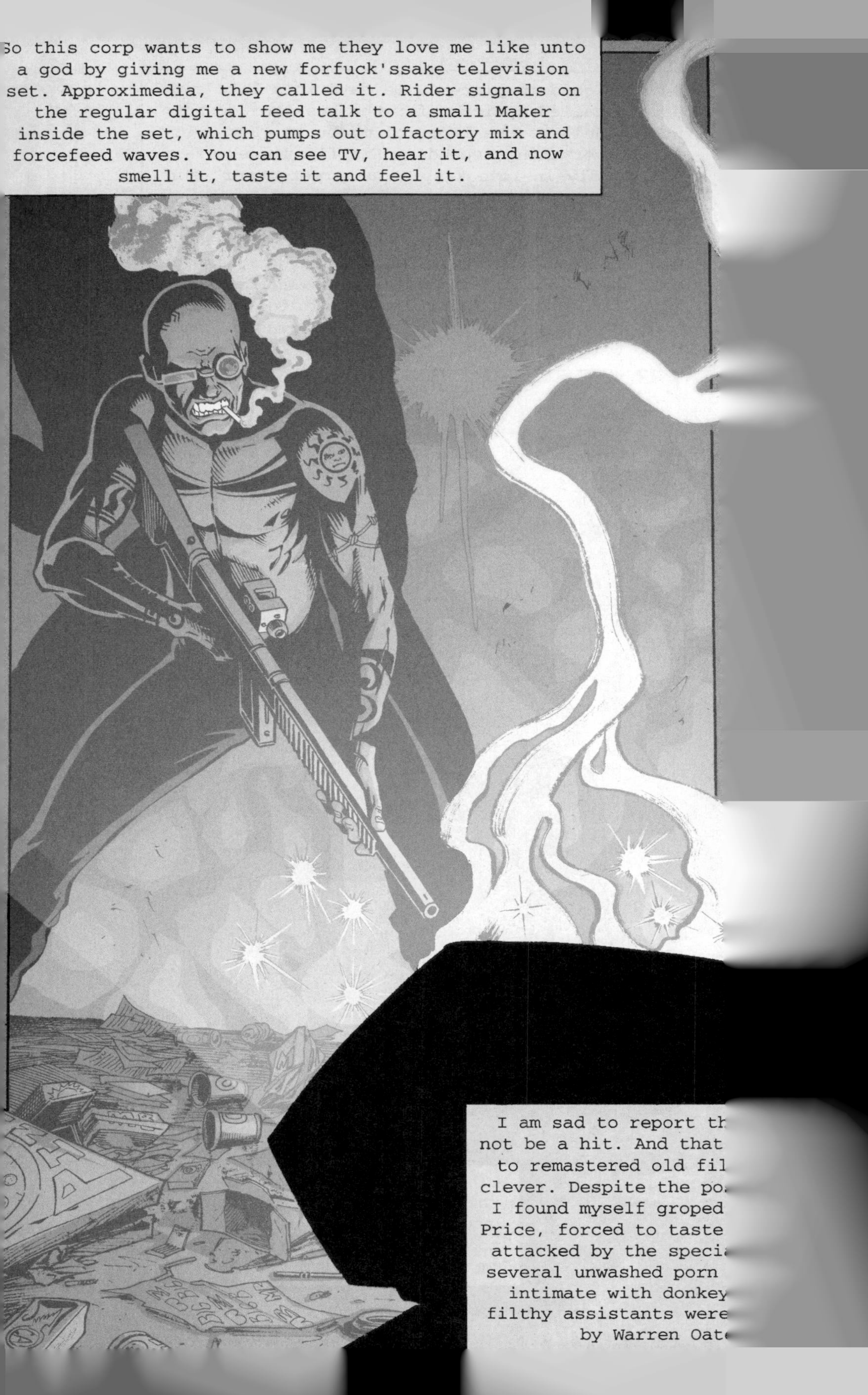
So this corp wants to show me they love me like unto a god by giving me a new forfuck'ssake television set. Approximedia, they called it. Rider signals on the regular digital feed talk to a small Maker inside the set, which pumps out olfactory mix and forcefeed waves. You can see TV, hear it, and now smell it, taste it and feel it.
I am sad to report th
not be a hit. And that
to remastered old fil
clever. Despite the po
I found myself groped
Price, forced to taste
attacked by the speci
several unwashed porn
intimate with donkey
filthy assistants were
by Warren Oat

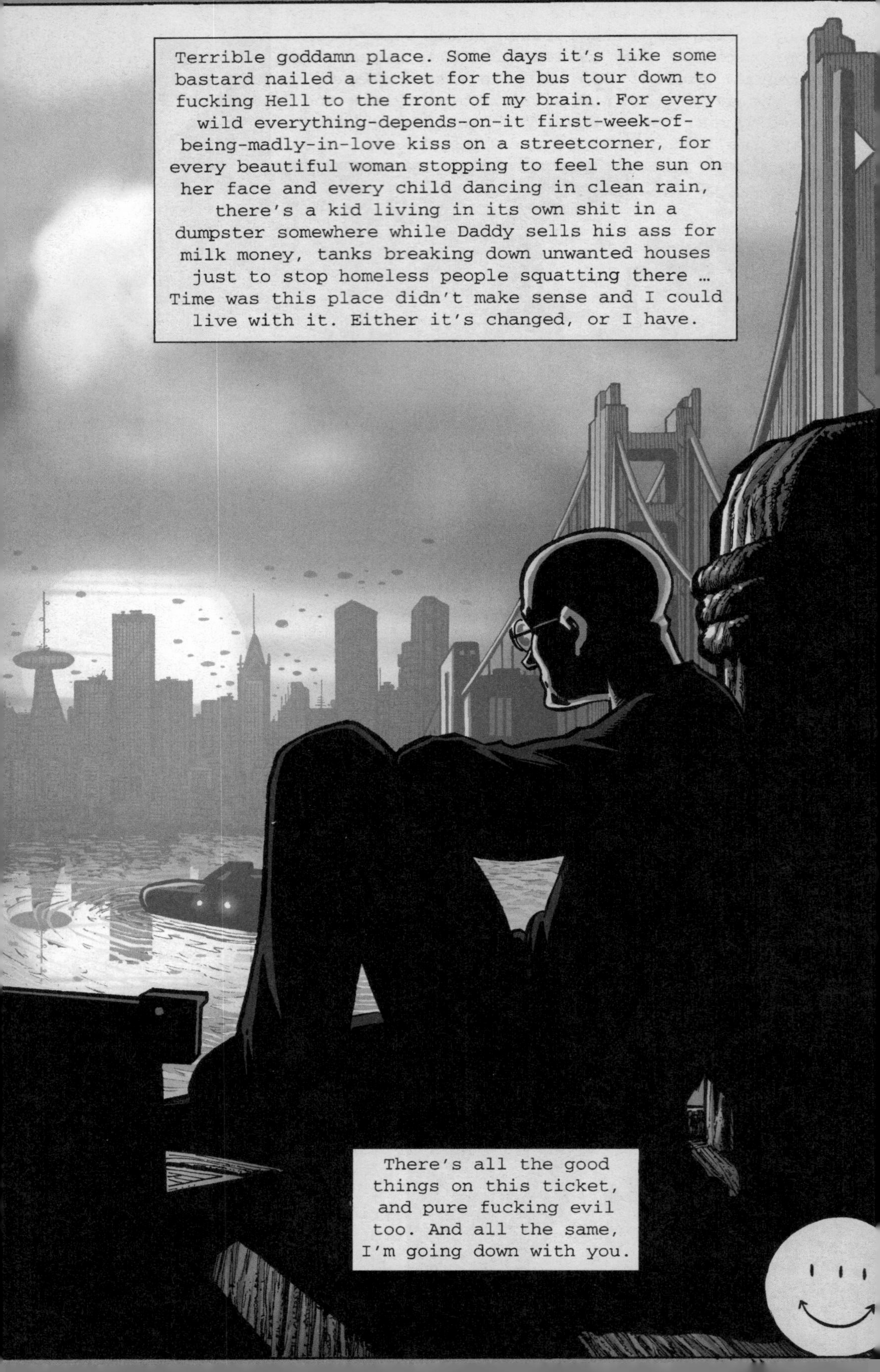
Terrible goddamn place. Some days it's like some bastard nailed a ticket for the bus tour down to fucking Hell to the front of my brain. For every wild everything-depends-on-it first-week-of-being-madly-in-love kiss on a streetcorner, for every beautiful woman stopping to feel the sun on her face and every child dancing in clean rain, there's a kid living in its own shit in a dumpster somewhere while Daddy sells his ass for milk money, tanks breaking down unwanted houses just to stop homeless people squatting there … Time was this place didn't make sense and I could live with it. Either it's changed, or I have.
There's all the good things on this ticket, and pure fucking evil too. And all the same, I'm going down with you.

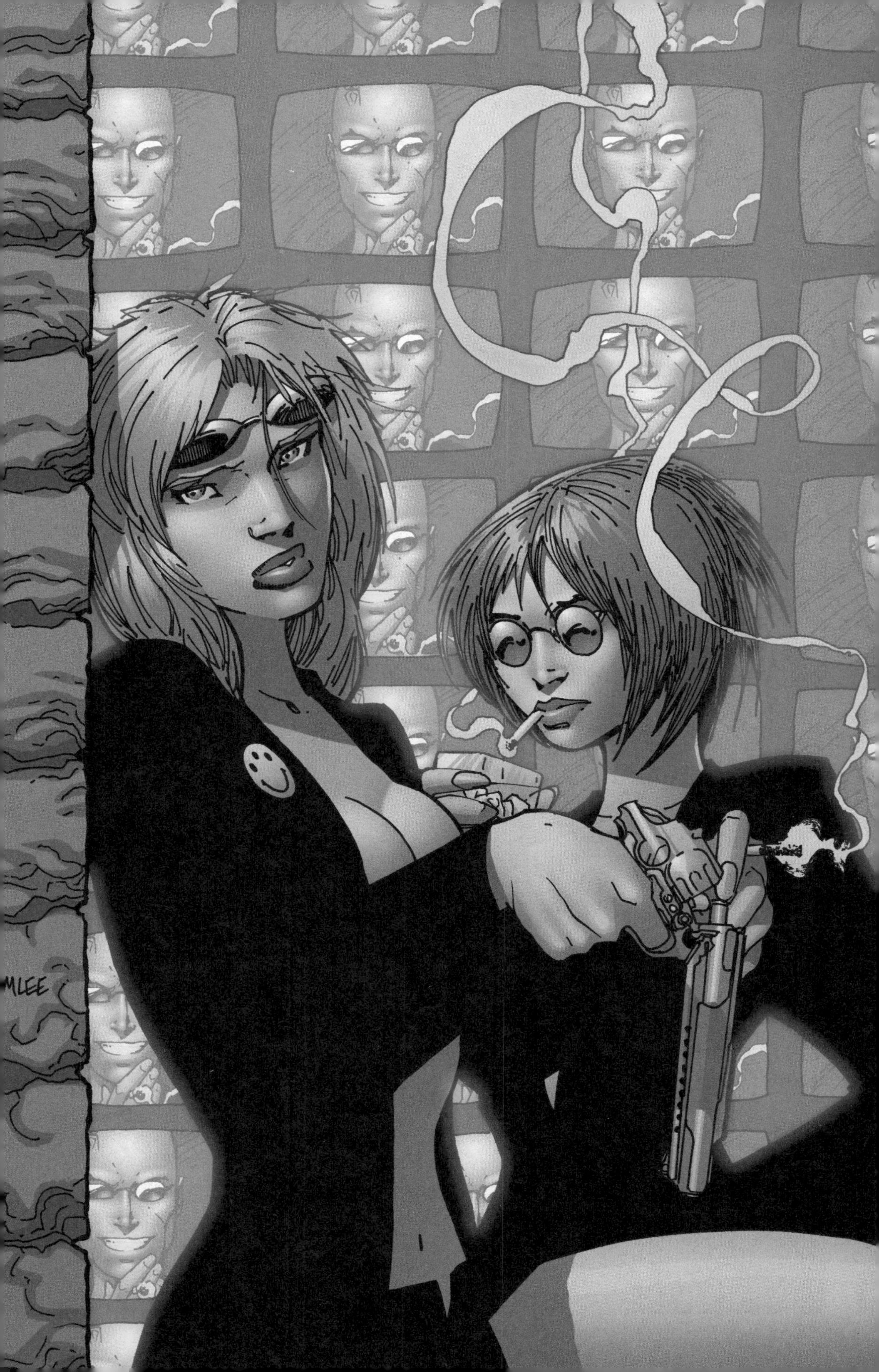
MLEE

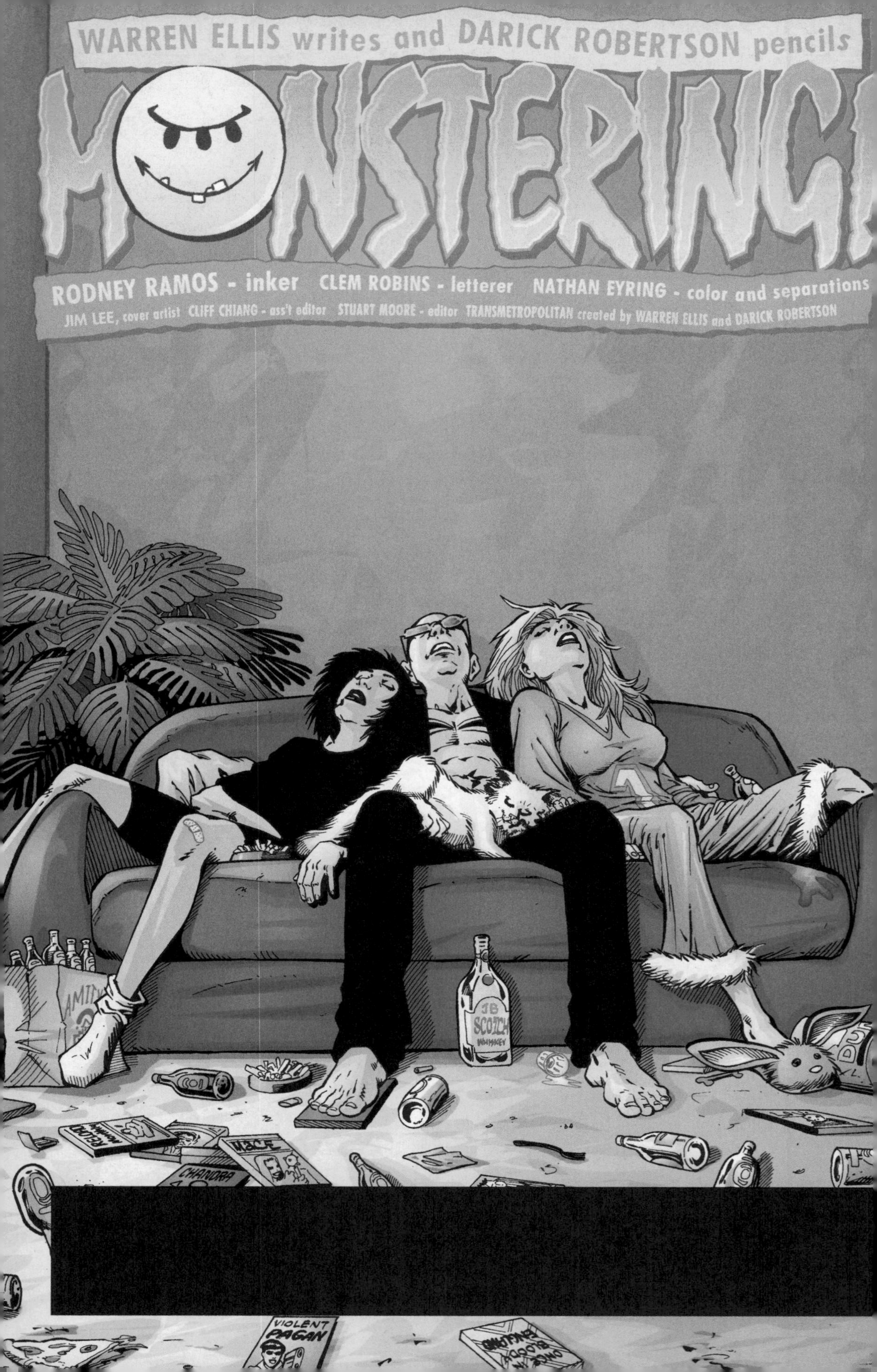
WARREN ELLIS writes and DARICK ROBERTSON pencils
MONSTERING
RODNEY RAMOS - inker CLEM ROBINS - letterer NATHAN EYRING - color and separations
JIM LEE, cover artist CLIFF CHIANG - ass't editor STUART MOORE - editor TRANSMETROPOLITAN created by WARREN ELLIS and DARICK ROBERTSON
JB SCOTCH WHISKEY
CHANDRA
VIOLENT PAGAN

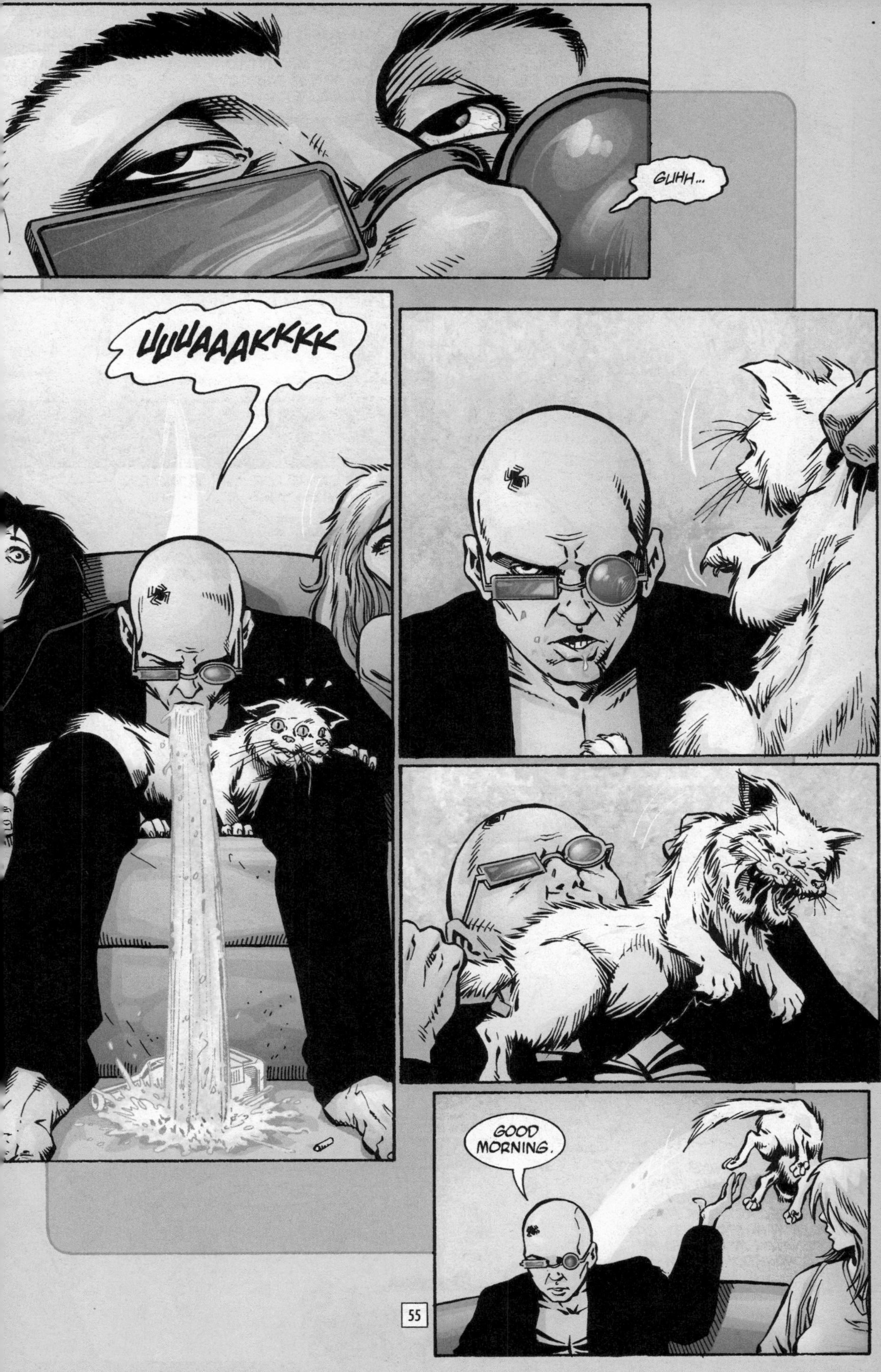
GUHH...
UUUAAAKKKK
GOOD MORNING.

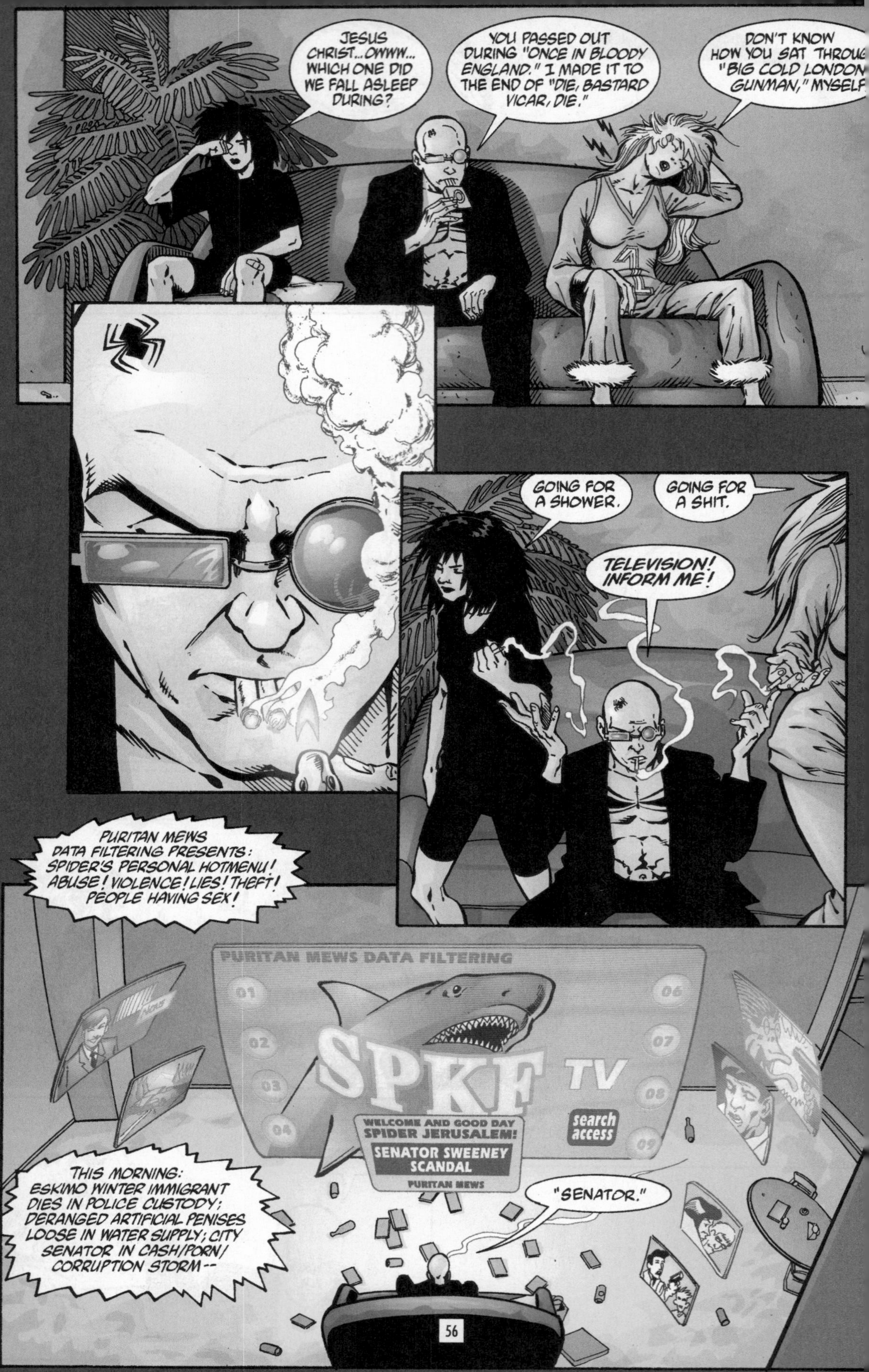
JESUS CHRIST...OWWW... WHICH ONE DID WE FALL ASLEEP DURING?
YOU PASSED OUT DURING "ONCE IN BLOODY ENGLAND." I MADE IT TO THE END OF "DIE, BASTARD VICAR, DIE."
DON'T KNOW HOW YOU SAT THROUG "BIG COLD LONDON GUNMAN," MYSELF.
GOING FOR A SHOWER.
GOING FOR A SHIT.
TELEVISION! INFORM ME!
PURITAN MEWS DATA FILTERING PRESENTS: SPIDER'S PERSONAL HOTMENU! ABUSE! VIOLENCE! LIES! THEFT! PEOPLE HAVING SEX!
PURITAN MEWS DATA FILTERING
SPKF TV
WELCOME AND GOOD DAY SPIDER JERUSALEM!
SENATOR SWEENEY SCANDAL
PURITAN MEWS
search access
THIS MORNING: ESKIMO WINTER IMMIGRANT DIES IN POLICE CUSTODY; DERANGED ARTIFICIAL PENISES LOOSE IN WATER SUPPLY; CITY SENATOR IN CASH/PORN/ CORRUPTION STORM --
"SENATOR."

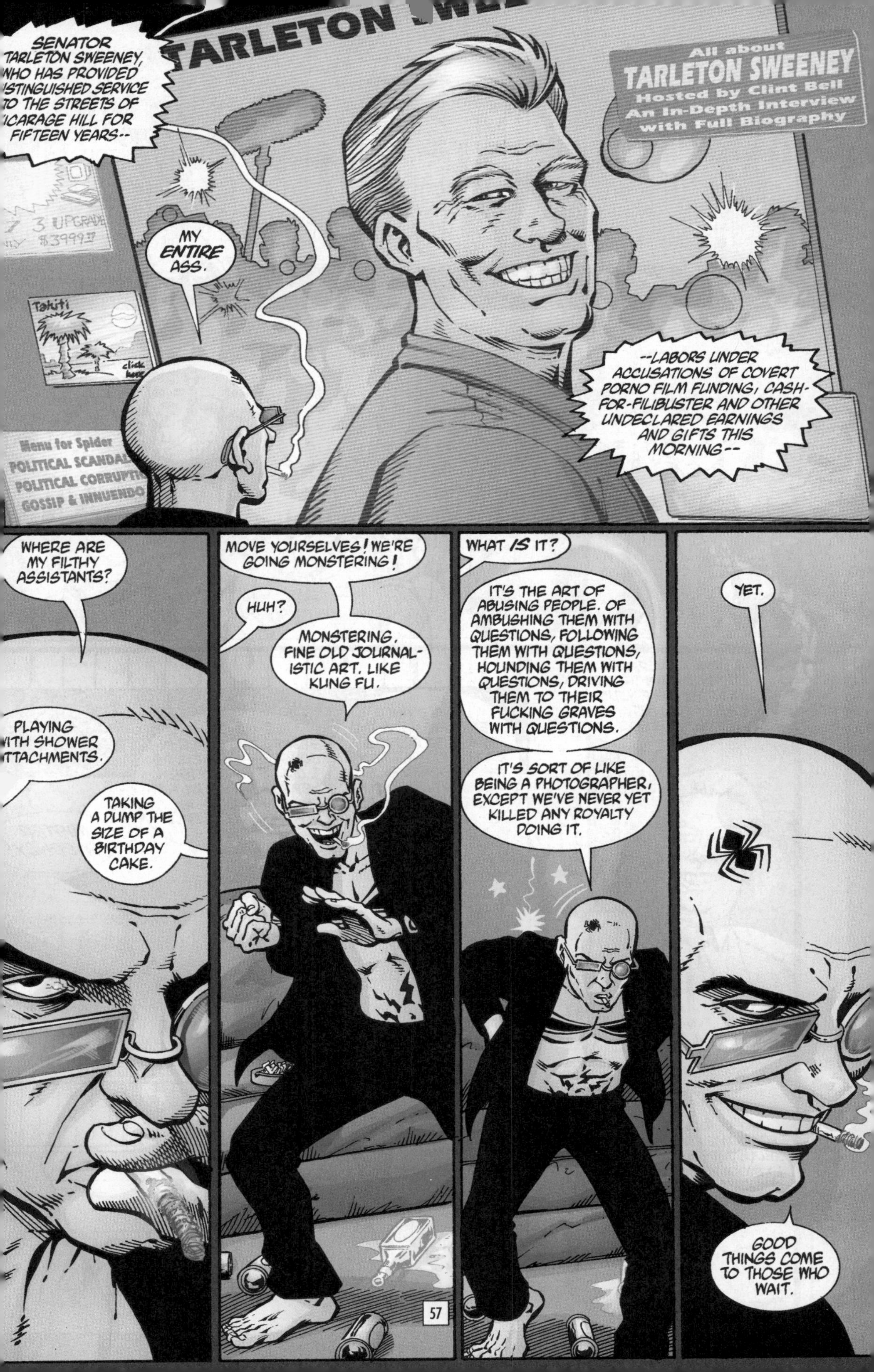

TARLETON SWE
All about
TARLETON SWEENEY
Hosted by Clint Bell
An In-Depth Interview
with Full Biography
SENATOR TARLETON SWEENEY, WHO HAS PROVIDED DISTINGUISHED SERVICE TO THE STREETS OF VICARAGE HILL FOR FIFTEEN YEARS--
MY ENTIRE ASS.
--LABORS UNDER ACCUSATIONS OF COVERT PORNO FILM FUNDING, CASH-FOR-FILIBUSTER AND OTHER UNDECLARED EARNINGS AND GIFTS THIS MORNING--
3 UPGRADE
$3999
Tahiti
click here
Menu for Spider
POLITICAL SCANDAL
POLITICAL CORRUPTION
GOSSIP & INNUENDO
WHERE ARE MY FILTHY ASSISTANTS?
PLAYING WITH SHOWER ATTACHMENTS.
TAKING A DUMP THE SIZE OF A BIRTHDAY CAKE.
MOVE YOURSELVES! WE'RE GOING MONSTERING!
HUH?
MONSTERING. FINE OLD JOURNALISTIC ART. LIKE KUNG FU.
WHAT IS IT?
IT'S THE ART OF ABUSING PEOPLE. OF AMBUSHING THEM WITH QUESTIONS, FOLLOWING THEM WITH QUESTIONS, HOUNDING THEM WITH QUESTIONS, DRIVING THEM TO THEIR FUCKING GRAVES WITH QUESTIONS.
IT'S SORT OF LIKE BEING A PHOTOGRAPHER, EXCEPT WE'VE NEVER YET KILLED ANY ROYALTY DOING IT.
YET.
GOOD THINGS COME TO THOSE WHO WAIT.

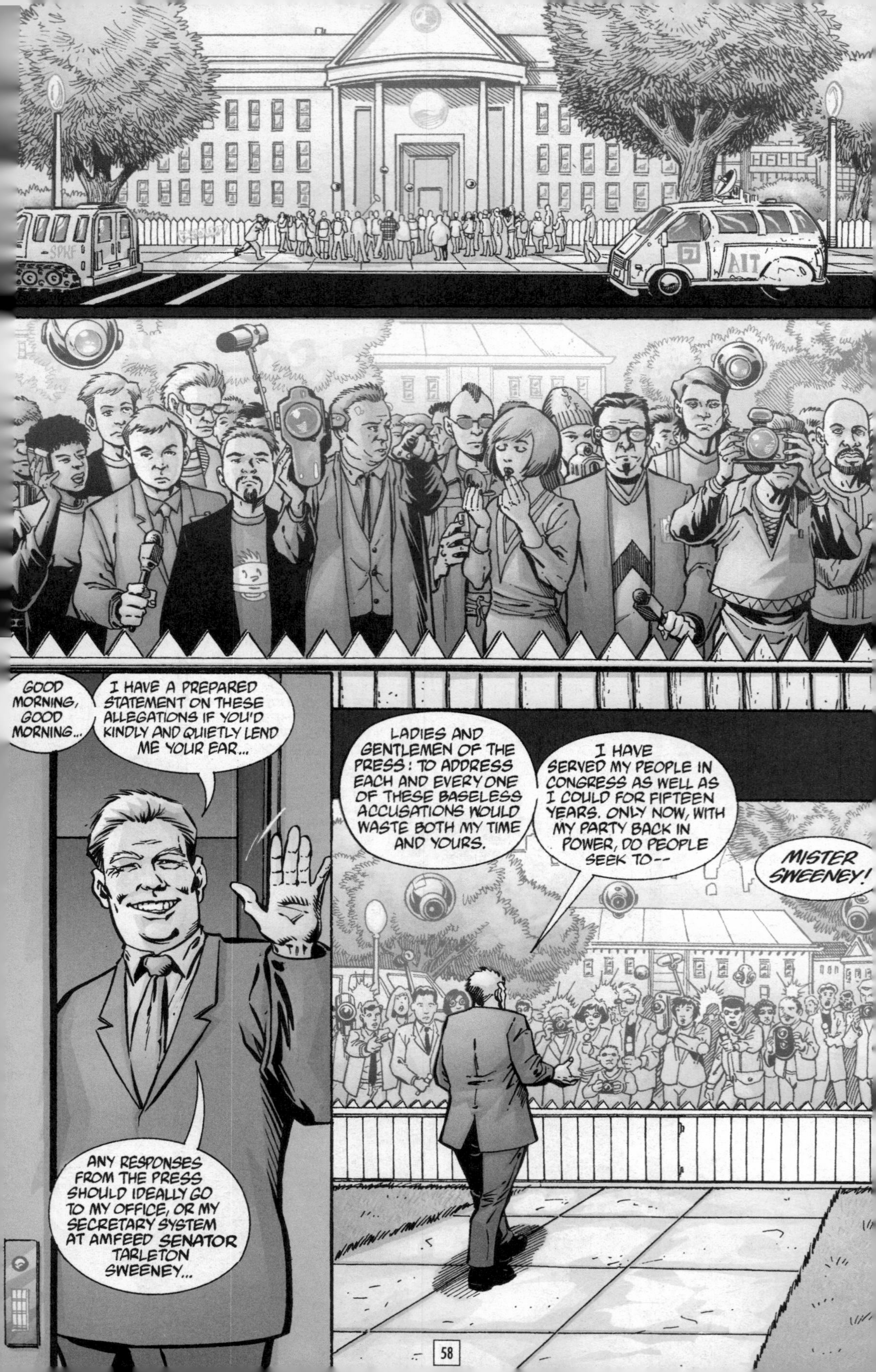

SPHF
AIT
GOOD MORNING, GOOD MORNING...
I HAVE A PREPARED STATEMENT ON THESE ALLEGATIONS IF YOU'D KINDLY AND QUIETLY LEND ME YOUR EAR...
ANY RESPONSES FROM THE PRESS SHOULD IDEALLY GO TO MY OFFICE, OR MY SECRETARY SYSTEM AT AMFEED SENATOR TARLETON SWEENEY...
LADIES AND GENTLEMEN OF THE PRESS: TO ADDRESS EACH AND EVERY ONE OF THESE BASELESS ACCUSATIONS WOULD WASTE BOTH MY TIME AND YOURS.
I HAVE SERVED MY PEOPLE IN CONGRESS AS WELL AS I COULD FOR FIFTEEN YEARS. ONLY NOW, WITH MY PARTY BACK IN POWER, DO PEOPLE SEEK TO--
MISTER SWEENEY!

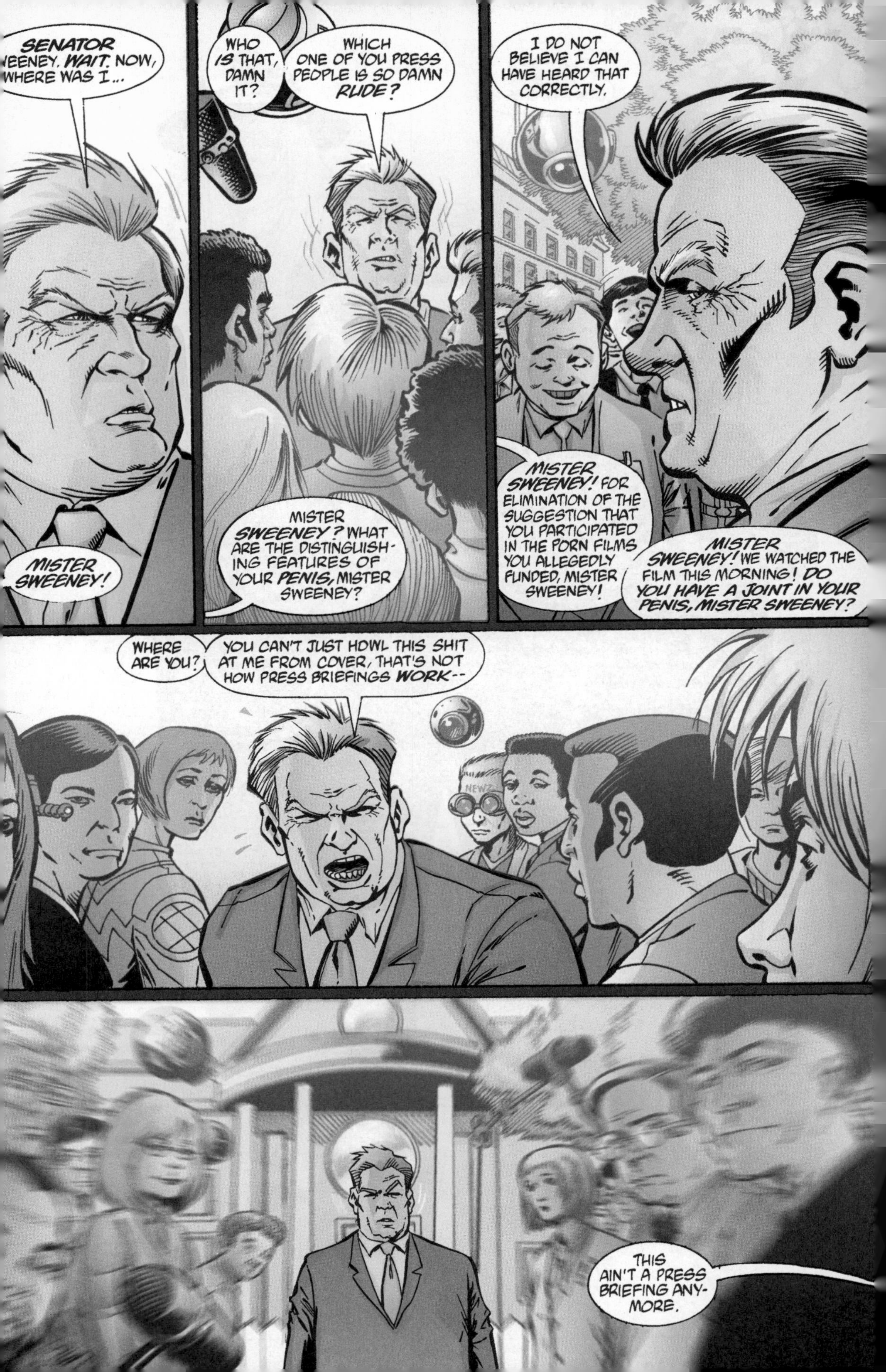
SENATOR SWEENEY. WAIT. NOW, WHERE WAS I...
MISTER SWEENEY!
WHO IS THAT, DAMN IT?
WHICH ONE OF YOU PRESS PEOPLE IS SO DAMN RUDE?
MISTER SWEENEY? WHAT ARE THE DISTINGUISHING FEATURES OF YOUR PENIS, MISTER SWEENEY?
I DO NOT BELIEVE I CAN HAVE HEARD THAT CORRECTLY.
MISTER SWEENEY! FOR ELIMINATION OF THE SUGGESTION THAT YOU PARTICIPATED IN THE PORN FILMS YOU ALLEGEDLY FUNDED, MISTER SWEENEY!
MISTER SWEENEY! WE WATCHED THE FILM THIS MORNING! DO YOU HAVE A JOINT IN YOUR PENIS, MISTER SWEENEY?
WHERE ARE YOU?
YOU CAN'T JUST HOWL THIS SHIT AT ME FROM COVER, THAT'S NOT HOW PRESS BRIEFINGS WORK--
NEWZ
THIS AIN'T A PRESS BRIEFING ANY-MORE.

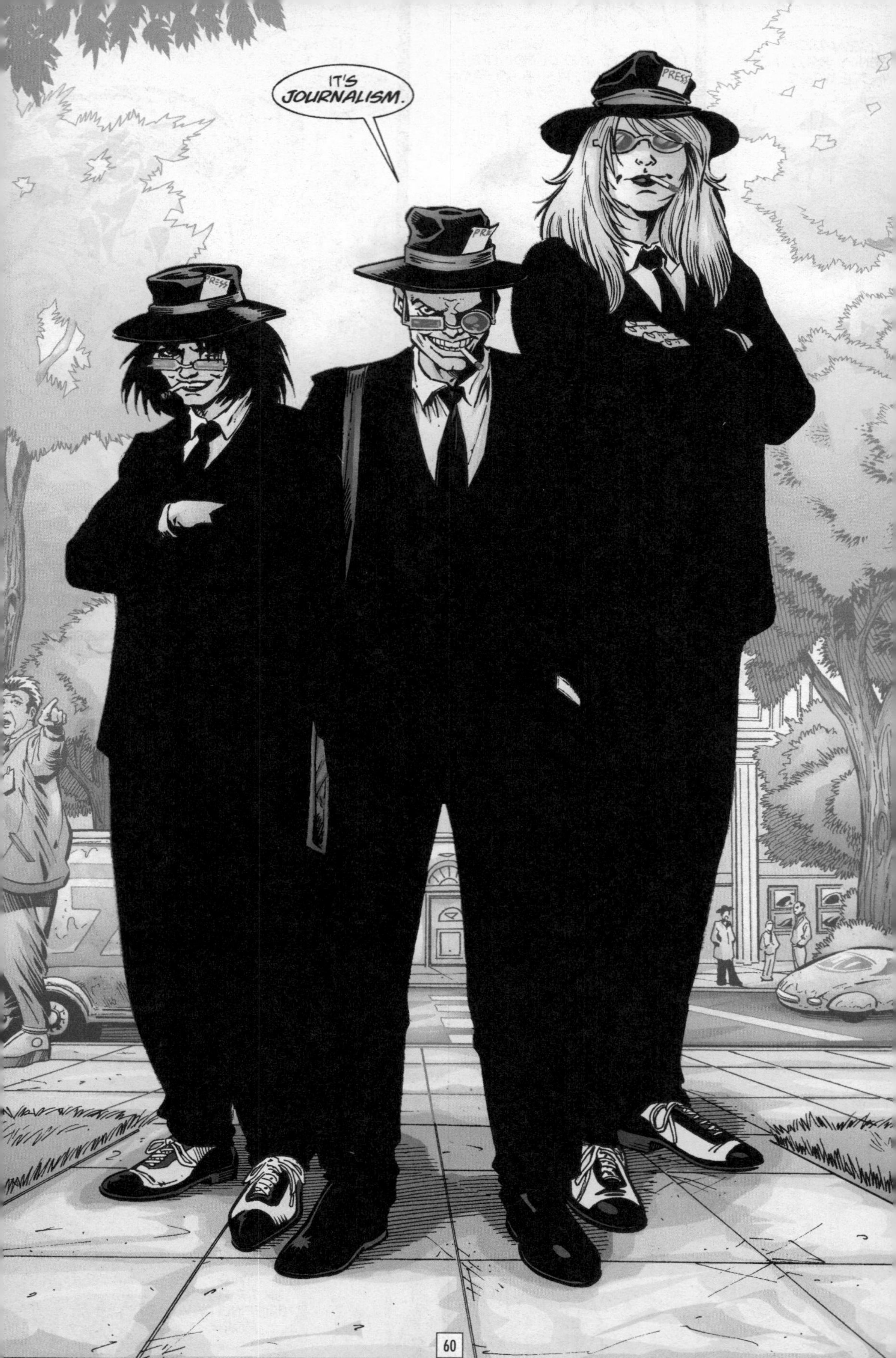
IT'S JOURNALISM.
PRESS
PRESS
PRESS

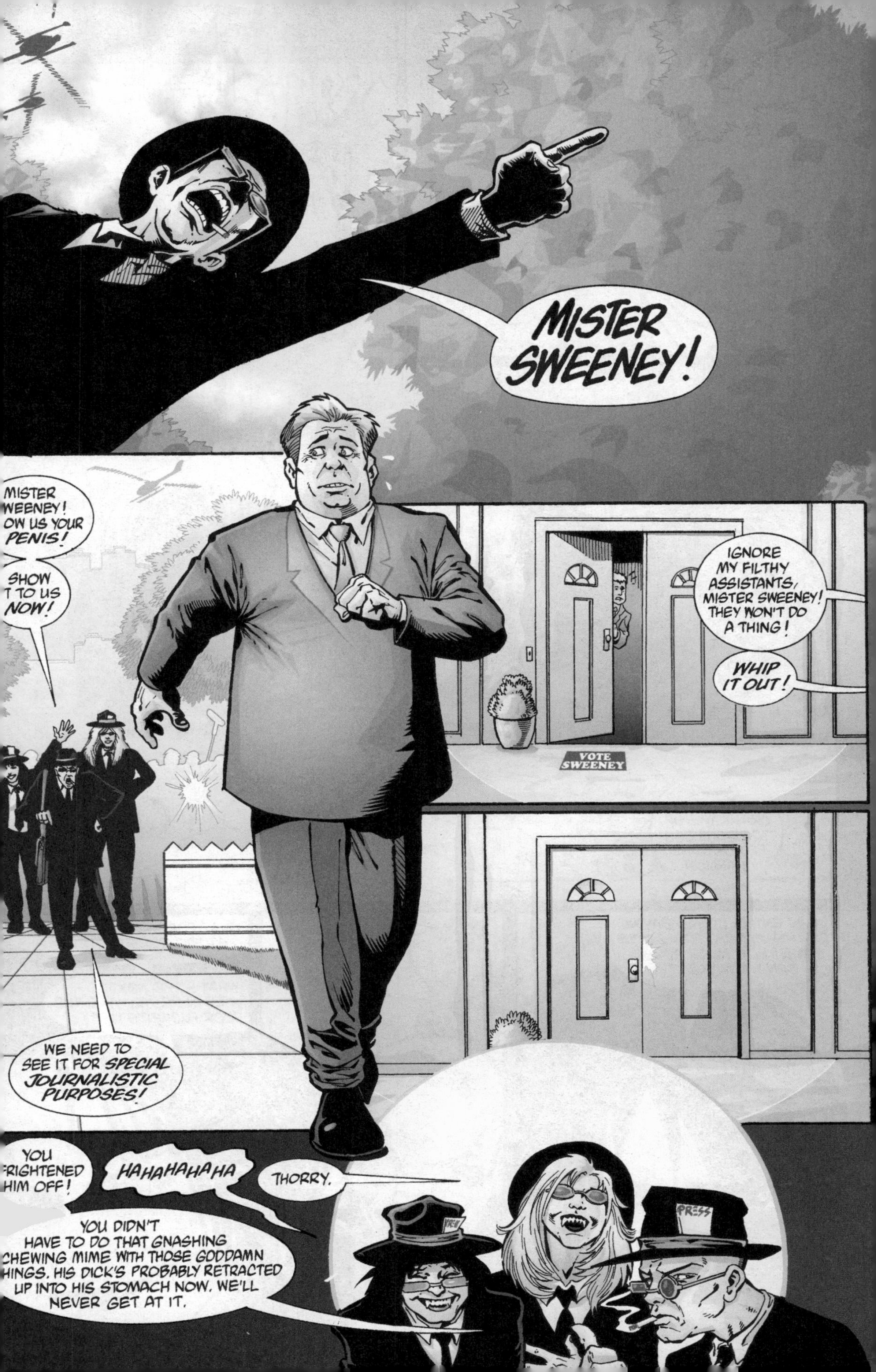

MISTER SWEENEY!
MISTER WEENEY! OW US YOUR PENIS!
SHOW T TO US NOW!
IGNORE MY FILTHY ASSISTANTS, MISTER SWEENEY! THEY WON'T DO A THING!
WHIP IT OUT!
VOTE SWEENEY
WE NEED TO SEE IT FOR SPECIAL JOURNALISTIC PURPOSES!
YOU FRIGHTENED HIM OFF!
HAHAHAHAHAHA
THORRY.
YOU DIDN'T HAVE TO DO THAT GNASHING CHEWING MIME WITH THOSE GODDAMN HINGS. HIS DICK'S PROBABLY RETRACTED UP INTO HIS STOMACH NOW. WE'LL NEVER GET AT IT.
PRESS

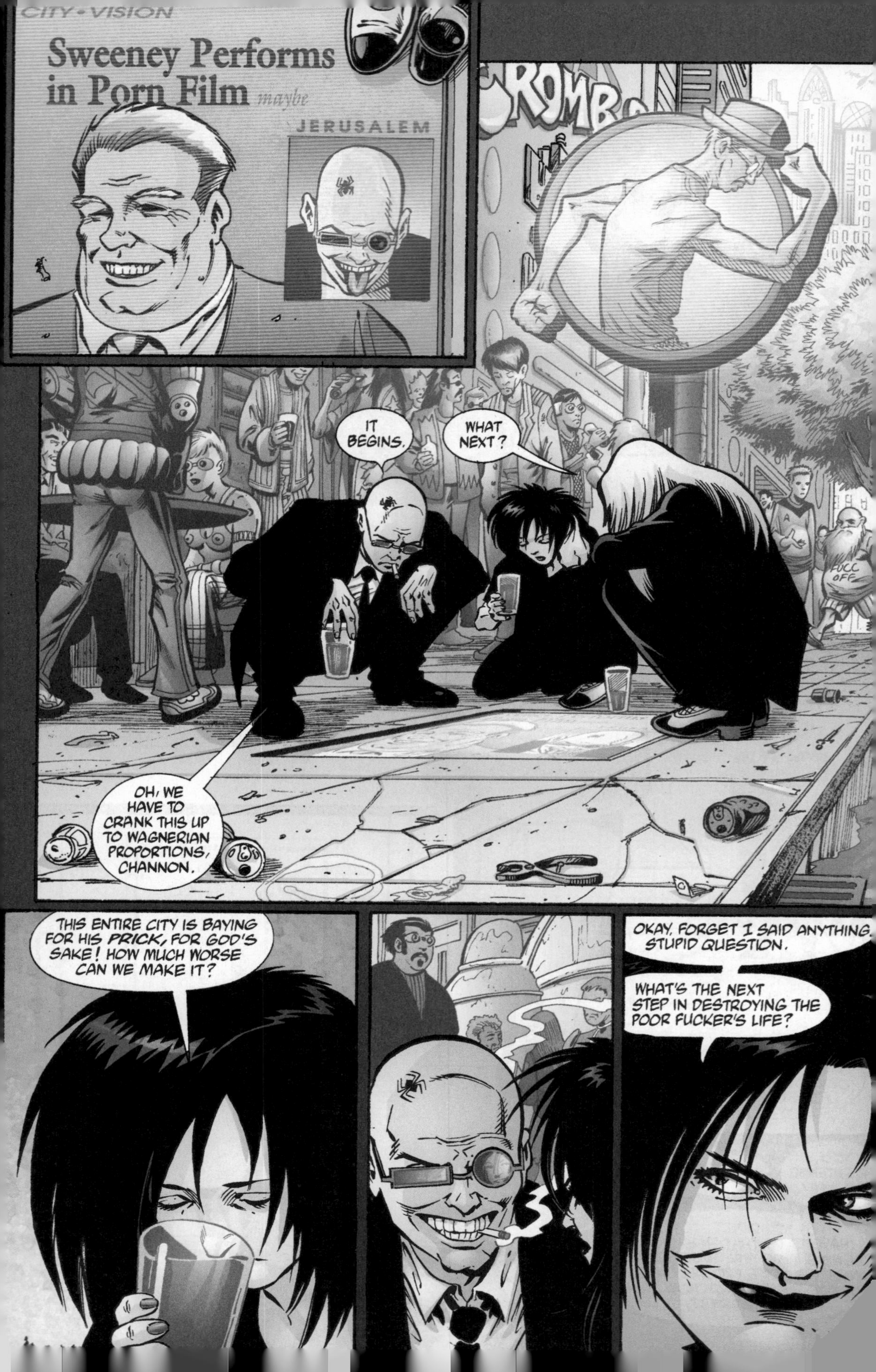
CITY • VISION
Sweeney Performs in Porn Film maybe
JERUSALEM
IT BEGINS.
WHAT NEXT?
OH, WE HAVE TO CRANK THIS UP TO WAGNERIAN PROPORTIONS, CHANNON.
THIS ENTIRE CITY IS BAYING FOR HIS PRICK, FOR GOD'S SAKE! HOW MUCH WORSE CAN WE MAKE IT?
OKAY, FORGET I SAID ANYTHING. STUPID QUESTION.
WHAT'S THE NEXT STEP IN DESTROYING THE POOR FUCKER'S LIFE?

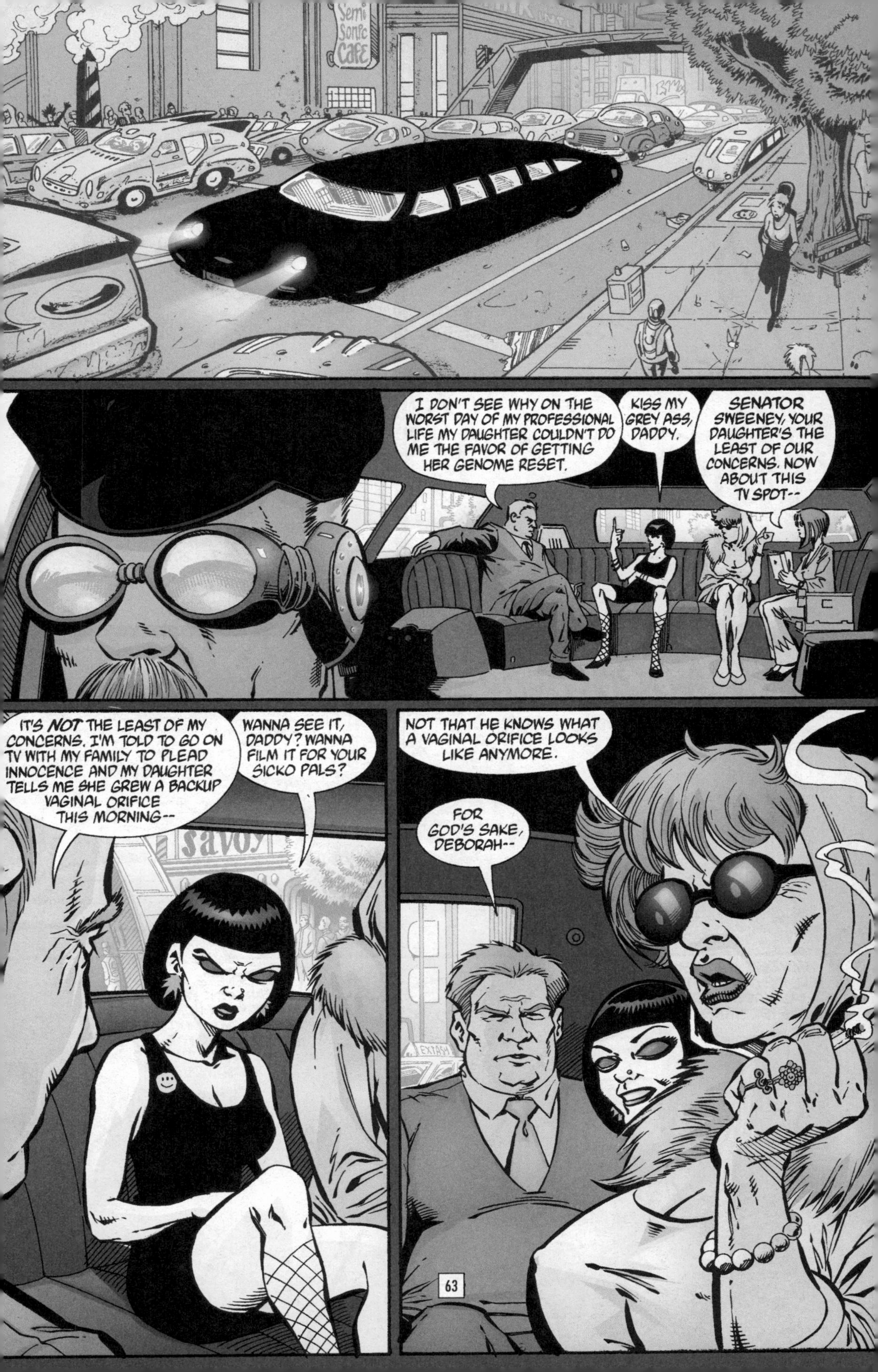

SEMI SONIC CAFE
I DON'T SEE WHY ON THE WORST DAY OF MY PROFESSIONAL LIFE MY DAUGHTER COULDN'T DO ME THE FAVOR OF GETTING HER GENOME RESET.
KISS MY GREY ASS, DADDY.
SENATOR SWEENEY, YOUR DAUGHTER'S THE LEAST OF OUR CONCERNS. NOW ABOUT THIS TV SPOT--
IT'S *NOT* THE LEAST OF MY CONCERNS. I'M TOLD TO GO ON TV WITH MY FAMILY TO PLEAD INNOCENCE AND MY DAUGHTER TELLS ME SHE GREW A BACKUP VAGINAL ORIFICE THIS MORNING--
WANNA SEE IT, DADDY? WANNA FILM IT FOR YOUR SICKO PALS?
SAVOY
NOT THAT HE KNOWS WHAT A VAGINAL ORIFICE LOOKS LIKE ANYMORE.
FOR GOD'S SAKE, DEBORAH--
EXTASY

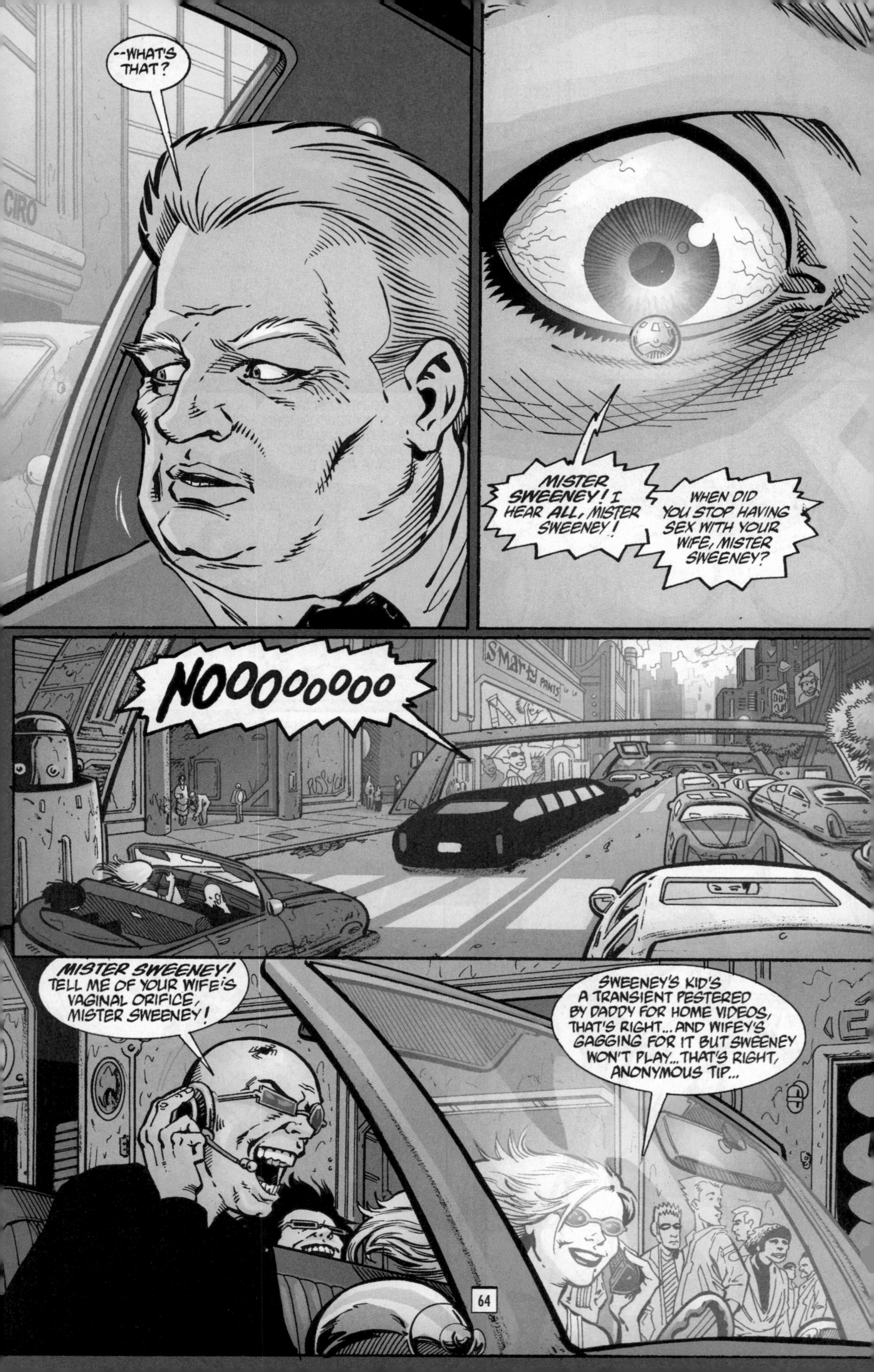

--WHAT'S THAT?
MISTER SWEENEY! I HEAR ALL, MISTER SWEENEY!
WHEN DID YOU STOP HAVING SEX WITH YOUR WIFE, MISTER SWEENEY?
NOOOOOOOO
MISTER SWEENEY! TELL ME OF YOUR WIFE'S VAGINAL ORIFICE, MISTER SWEENEY!
SWEENEY'S KID'S A TRANSIENT PESTERED BY DADDY FOR HOME VIDEOS, THAT'S RIGHT... AND WIFEY'S GAGGING FOR IT BUT SWEENEY WON'T PLAY... THAT'S RIGHT, ANONYMOUS TIP...

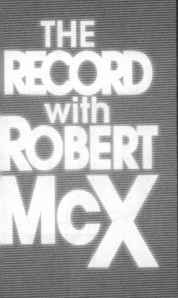

THE
RECORD
with
ROBERT
McX

SENATOR SWEENEY, I'D LIKE TO THANK YOU AND YOUR WONDERFUL FAMILY FOR JOINING ME HERE TODAY.

OUR PLEASURE, ROBERT. GLAD TO BE HERE ON THE RECORD, TO SET THE RECORD STRAIGHT.

INDEED.

SO... WHEN DID YOU STOP HAVING SEX WITH YOUR WIFE, AND DOES THIS HAVE ANY BEARING ON YOUR ALLEGED PORN BUSINESS?

ROBERT McX

WHAT NEXT?

SOME ACTUAL JOURNALISM, I THINK.

ACTUAL JOURNALISM? IS THAT WHEN YOU DON'T COMMIT CRIMES?

HELL, NO. IT'S WHEN WE COMMIT REALLY GOOD CRIMES.

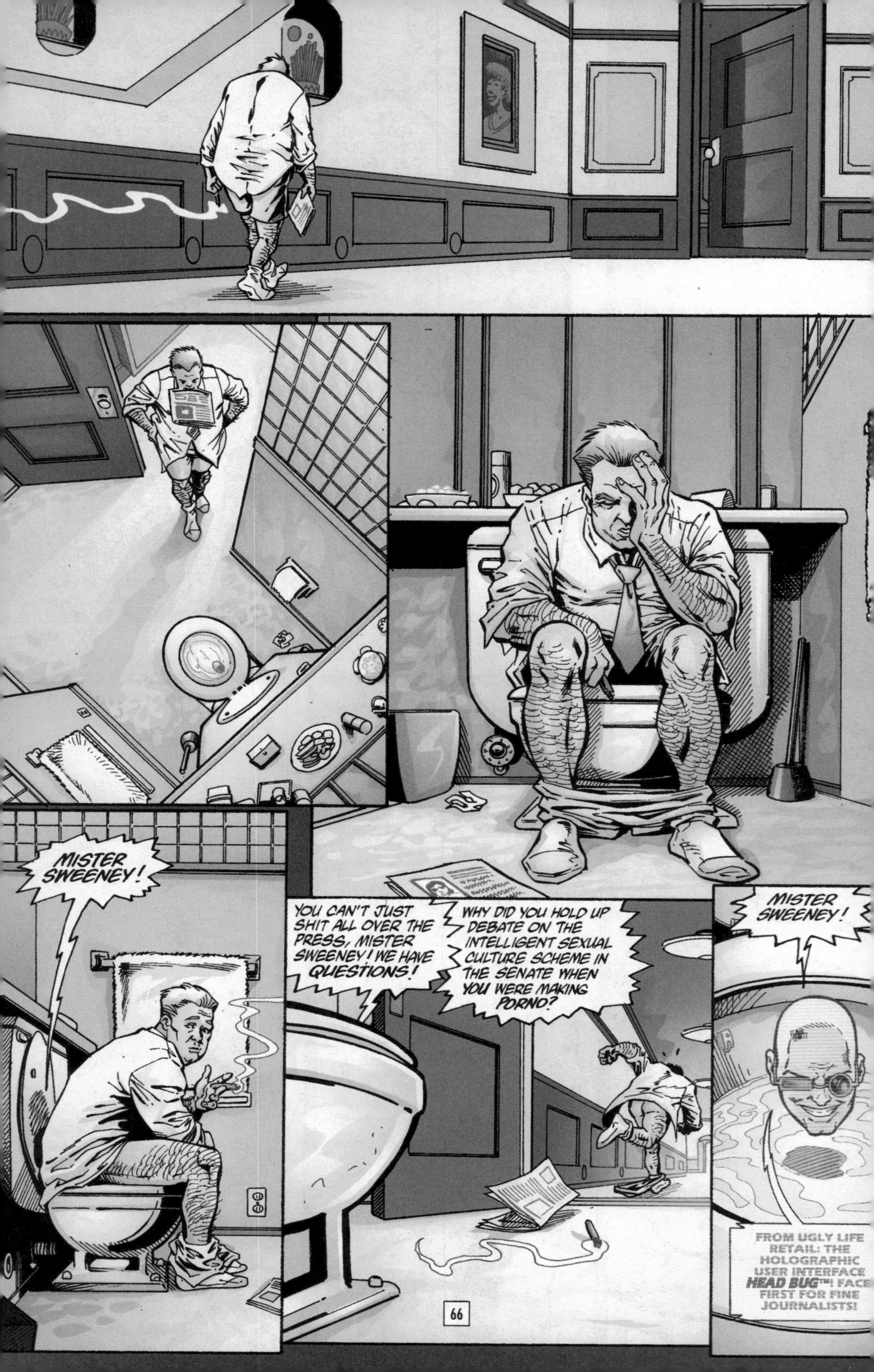
MISTER SWEENEY!
YOU CAN'T JUST SHIT ALL OVER THE PRESS, MISTER SWEENEY! WE HAVE QUESTIONS!
WHY DID YOU HOLD UP DEBATE ON THE INTELLIGENT SEXUAL CULTURE SCHEME IN THE SENATE WHEN YOU WERE MAKING PORNO?
MISTER SWEENEY!
FROM UGLY LIFE RETAIL: THE HOLOGRAPHIC USER INTERFACE HEAD BUG™! FACE FIRST FOR FINE JOURNALISTS!

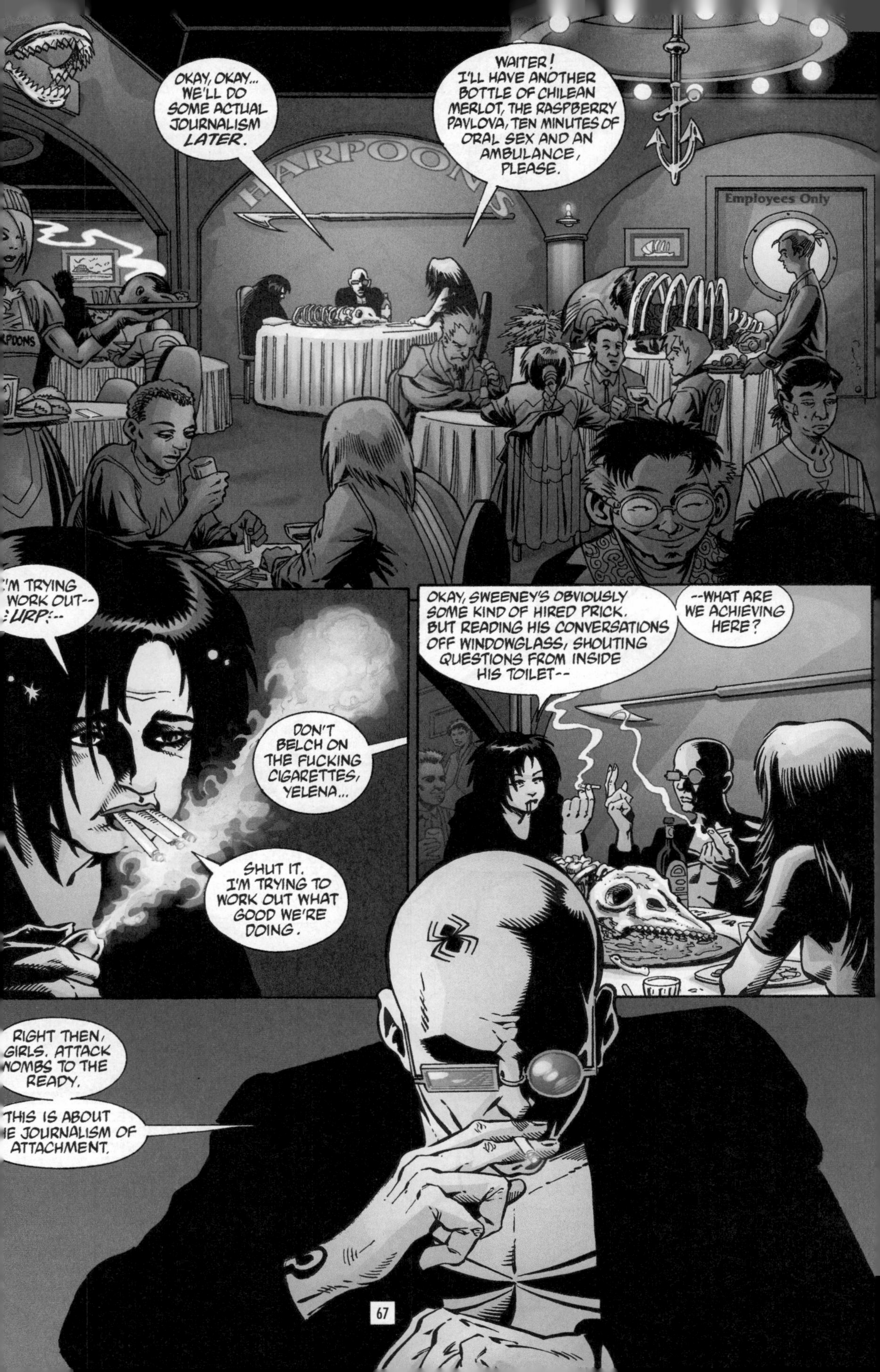
OKAY, OKAY... WE'LL DO SOME ACTUAL JOURNALISM LATER.
WAITER! I'LL HAVE ANOTHER BOTTLE OF CHILEAN MERLOT, THE RASPBERRY PAVLOVA, TEN MINUTES OF ORAL SEX AND AN AMBULANCE, PLEASE.
HARPOONS
Employees Only
'M TRYING WORK OUT-- URP!--
DON'T BELCH ON THE FUCKING CIGARETTES, YELENA...
SHUT IT. I'M TRYING TO WORK OUT WHAT GOOD WE'RE DOING.
OKAY, SWEENEY'S OBVIOUSLY SOME KIND OF HIRED PRICK. BUT READING HIS CONVERSATIONS OFF WINDOWGLASS, SHOUTING QUESTIONS FROM INSIDE HIS TOILET--
--WHAT ARE WE ACHIEVING HERE?
RIGHT THEN, GIRLS. ATTACK WOMBS TO THE READY.
THIS IS ABOUT E JOURNALISM OF ATTACHMENT.

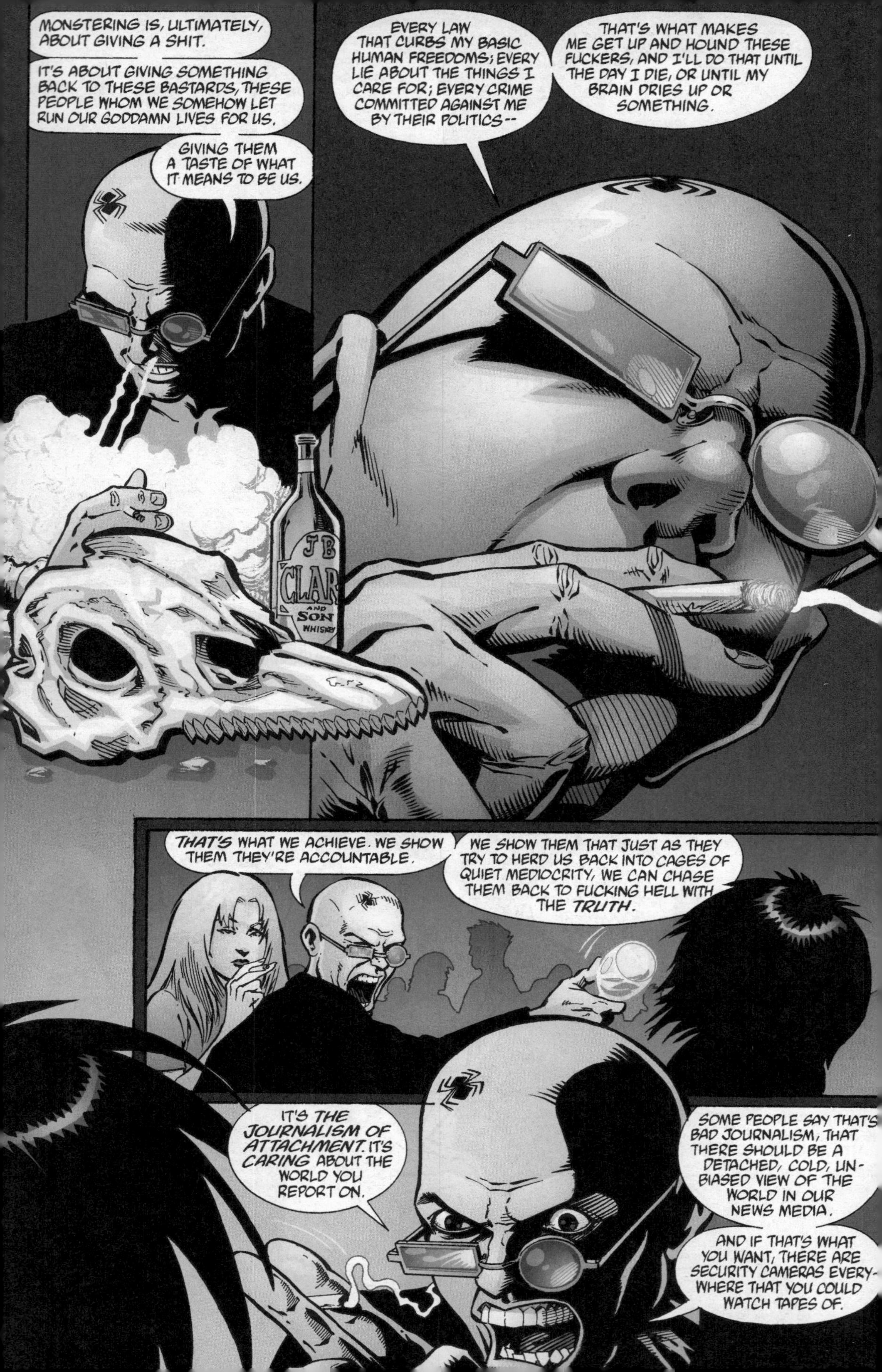
MONSTERING IS, ULTIMATELY, ABOUT GIVING A SHIT.
IT'S ABOUT GIVING SOMETHING BACK TO THESE BASTARDS, THESE PEOPLE WHOM WE SOMEHOW LET RUN OUR GODDAMN LIVES FOR US.
GIVING THEM A TASTE OF WHAT IT MEANS TO BE US.
EVERY LAW THAT CURBS MY BASIC HUMAN FREEDOMS; EVERY LIE ABOUT THE THINGS I CARE FOR; EVERY CRIME COMMITTED AGAINST ME BY THEIR POLITICS--
THAT'S WHAT MAKES ME GET UP AND HOUND THESE FUCKERS, AND I'LL DO THAT UNTIL THE DAY I DIE, OR UNTIL MY BRAIN DRIES UP OR SOMETHING.
JB
CLAR
AND
SON
WHISKEY
THAT'S WHAT WE ACHIEVE. WE SHOW THEM THEY'RE ACCOUNTABLE.
WE SHOW THEM THAT JUST AS THEY TRY TO HERD US BACK INTO CAGES OF QUIET MEDIOCRITY, WE CAN CHASE THEM BACK TO FUCKING HELL WITH THE TRUTH.
IT'S THE JOURNALISM OF ATTACHMENT. IT'S CARING ABOUT THE WORLD YOU REPORT ON.
SOME PEOPLE SAY THAT'S BAD JOURNALISM, THAT THERE SHOULD BE A DETACHED, COLD, UNBIASED VIEW OF THE WORLD IN OUR NEWS MEDIA.
AND IF THAT'S WHAT YOU WANT, THERE ARE SECURITY CAMERAS EVERYWHERE THAT YOU COULD WATCH TAPES OF.

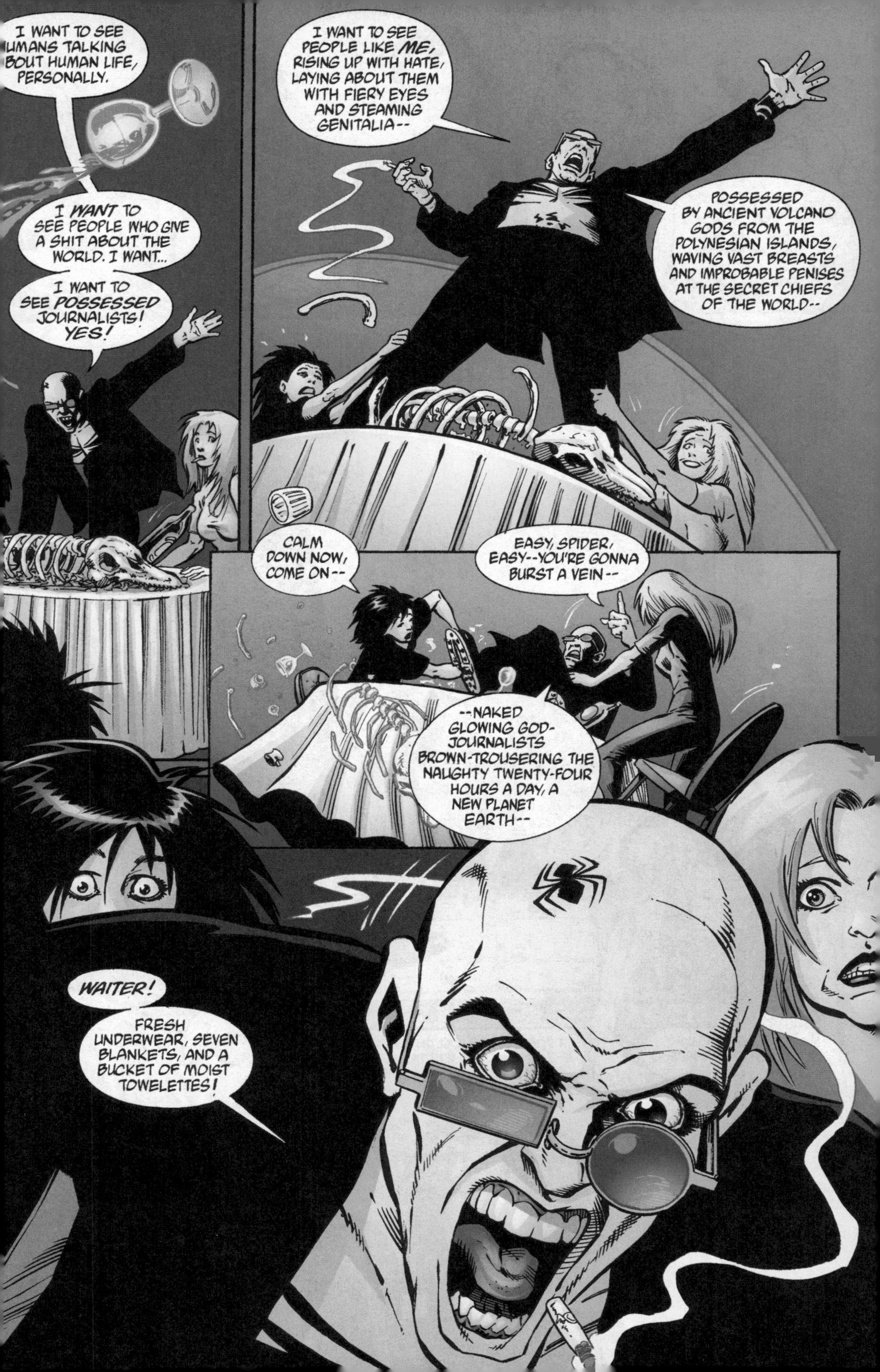
I WANT TO SEE
UMANS TALKING
BOUT HUMAN LIFE,
PERSONALLY.
I WANT TO SEE PEOPLE WHO GIVE A SHIT ABOUT THE WORLD. I WANT...
I WANT TO SEE POSSESSED JOURNALISTS! YES!
I WANT TO SEE PEOPLE LIKE ME, RISING UP WITH HATE, LAYING ABOUT THEM WITH FIERY EYES AND STEAMING GENITALIA--
POSSESSED BY ANCIENT VOLCANO GODS FROM THE POLYNESIAN ISLANDS, WAVING VAST BREASTS AND IMPROBABLE PENISES AT THE SECRET CHIEFS OF THE WORLD--
CALM DOWN NOW, COME ON--
EASY, SPIDER, EASY--YOU'RE GONNA BURST A VEIN--
--NAKED GLOWING GOD-JOURNALISTS BROWN-TROUSERING THE NAUGHTY TWENTY-FOUR HOURS A DAY, A NEW PLANET EARTH--
WAITER!
FRESH UNDERWEAR, SEVEN BLANKETS, AND A BUCKET OF MOIST TOWELETTES!

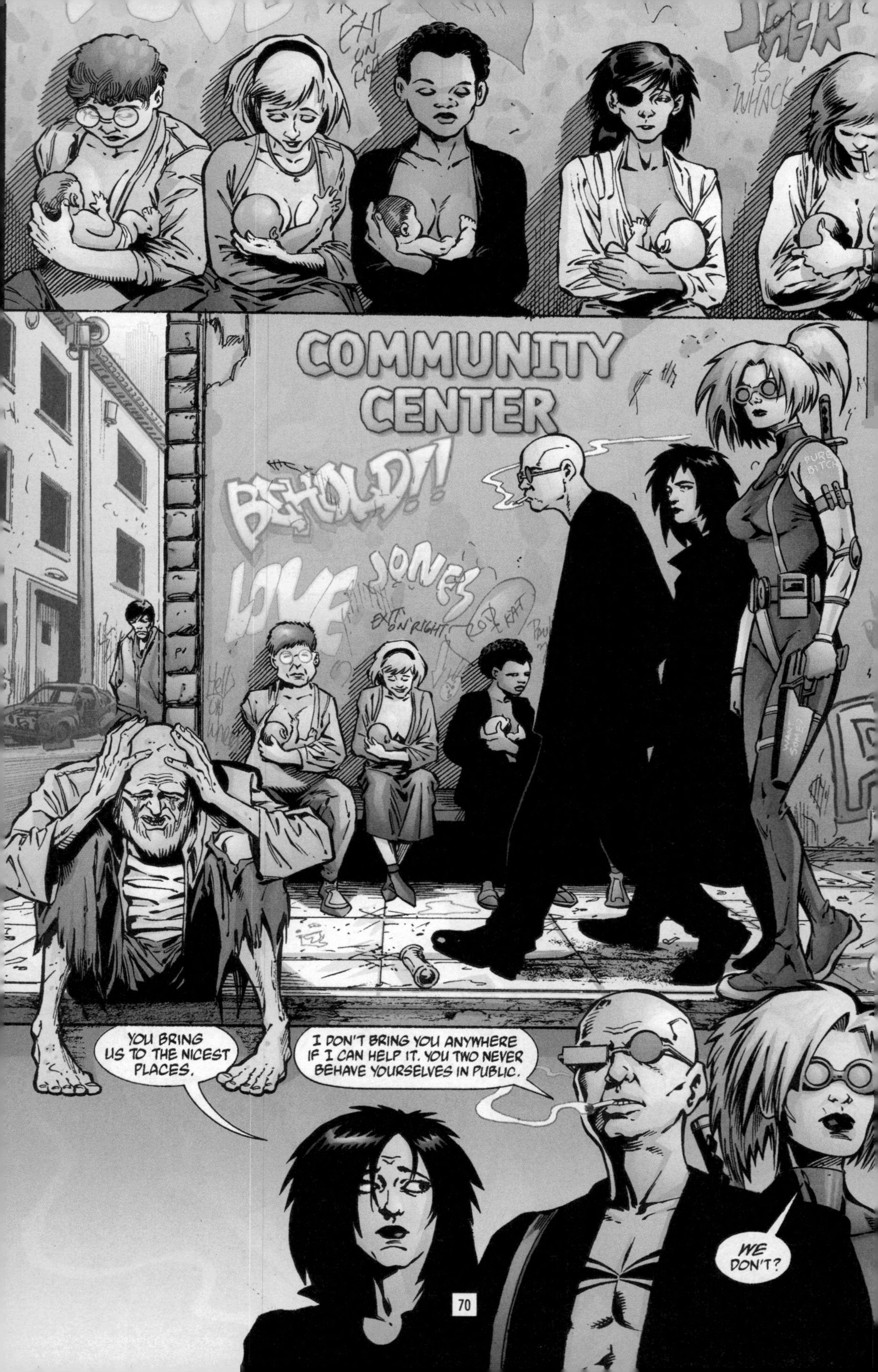
COMMUNITY CENTER
YOU BRING US TO THE NICEST PLACES.
I DON'T BRING YOU ANYWHERE IF I CAN HELP IT. YOU TWO NEVER BEHAVE YOURSELVES IN PUBLIC.
WE DON'T?

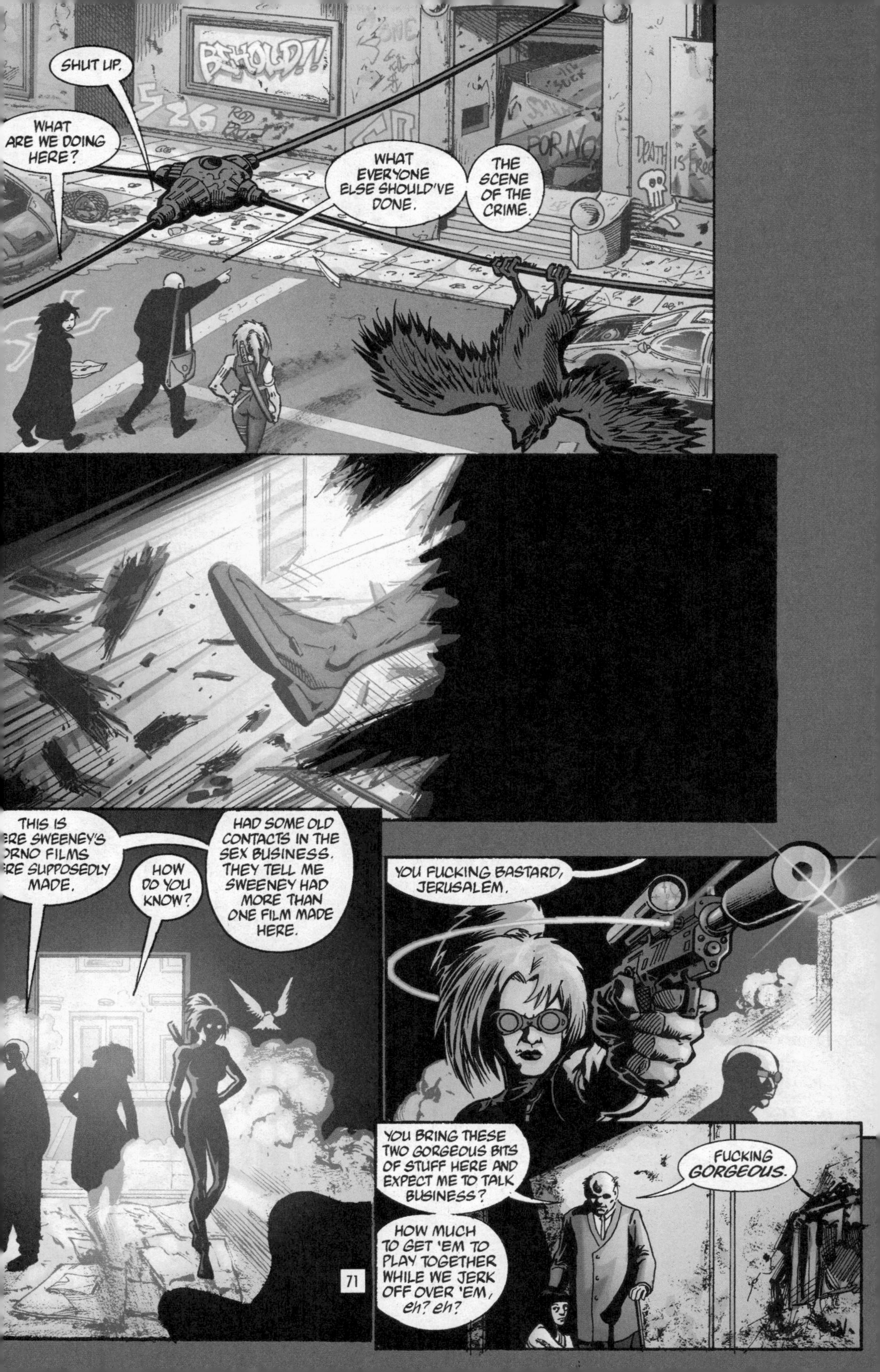
SHUT UP.
WHAT ARE WE DOING HERE?
WHAT EVERYONE ELSE SHOULD'VE DONE.
THE SCENE OF THE CRIME.
BEHOLD!!
PORNO
DEATH IS FREE
THIS IS ...ERE SWEENEY'S ...ORNO FILMS ...ERE SUPPOSEDLY MADE.
HOW DO YOU KNOW?
HAD SOME OLD CONTACTS IN THE SEX BUSINESS. THEY TELL ME SWEENEY HAD MORE THAN ONE FILM MADE HERE.
YOU FUCKING BASTARD, JERUSALEM.
YOU BRING THESE TWO GORGEOUS BITS OF STUFF HERE AND EXPECT ME TO TALK BUSINESS?
HOW MUCH TO GET 'EM TO PLAY TOGETHER WHILE WE JERK OFF OVER 'EM, eh? eh?
FUCKING GORGEOUS.

FILTHY ASSISTANTS, MEET MR. GRISHAM.

GRISHAM HAS BEEN THE CITY'S CHIEF PORNOGRAPHER FOR SOMETHING LIKE A HUNDRED AND FIFTY YEARS NOW.

NO ONE GETS OFF IN THIS TOWN WITHOUT HIM KNOWING ABOUT IT.

AH, BUT YOU WANTED TO MEET ME OUT OF YOUR PROFOUND CONCERN FOR THE CONDITION OF POLITICS IN THE CITY TODAY. AND SO SOON AFTER THE ELECTION, TOO.

"DEMOCRACY IS THE THEORY THAT HOLDS THAT THE COMMON PEOPLE KNOW WHAT THEY WANT. AND DESERVE TO GET IT GOOD AND HARD."

MENCKEN.

AND, THANKS TO HIS ROGUE SECRETION-DWELLING NANOSENSORS, THAT IS LITERALLY TRUE IN OVER EIGHTEEN CITY DISTRICTS.

SO, IT OCCURRED TO ME, IF A CLEVER MAN REALLY WAS FUNDING PORNO WHILE TRYING TO FILIBUSTER SEX LEGISLATION OUT OF EXISTENCE, AND THAT GOT LEAKED--

I LEAKED IT. BECAUSE NO ONE ELSE WOULD KNOW SHIT ABOUT IT.

BUSTED. LET'S GO--

NO. THIS IS BACKGROUND. STRICTLY OFF THE RECORD. THAT'S ALWAYS BEEN MY DEAL WITH GRISHAM.

WE HAVE JOURNALISTIC ETHICS, YELENA. PUT YOUR ATTACK WOMB AWAY.

MEET MELISSA. SHE LIVES IN THIS HOUSE. THIS IS THE BERLITZ-ABRAMS DISTRICT. THAT RING ANY BELLS, LADIES?

ROUND ABOUT THE TIME WHEN MELISSA HAD JUST GOTTEN OLD ENOUGH TO GET HERSELF DRINKS OF WATER FROM THE FAUCET, AN AUTONOMY-TERRORIST GROUP DROPPED INTELLECT SUPPRESSANT INTO THE WATER SUPPLY.

SHE'S NOT BRIGHT. SHE DOESN'T UNDERSTAND MUCH. SHE'S POOR AND SHE GETS FUCKED UP A LOT.

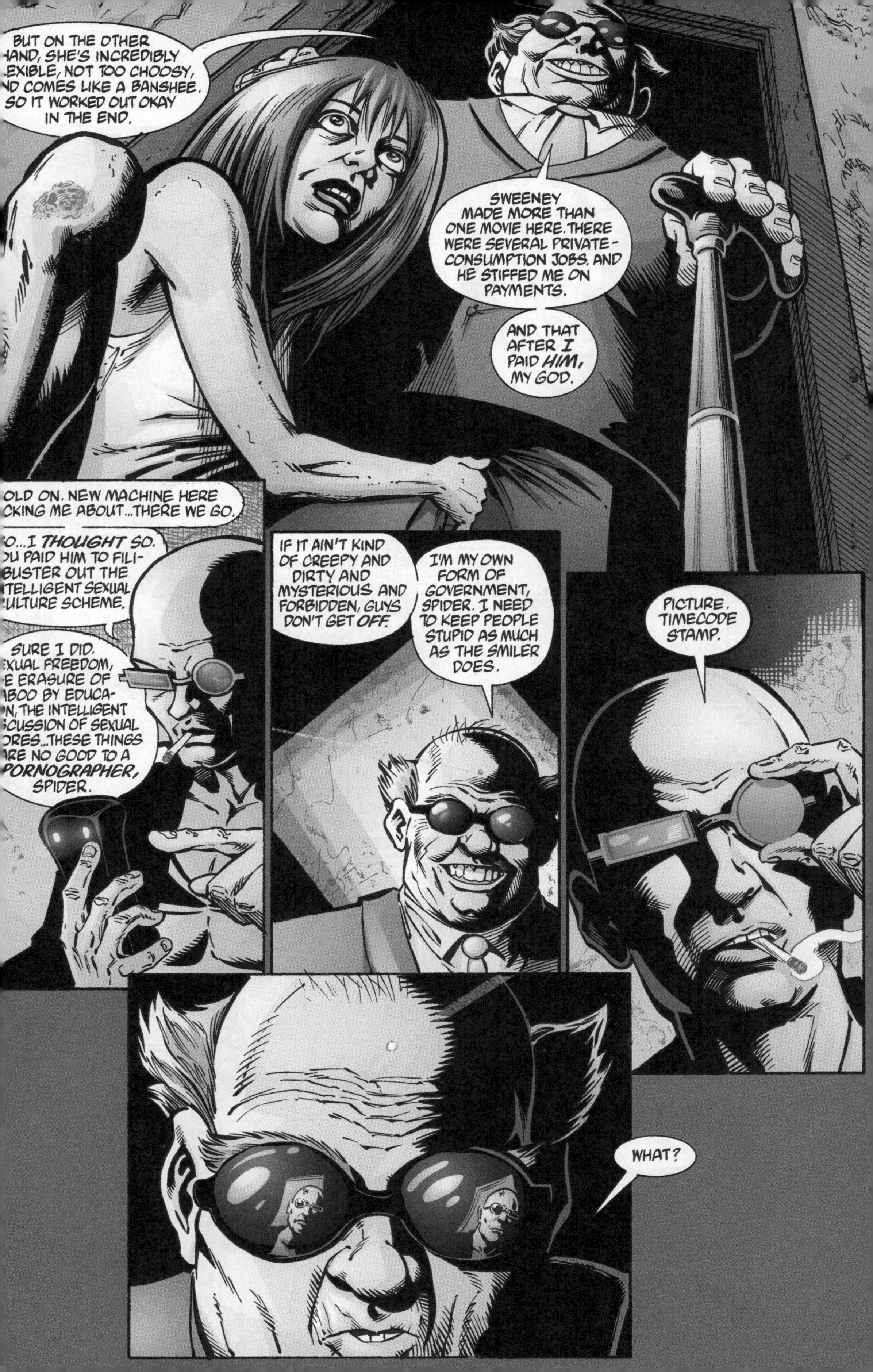
BUT ON THE OTHER HAND, SHE'S INCREDIBLY LEXIBLE, NOT TOO CHOOSY, ND COMES LIKE A BANSHEE. SO IT WORKED OUT OKAY IN THE END.
SWEENEY MADE MORE THAN ONE MOVIE HERE. THERE WERE SEVERAL PRIVATE-CONSUMPTION JOBS. AND HE STIFFED ME ON PAYMENTS.
AND THAT AFTER I PAID HIM, MY GOD.
OLD ON. NEW MACHINE HERE CKING ME ABOUT...THERE WE GO.
O...I THOUGHT SO. OU PAID HIM TO FILIBUSTER OUT THE NTELLIGENT SEXUAL ULTURE SCHEME.
SURE I DID. EXUAL FREEDOM, E ERASURE OF ABOO BY EDUCA- N, THE INTELLIGENT CUSSION OF SEXUAL ORES...THESE THINGS ARE NO GOOD TO A PORNOGRAPHER, SPIDER.
IF IT AIN'T KIND OF CREEPY AND DIRTY AND MYSTERIOUS AND FORBIDDEN, GUYS DON'T GET OFF.
I'M MY OWN FORM OF GOVERNMENT, SPIDER. I NEED TO KEEP PEOPLE STUPID AS MUCH AS THE SMILER DOES.
PICTURE. TIMECODE STAMP.
WHAT?

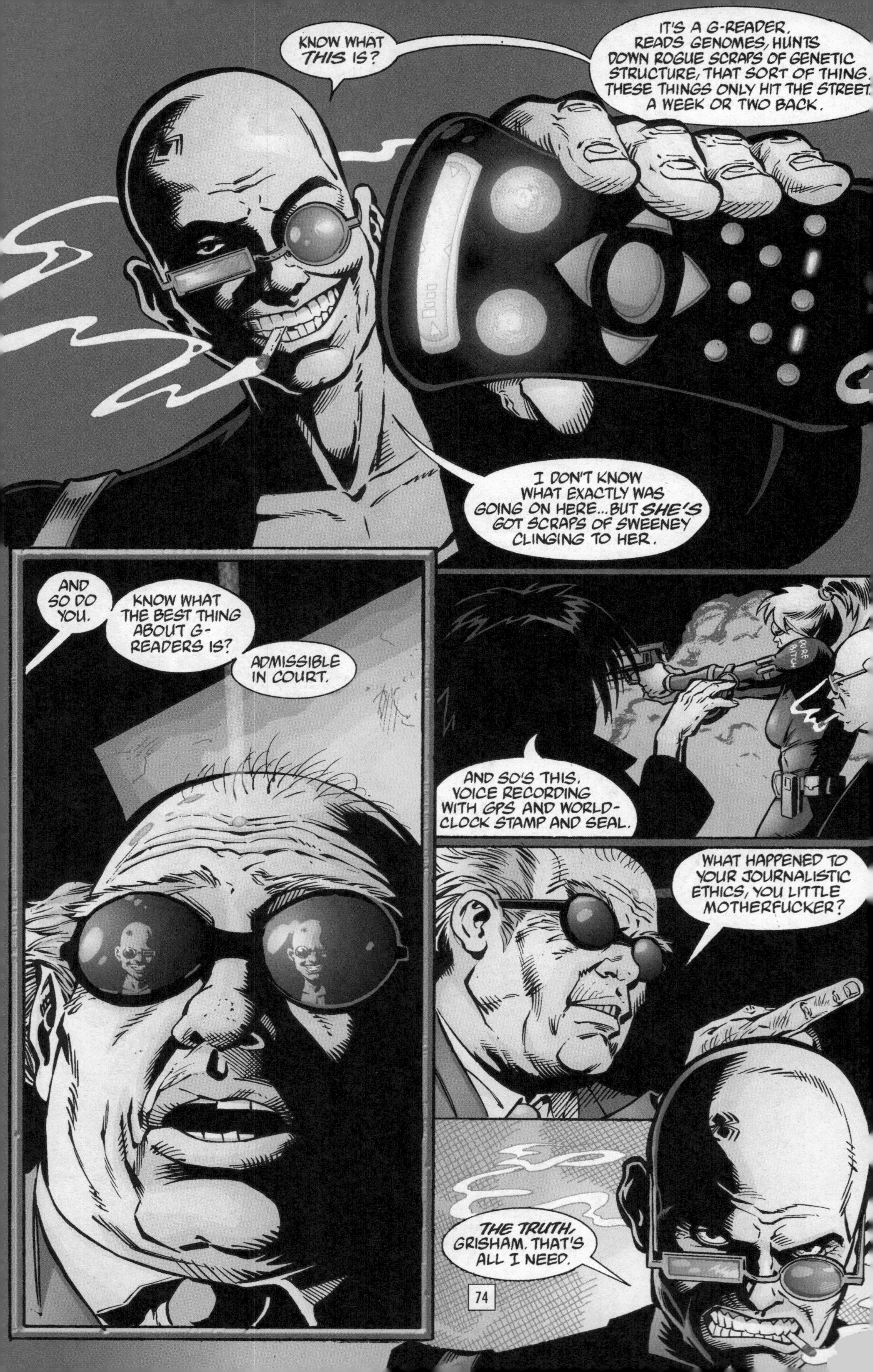
KNOW WHAT *THIS* IS?
IT'S A G-READER. READS GENOMES, HUNTS DOWN ROGUE SCRAPS OF GENETIC STRUCTURE, THAT SORT OF THING. THESE THINGS ONLY HIT THE STREET A WEEK OR TWO BACK.
I DON'T KNOW WHAT EXACTLY WAS GOING ON HERE...BUT *SHE'S* GOT SCRAPS OF SWEENEY CLINGING TO HER.
AND SO DO YOU.
KNOW WHAT THE BEST THING ABOUT G-READERS IS?
ADMISSIBLE IN COURT.
AND SO'S THIS. VOICE RECORDING WITH GPS AND WORLD-CLOCK STAMP AND SEAL.
WHAT HAPPENED TO YOUR JOURNALISTIC ETHICS, YOU LITTLE MOTHERFUCKER?
THE TRUTH, GRISHAM. THAT'S ALL I NEED.

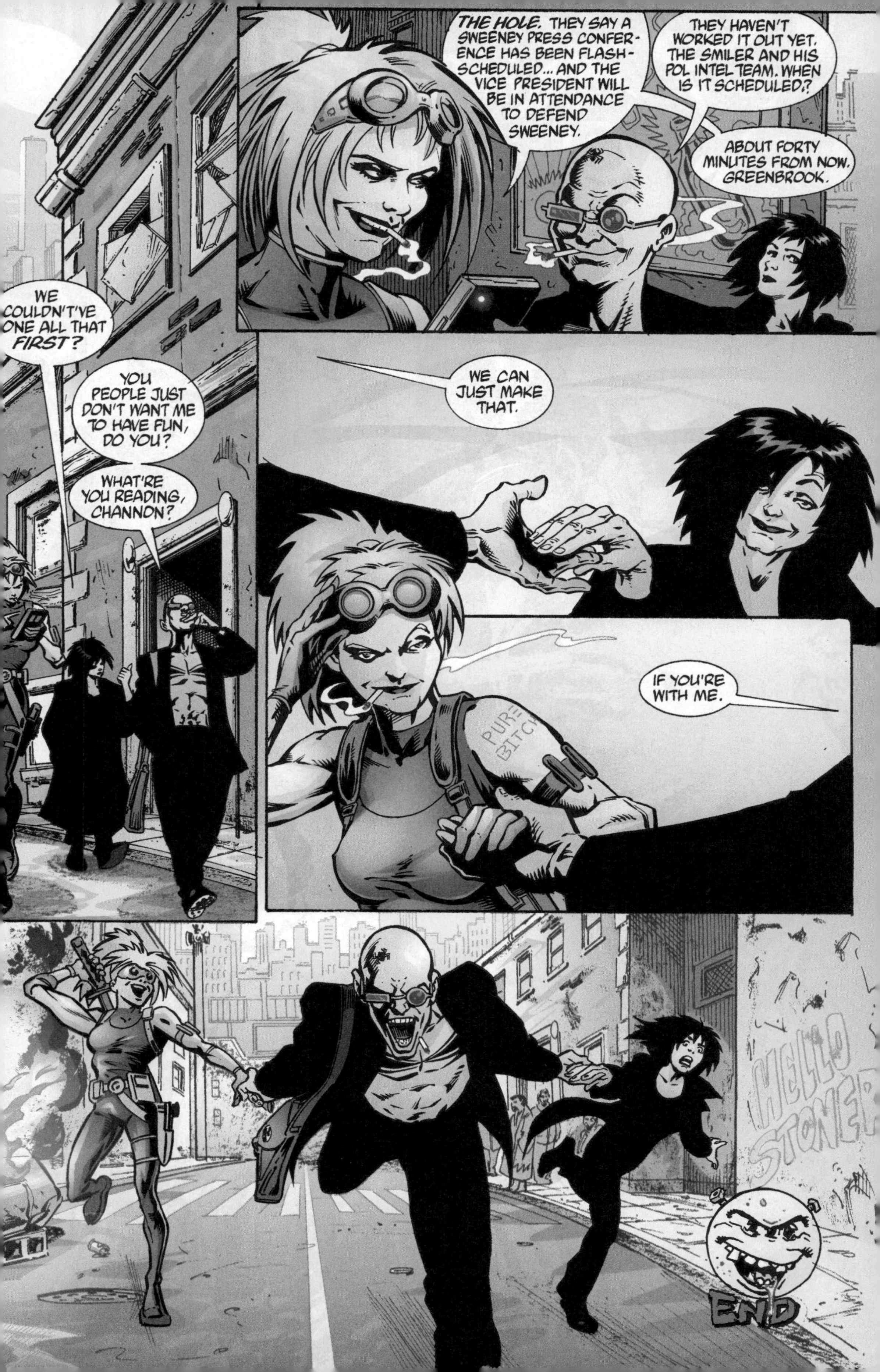
THE HOLE. THEY SAY A SWEENEY PRESS CONFERENCE HAS BEEN FLASH-SCHEDULED... AND THE VICE PRESIDENT WILL BE IN ATTENDANCE TO DEFEND SWEENEY.
THEY HAVEN'T WORKED IT OUT YET. THE SMILER AND HIS POL INTEL TEAM. WHEN IS IT SCHEDULED?
ABOUT FORTY MINUTES FROM NOW. GREENBROOK.
WE COULDN'T'VE ONE ALL THAT FIRST?
YOU PEOPLE JUST DON'T WANT ME TO HAVE FUN, DO YOU?
WHAT'RE YOU READING, CHANNON?
WE CAN JUST MAKE THAT.
IF YOU'RE WITH ME.
PURE BITCH
HELLO STONER
END

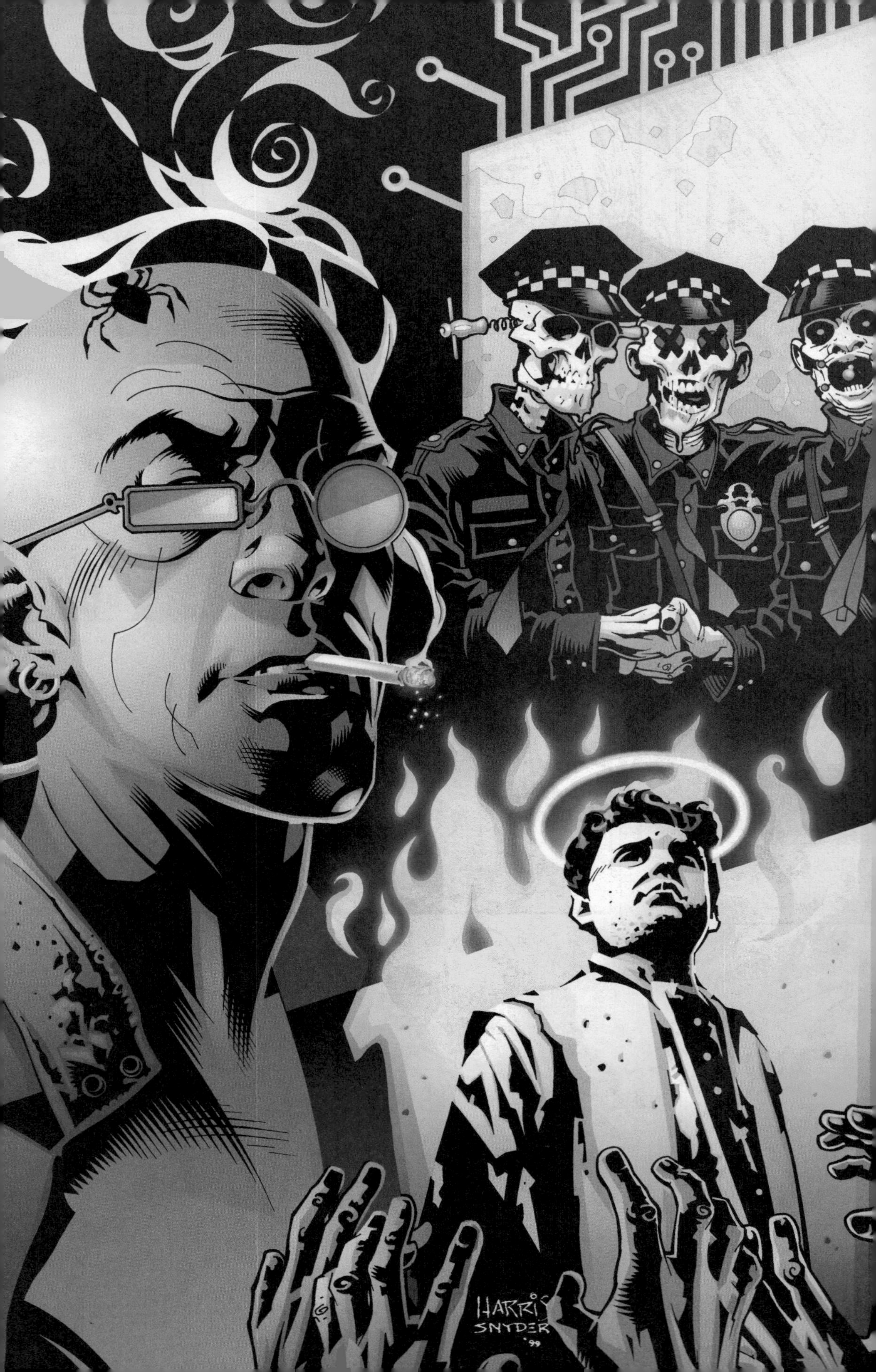
HARRIS
SNYDER
'99

LONELY CITY

CITY ™

PRODUCED IN CONJUNCTION WITH THE TV SHOW

teX

ESSAYS
SPONSORED BY
LONELY CITY ™
TELEVISION

SPIDER JERUSALEM

Warren Ellis writes & Darick Robertson pencils

LONELY CITY
one of three

Rodney Ramos	Clem Robins	Nathan Eyring	Tony Harris	Ray Snyder	Cliff Chiang	Stuart Moore
Inker	Letterer	Color & Seps	Cover Pencils	Cover Inks	Ass't Editor	Editor

TRANSMETROPOLITAN created by Warren Ellis and Darick Robertson

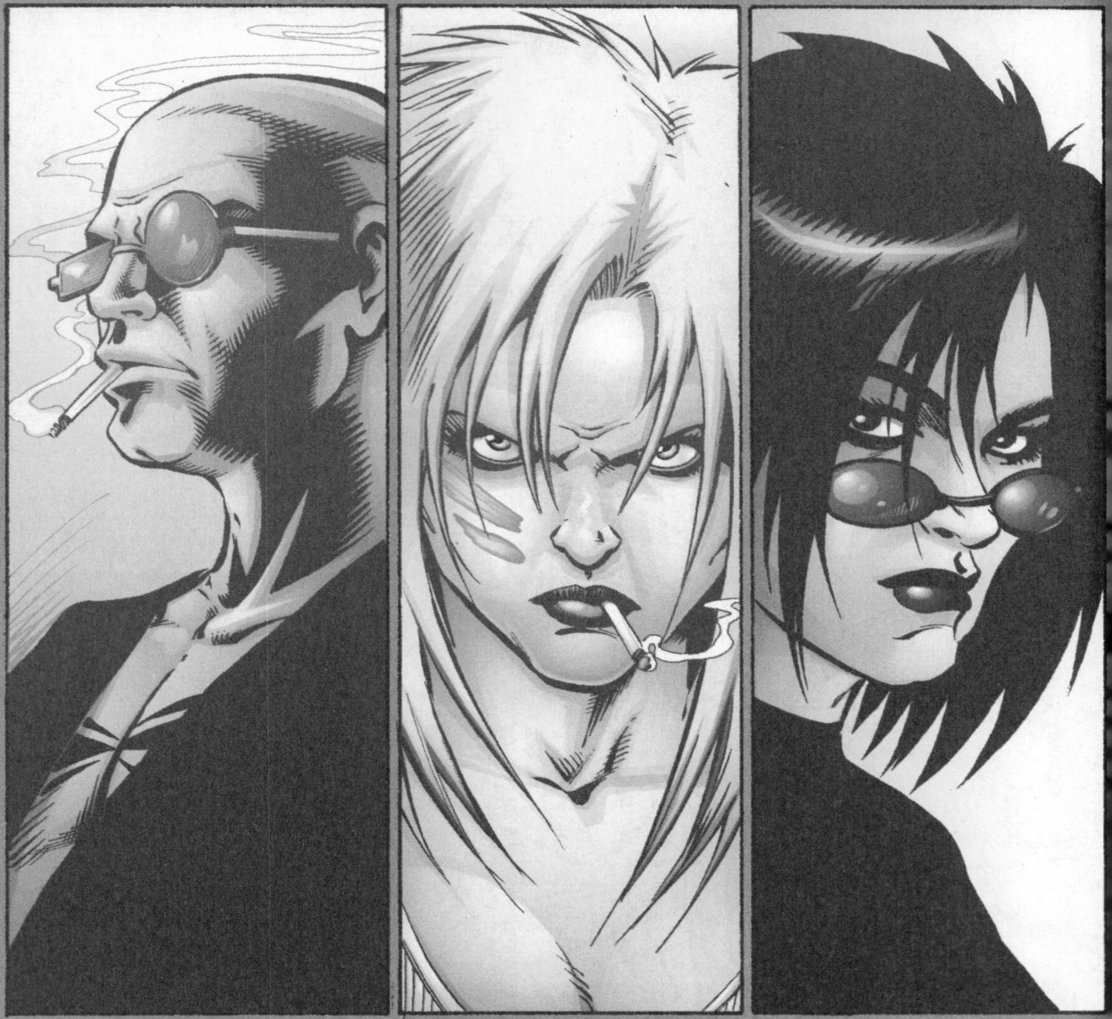

Spider Jerusalem is the acclaimed columnist for the major metropolitan newspaper "The Word." These are essays from the doomed streets he haunts in pursuit of the Truth.

Channon Yarrow, a one-time stripper and convicted pay-dacoit, is Mr. Jerusalem's personal bodyguard and long-time confidante, providing protection during the writing of the "Lonely City" series.

Yelena Rossini, daughter of one of the city's oldest political families, is Mr. Jerusalem's personal assistant in both his daily life and his relentless hunt for the Truth.

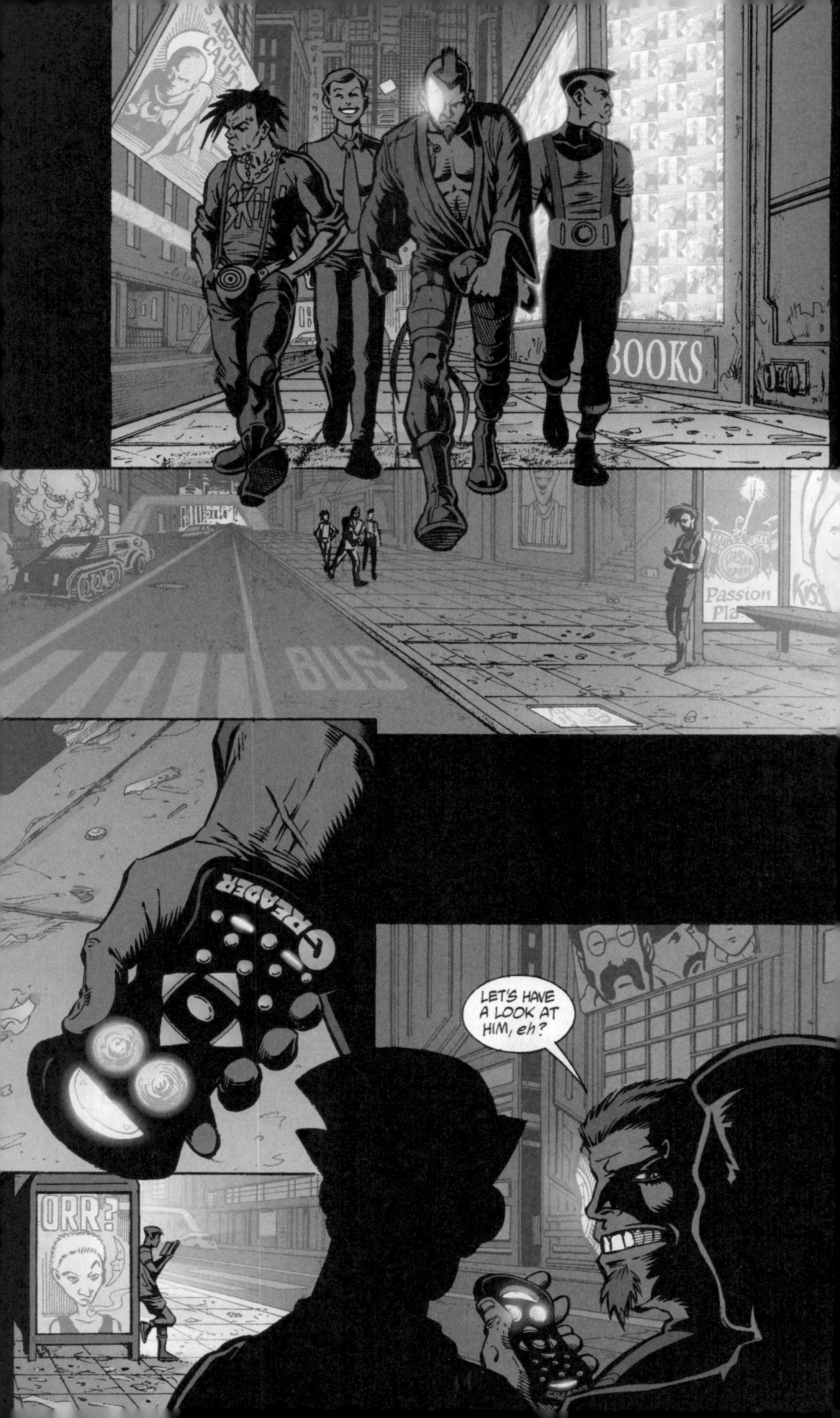

BOOKS
BUS
Passion Play
CREADER
LET'S HAVE A LOOK AT HIM, eh?
ORR?

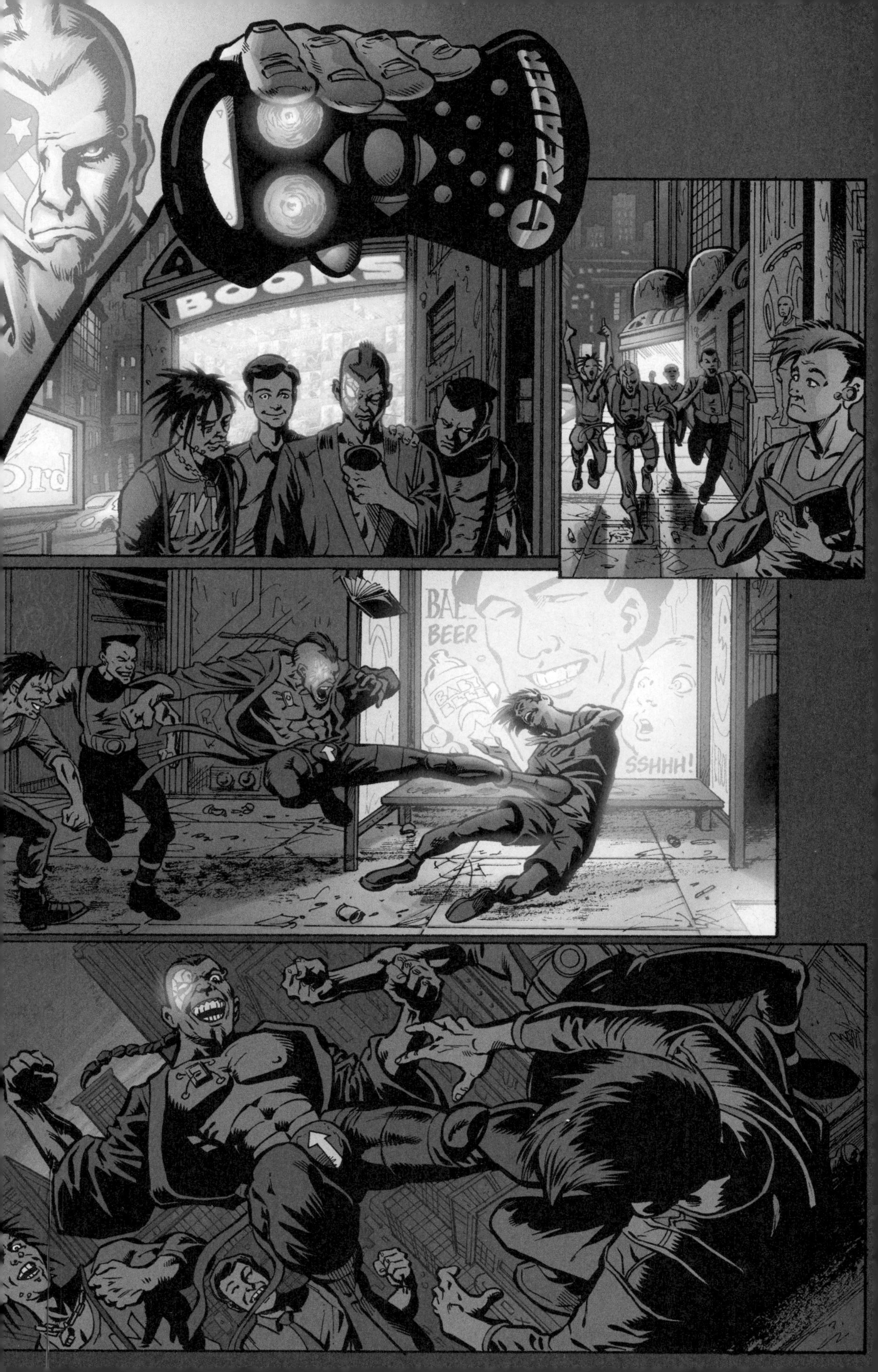
READER
BOOKS
BEER
SSHHH!

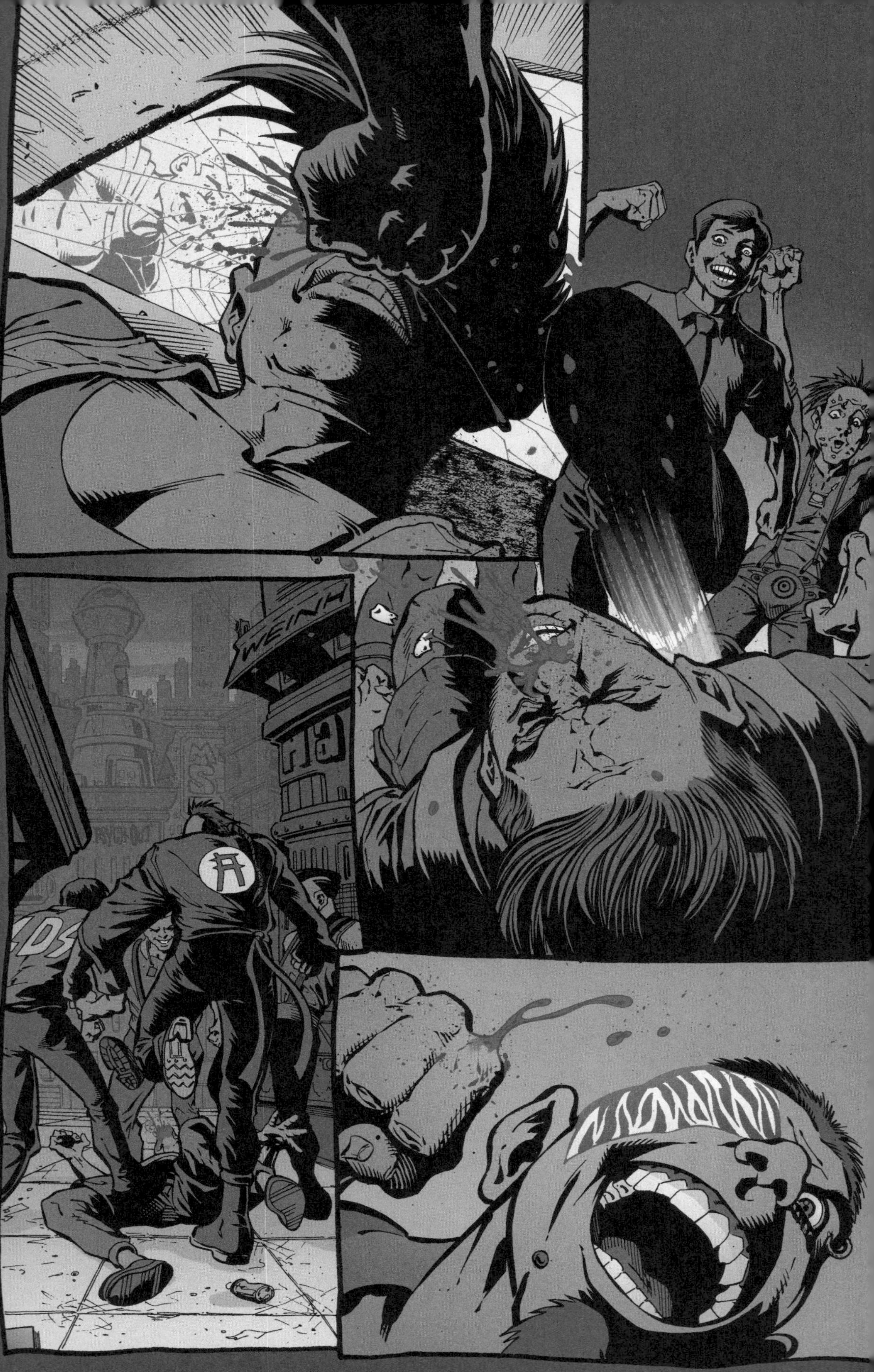

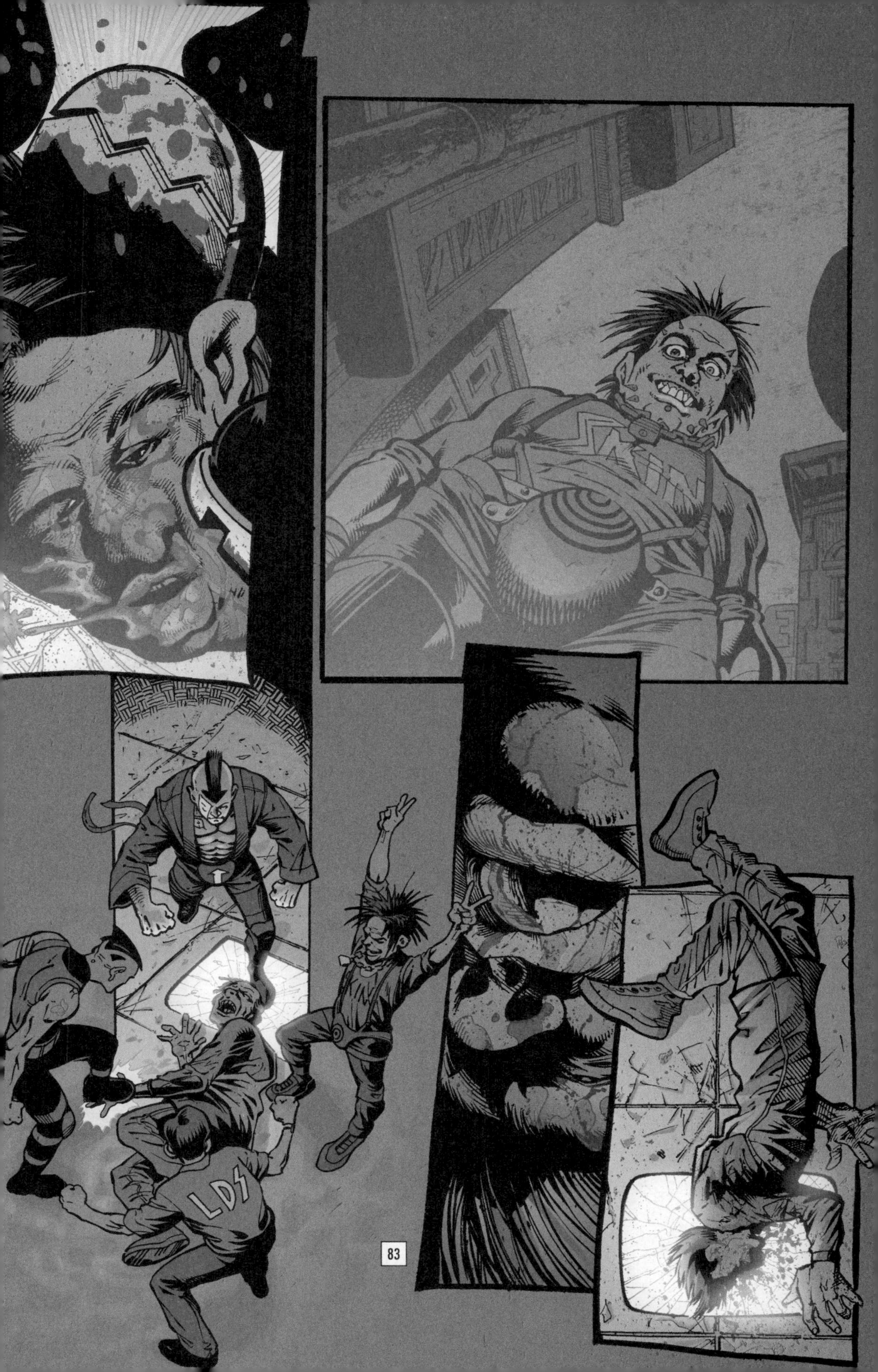
LDS

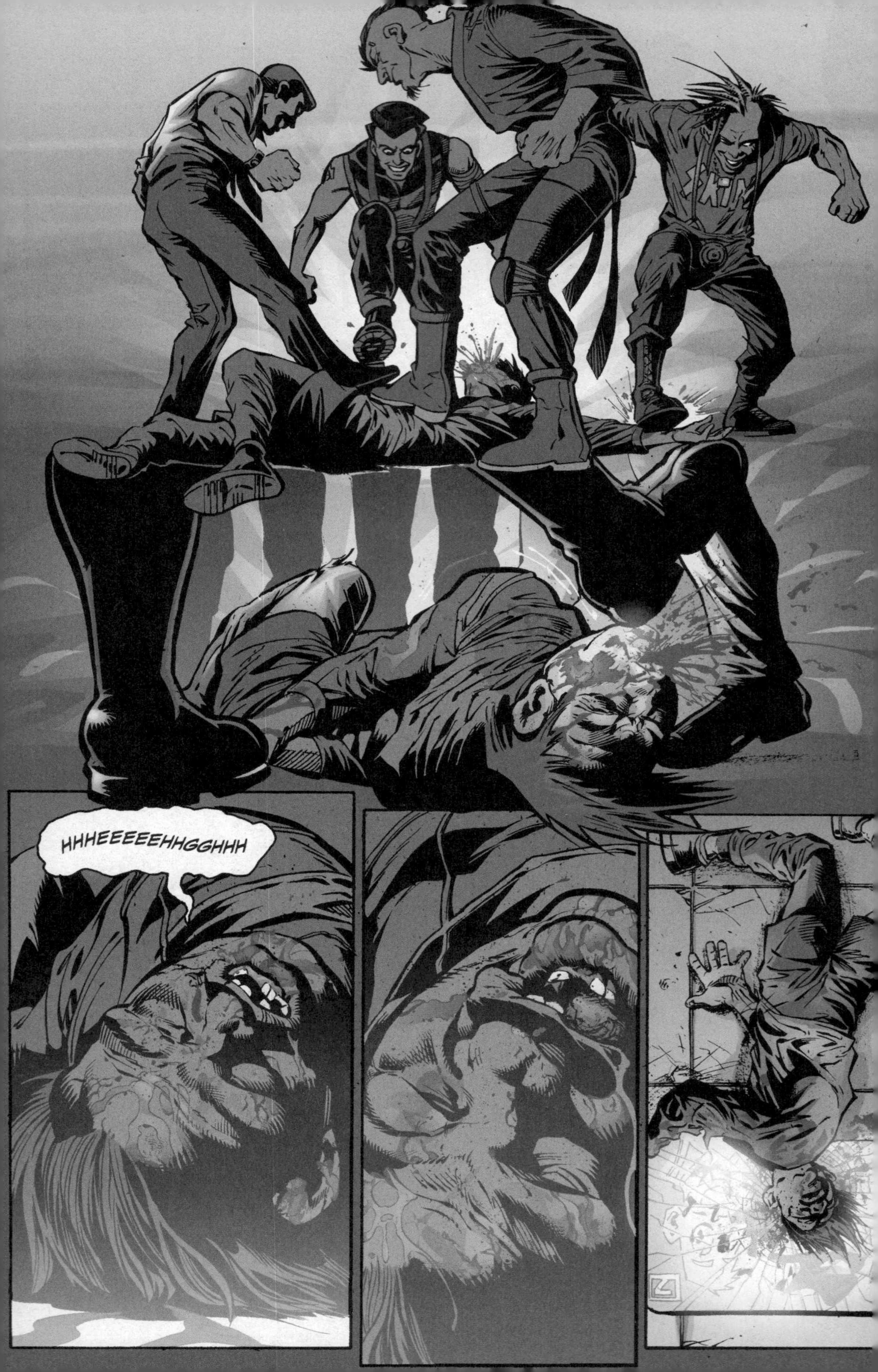
HHHEEEEEEHHGGHHH

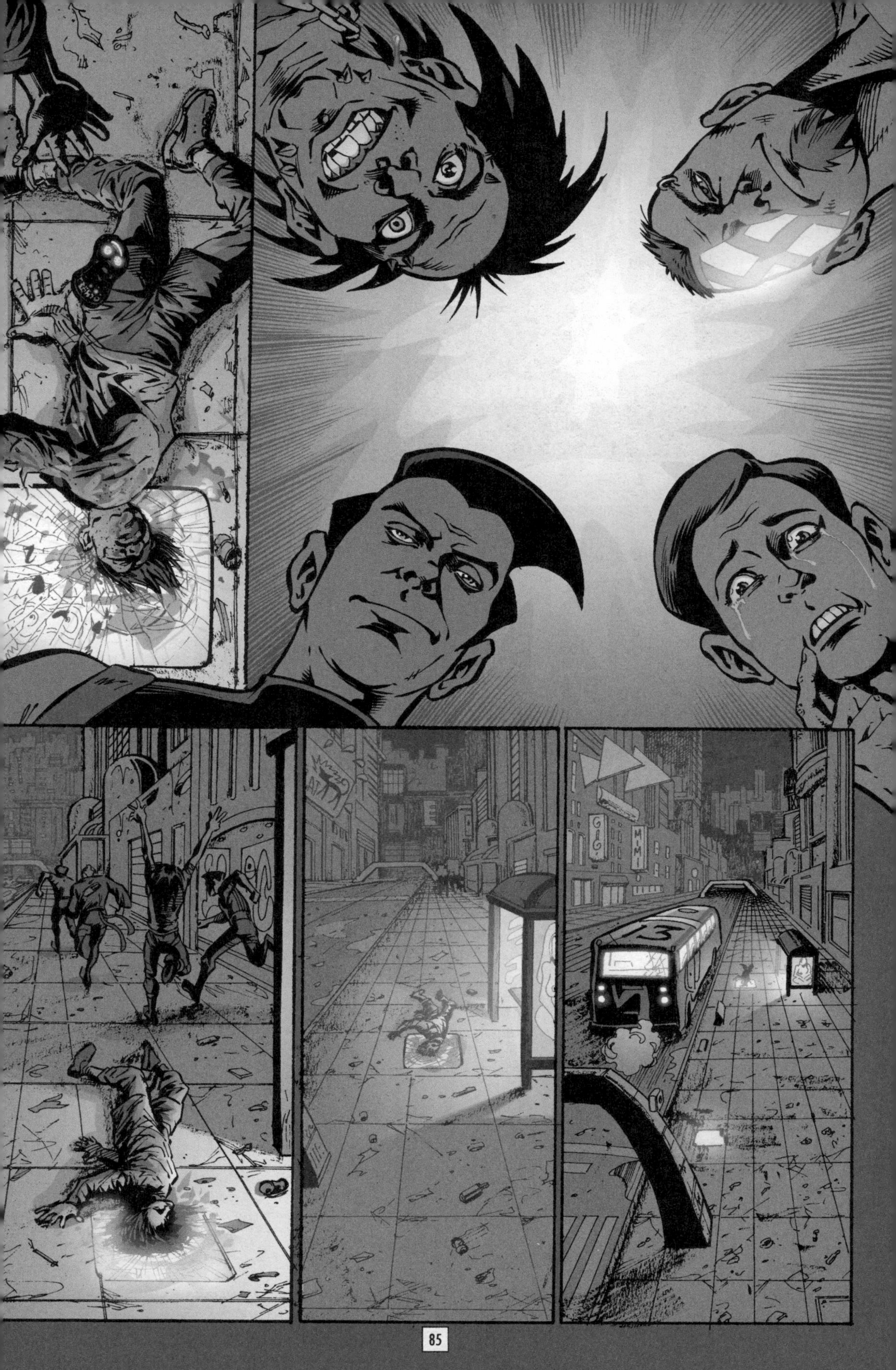
MIMI

Spider Jerusalem

HI. I'M SPIDER JERUSALEM.

amfeed

I SMOKE. I TAKE DRUGS. I DRINK. I WASH EVERY SIX WEEKS.

amfeed

I MASTURBATE CONSTANTLY AND FLING MY STEAMING POISON SEMEN DOWN FROM MY WINDOW INTO YOUR HAIR AND FOOD.

amfeed

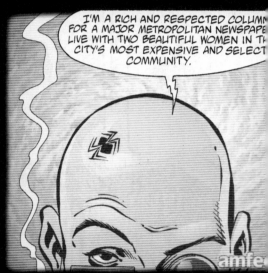

I'M A RICH AND RESPECTED COLUMN FOR A MAJOR METROPOLITAN NEWSPAPE LIVE WITH TWO BEAUTIFUL WOMEN IN TH CITY'S MOST EXPENSIVE AND SELECT COMMUNITY.

amfeed

BEING A BASTARD WORKS.

amfeed

The City
Careers Servic

Call us now.
No matter how
much of a fuck
you are.

amfeed

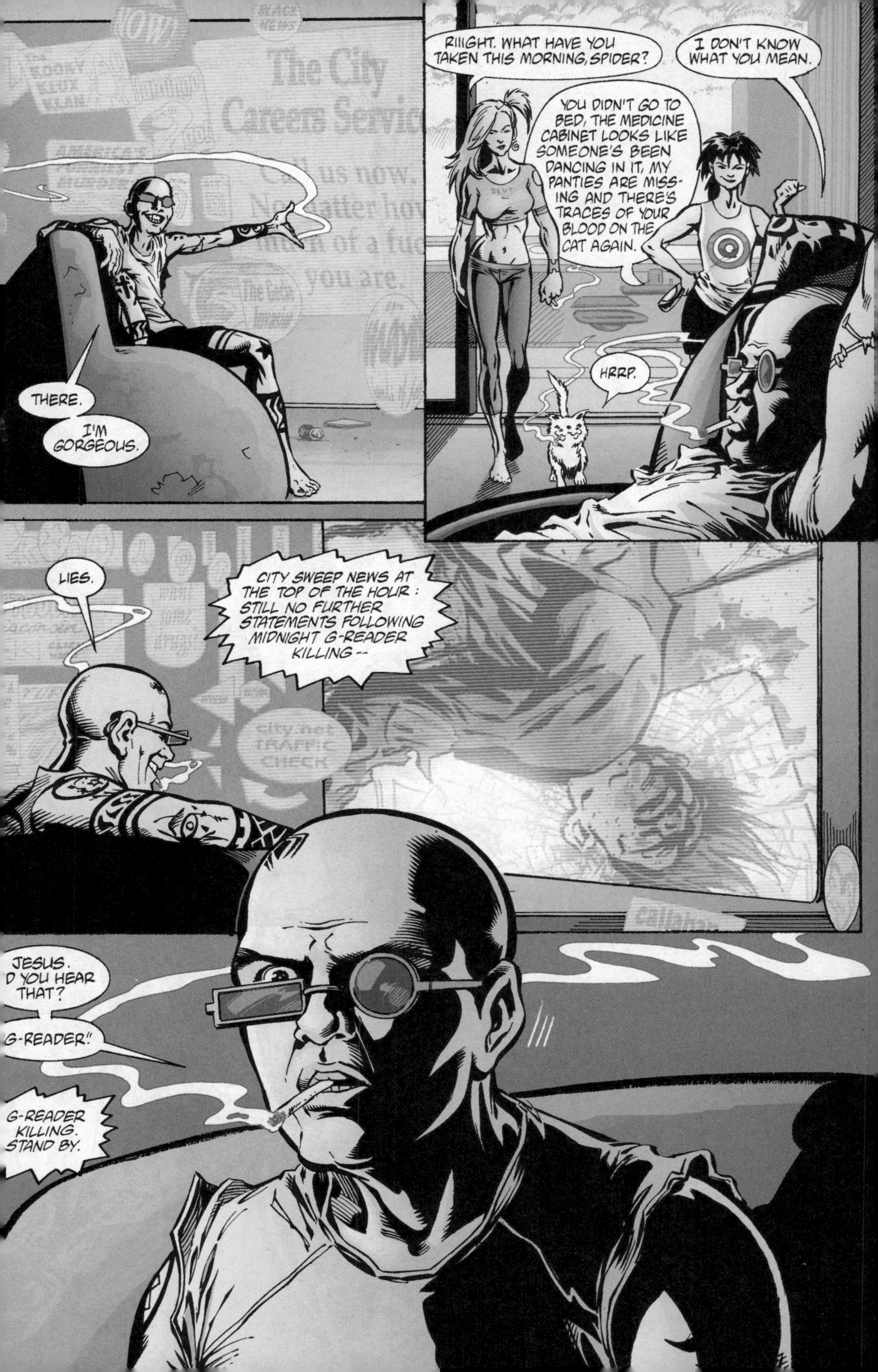
THERE.
I'M GORGEOUS.
RIIIGHT. WHAT HAVE YOU TAKEN THIS MORNING, SPIDER?
I DON'T KNOW WHAT YOU MEAN.
YOU DIDN'T GO TO BED, THE MEDICINE CABINET LOOKS LIKE SOMEONE'S BEEN DANCING IN IT, MY PANTIES ARE MISSING AND THERE'S TRACES OF YOUR BLOOD ON THE CAT AGAIN.
HRRP.
LIES.
CITY SWEEP NEWS AT THE TOP OF THE HOUR : STILL NO FURTHER STATEMENTS FOLLOWING MIDNIGHT G-READER KILLING --
city.net TRAFFIC CHECK
JESUS.
D YOU HEAR THAT?
G-READER."
G-READER KILLING. STAND BY.

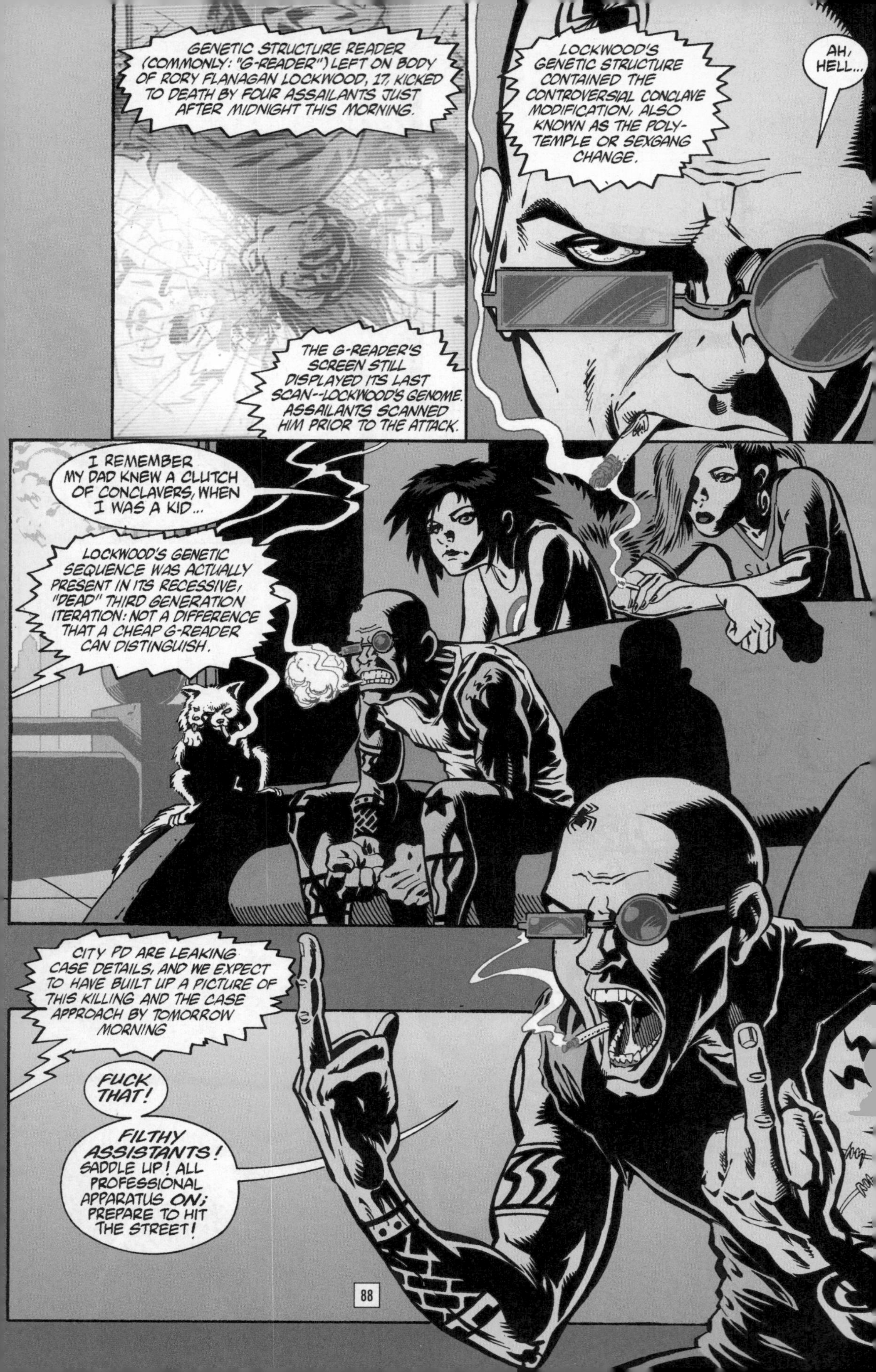
GENETIC STRUCTURE READER (COMMONLY: "G-READER") LEFT ON BODY OF RORY FLANAGAN LOCKWOOD, 17, KICKED TO DEATH BY FOUR ASSAILANTS JUST AFTER MIDNIGHT THIS MORNING.
LOCKWOOD'S GENETIC STRUCTURE CONTAINED THE CONTROVERSIAL CONCLAVE MODIFICATION, ALSO KNOWN AS THE POLY-TEMPLE OR SEXGANG CHANGE.
AH, HELL...
THE G-READER'S SCREEN STILL DISPLAYED ITS LAST SCAN--LOCKWOOD'S GENOME. ASSAILANTS SCANNED HIM PRIOR TO THE ATTACK.
I REMEMBER MY DAD KNEW A CLUTCH OF CONCLAVERS, WHEN I WAS A KID...
LOCKWOOD'S GENETIC SEQUENCE WAS ACTUALLY PRESENT IN ITS RECESSIVE, "DEAD" THIRD GENERATION ITERATION: NOT A DIFFERENCE THAT A CHEAP G-READER CAN DISTINGUISH.
CITY PD ARE LEAKING CASE DETAILS, AND WE EXPECT TO HAVE BUILT UP A PICTURE OF THIS KILLING AND THE CASE APPROACH BY TOMORROW MORNING
FUCK THAT!
FILTHY ASSISTANTS! SADDLE UP! ALL PROFESSIONAL APPARATUS ON; PREPARE TO HIT THE STREET!

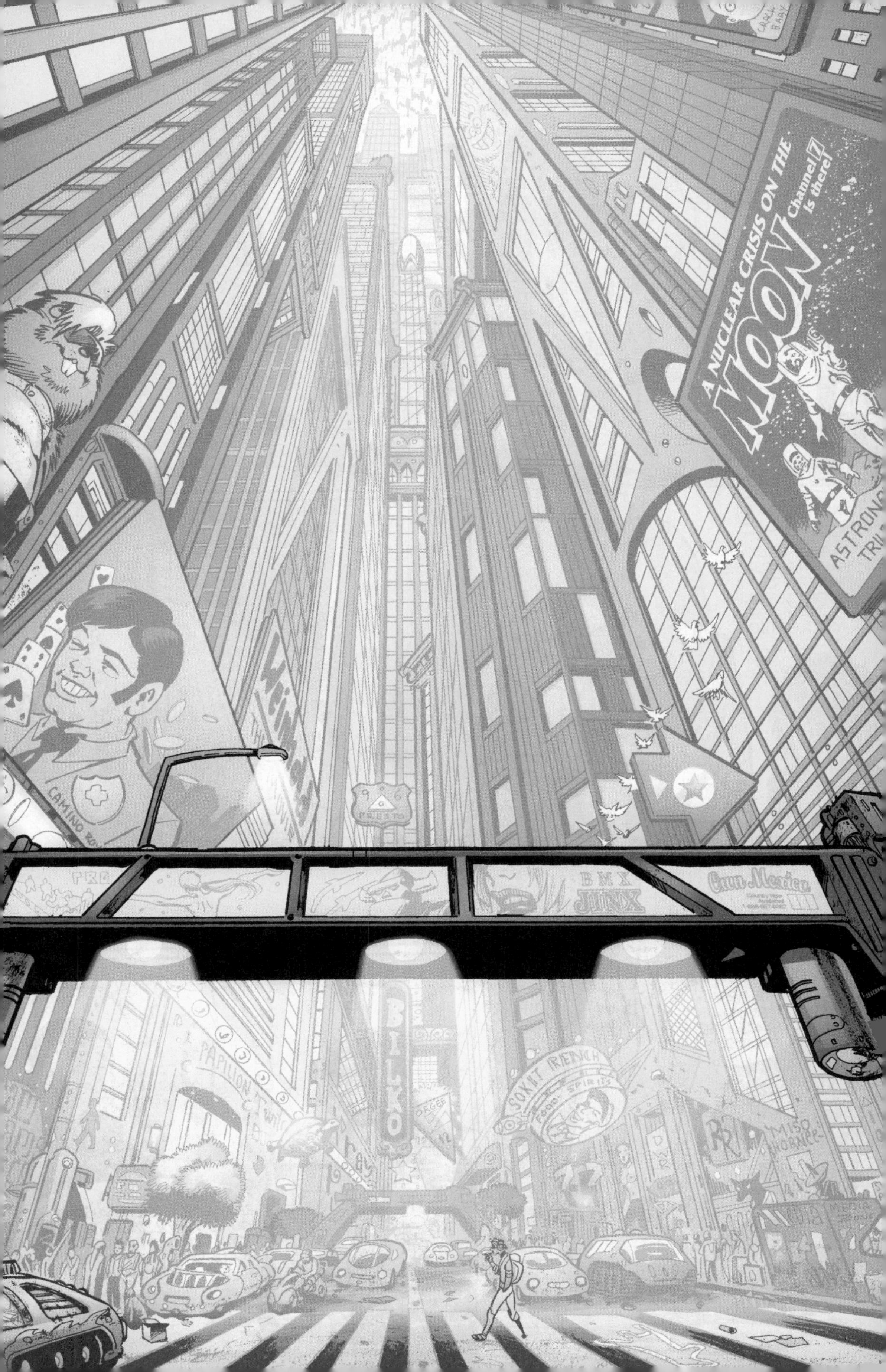

A NUCLEAR CRISIS ON THE MOON
Channel 7 Is there!
BMX
JINX
PRESTO
BILKO
FOOD · SPIRITS
PAPILLON
MEDIA ZONE

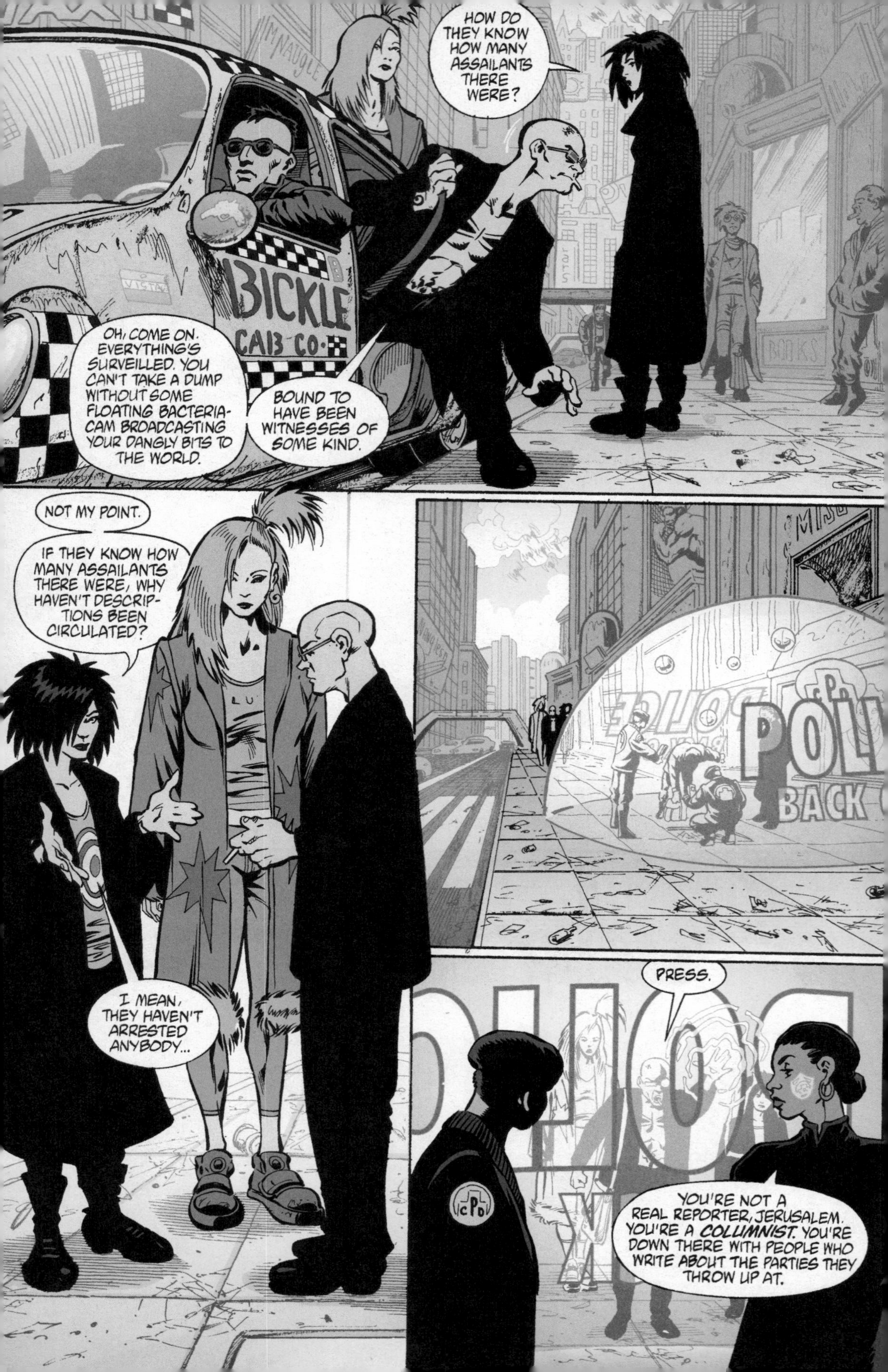
HOW DO THEY KNOW HOW MANY ASSAILANTS THERE WERE?
BICKLE CAB CO.
OH, COME ON. EVERYTHING'S SURVEILLED. YOU CAN'T TAKE A DUMP WITHOUT SOME FLOATING BACTERIA-CAM BROADCASTING YOUR DANGLY BITS TO THE WORLD.
BOUND TO HAVE BEEN WITNESSES OF SOME KIND.
BOOKS
NOT MY POINT.
IF THEY KNOW HOW MANY ASSAILANTS THERE WERE, WHY HAVEN'T DESCRIPTIONS BEEN CIRCULATED?
I MEAN, THEY HAVEN'T ARRESTED ANYBODY...
POLI
BACK
PRESS.
YOU'RE NOT A REAL REPORTER, JERUSALEM. YOU'RE A *COLUMNIST.* YOU'RE DOWN THERE WITH PEOPLE WHO WRITE ABOUT THE PARTIES THEY THROW UP AT.

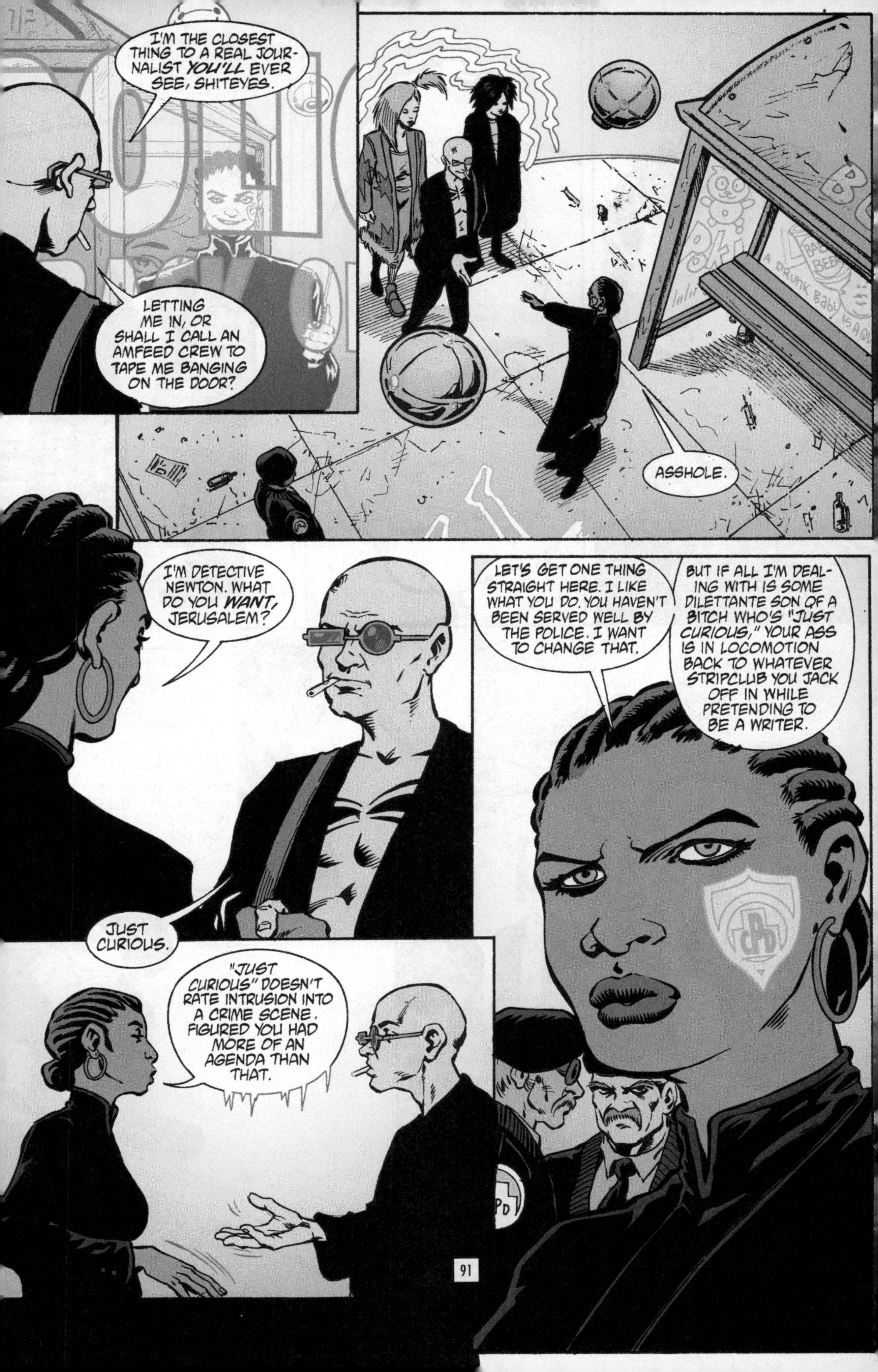
I'M THE CLOSEST THING TO A REAL JOURNALIST YOU'LL EVER SEE, SHITEYES.
LETTING ME IN, OR SHALL I CALL AN AMFEED CREW TO TAPE ME BANGING ON THE DOOR?
ASSHOLE.
I'M DETECTIVE NEWTON. WHAT DO YOU WANT, JERUSALEM?
JUST CURIOUS.
"JUST CURIOUS" DOESN'T RATE INTRUSION INTO A CRIME SCENE. FIGURED YOU HAD MORE OF AN AGENDA THAN THAT.
LET'S GET ONE THING STRAIGHT HERE. I LIKE WHAT YOU DO. YOU HAVEN'T BEEN SERVED WELL BY THE POLICE. I WANT TO CHANGE THAT.
BUT IF ALL I'M DEALING WITH IS SOME DILETTANTE SON OF A BITCH WHO'S "JUST CURIOUS," YOUR ASS IS IN LOCOMOTION BACK TO WHATEVER STRIPCLUB YOU JACK OFF IN WHILE PRETENDING TO BE A WRITER.

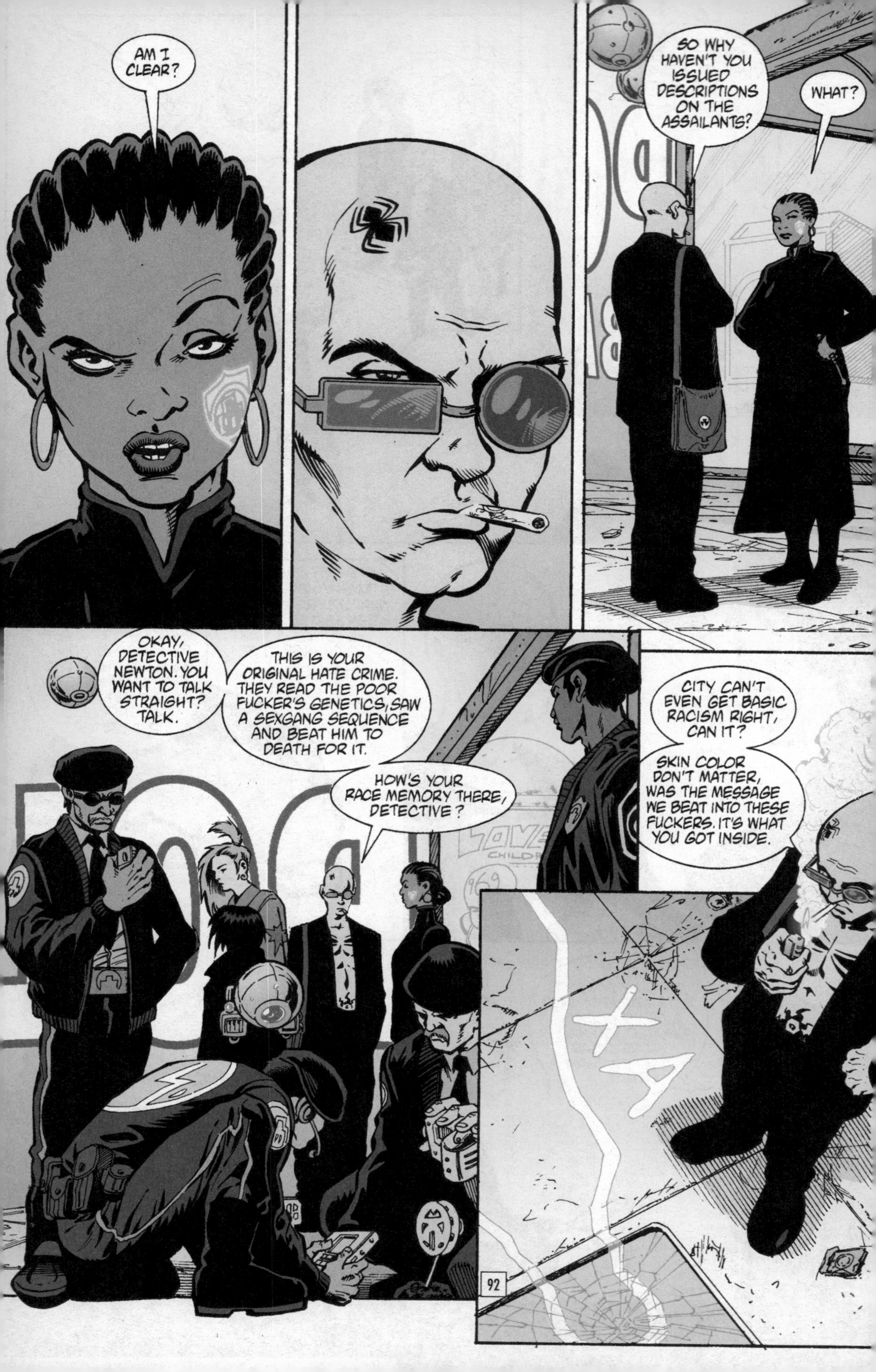
AM I CLEAR?
SO WHY HAVEN'T YOU ISSUED DESCRIPTIONS ON THE ASSAILANTS?
WHAT?
OKAY, DETECTIVE NEWTON. YOU WANT TO TALK STRAIGHT? TALK.
THIS IS YOUR ORIGINAL HATE CRIME. THEY READ THE POOR FUCKER'S GENETICS, SAW A SEXGANG SEQUENCE AND BEAT HIM TO DEATH FOR IT.
HOW'S YOUR RACE MEMORY THERE, DETECTIVE?
CITY CAN'T EVEN GET BASIC RACISM RIGHT, CAN IT?
SKIN COLOR DON'T MATTER, WAS THE MESSAGE WE BEAT INTO THESE FUCKERS. IT'S WHAT YOU GOT INSIDE.

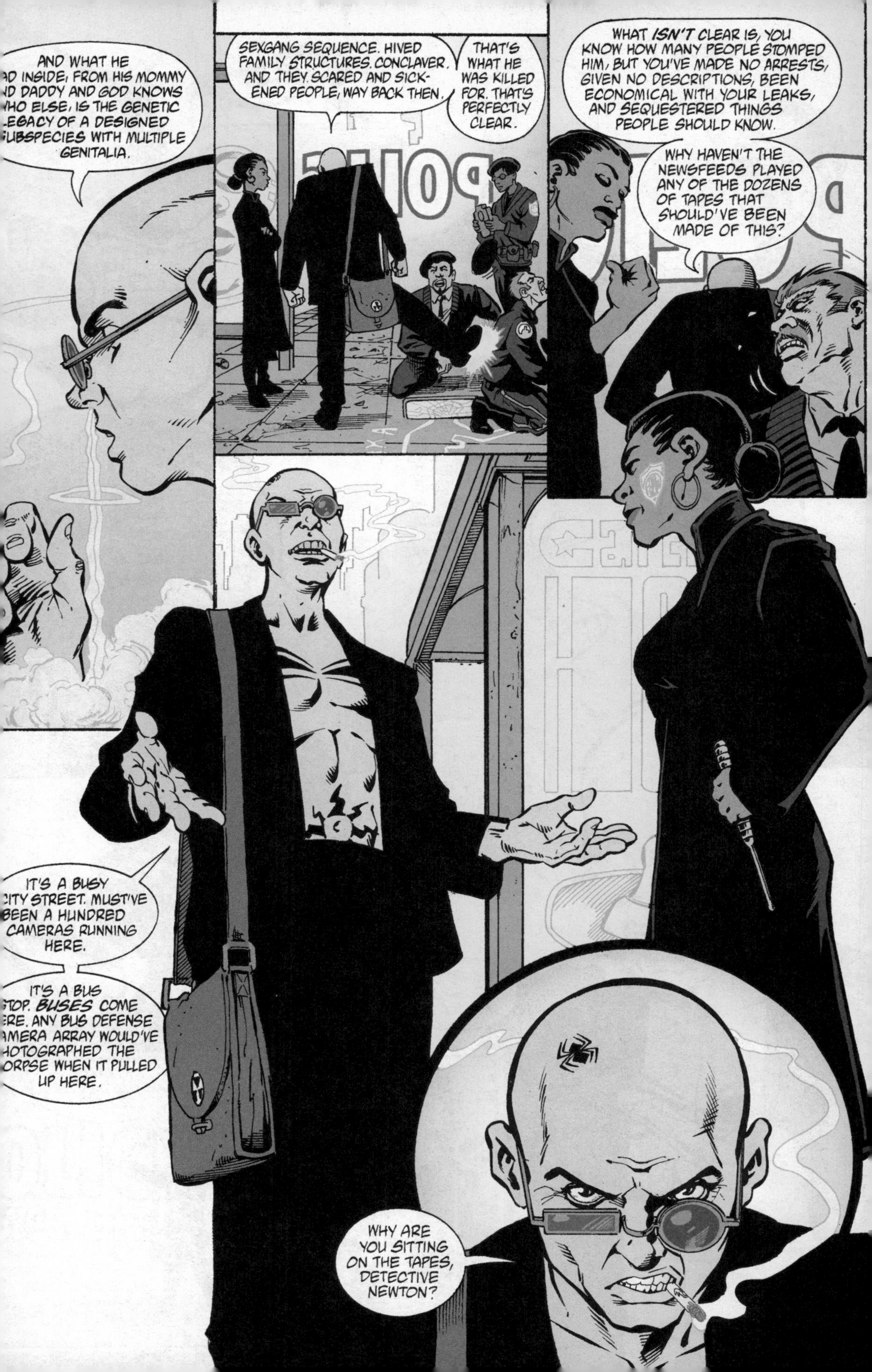
AND WHAT HE AD INSIDE, FROM HIS MOMMY ND DADDY AND GOD KNOWS WHO ELSE, IS THE GENETIC LEGACY OF A DESIGNED SUBSPECIES WITH MULTIPLE GENITALIA.
SEXGANG SEQUENCE. HIVED FAMILY STRUCTURES. CONCLAVER. AND THEY. SCARED AND SICK-ENED PEOPLE, WAY BACK THEN.
THAT'S WHAT HE WAS KILLED FOR. THAT'S PERFECTLY CLEAR.
WHAT ISN'T CLEAR IS, YOU KNOW HOW MANY PEOPLE STOMPED HIM, BUT YOU'VE MADE NO ARRESTS, GIVEN NO DESCRIPTIONS, BEEN ECONOMICAL WITH YOUR LEAKS, AND SEQUESTERED THINGS PEOPLE SHOULD KNOW.
WHY HAVEN'T THE NEWSFEEDS PLAYED ANY OF THE DOZENS OF TAPES THAT SHOULD'VE BEEN MADE OF THIS?
IT'S A BUSY CITY STREET. MUST'VE BEEN A HUNDRED CAMERAS RUNNING HERE.
IT'S A BUS STOP. BUSES COME ERE. ANY BUS DEFENSE AMERA ARRAY WOULD'VE HOTOGRAPHED THE ORPSE WHEN IT PULLED UP HERE.
WHY ARE YOU SITTING ON THE TAPES, DETECTIVE NEWTON?

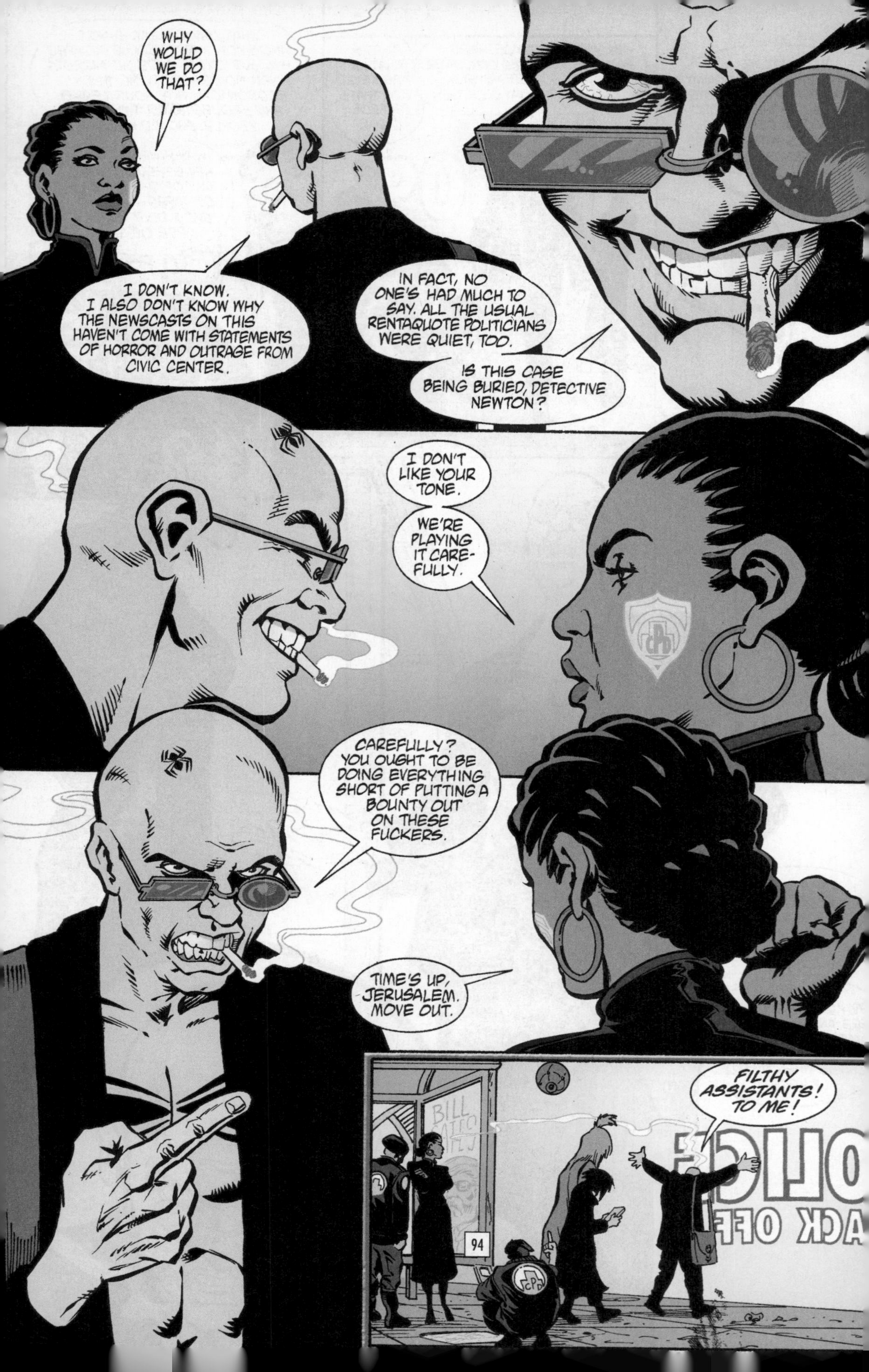
WHY WOULD WE DO THAT?
I DON'T KNOW. I ALSO DON'T KNOW WHY THE NEWSCASTS ON THIS HAVEN'T COME WITH STATEMENTS OF HORROR AND OUTRAGE FROM CIVIC CENTER.
IN FACT, NO ONE'S HAD MUCH TO SAY. ALL THE USUAL RENTAQUOTE POLITICIANS WERE QUIET, TOO.
IS THIS CASE BEING BURIED, DETECTIVE NEWTON?
I DON'T LIKE YOUR TONE.
WE'RE PLAYING IT CAREFULLY.
CAREFULLY? YOU OUGHT TO BE DOING EVERYTHING SHORT OF PUTTING A BOUNTY OUT ON THESE FUCKERS.
TIME'S UP, JERUSALEM. MOVE OUT.
FILTHY ASSISTANTS! TO ME!

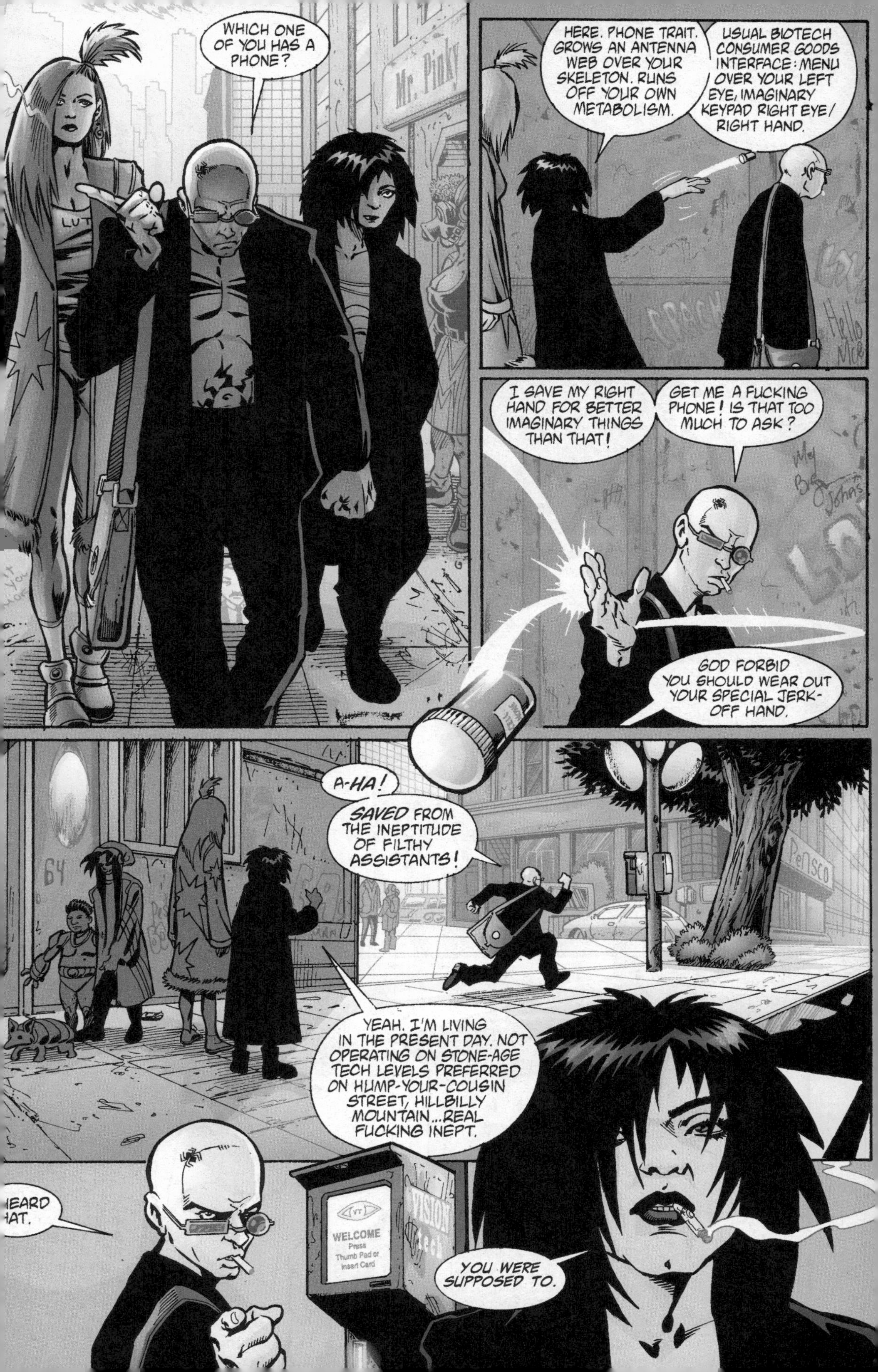
WHICH ONE OF YOU HAS A PHONE?
Mr. Pinky
HERE. PHONE TRAIT. GROWS AN ANTENNA WEB OVER YOUR SKELETON. RUNS OFF YOUR OWN METABOLISM.
USUAL BIOTECH CONSUMER GOODS INTERFACE: MENU OVER YOUR LEFT EYE, IMAGINARY KEYPAD RIGHT EYE/ RIGHT HAND.
I SAVE MY RIGHT HAND FOR BETTER IMAGINARY THINGS THAN THAT!
GET ME A FUCKING PHONE! IS THAT TOO MUCH TO ASK?
GOD FORBID YOU SHOULD WEAR OUT YOUR SPECIAL JERK-OFF HAND.
A-HA!
SAVED FROM THE INEPTITUDE OF FILTHY ASSISTANTS!
PeNSCO
YEAH. I'M LIVING IN THE PRESENT DAY. NOT OPERATING ON STONE-AGE TECH LEVELS PREFERRED ON HUMP-YOUR-COUSIN STREET, HILLBILLY MOUNTAIN...REAL FUCKING INEPT.
HEARD HAT.
VISION tech
WELCOME
Press Thumb Pad or Insert Card
YOU WERE SUPPOSED TO.

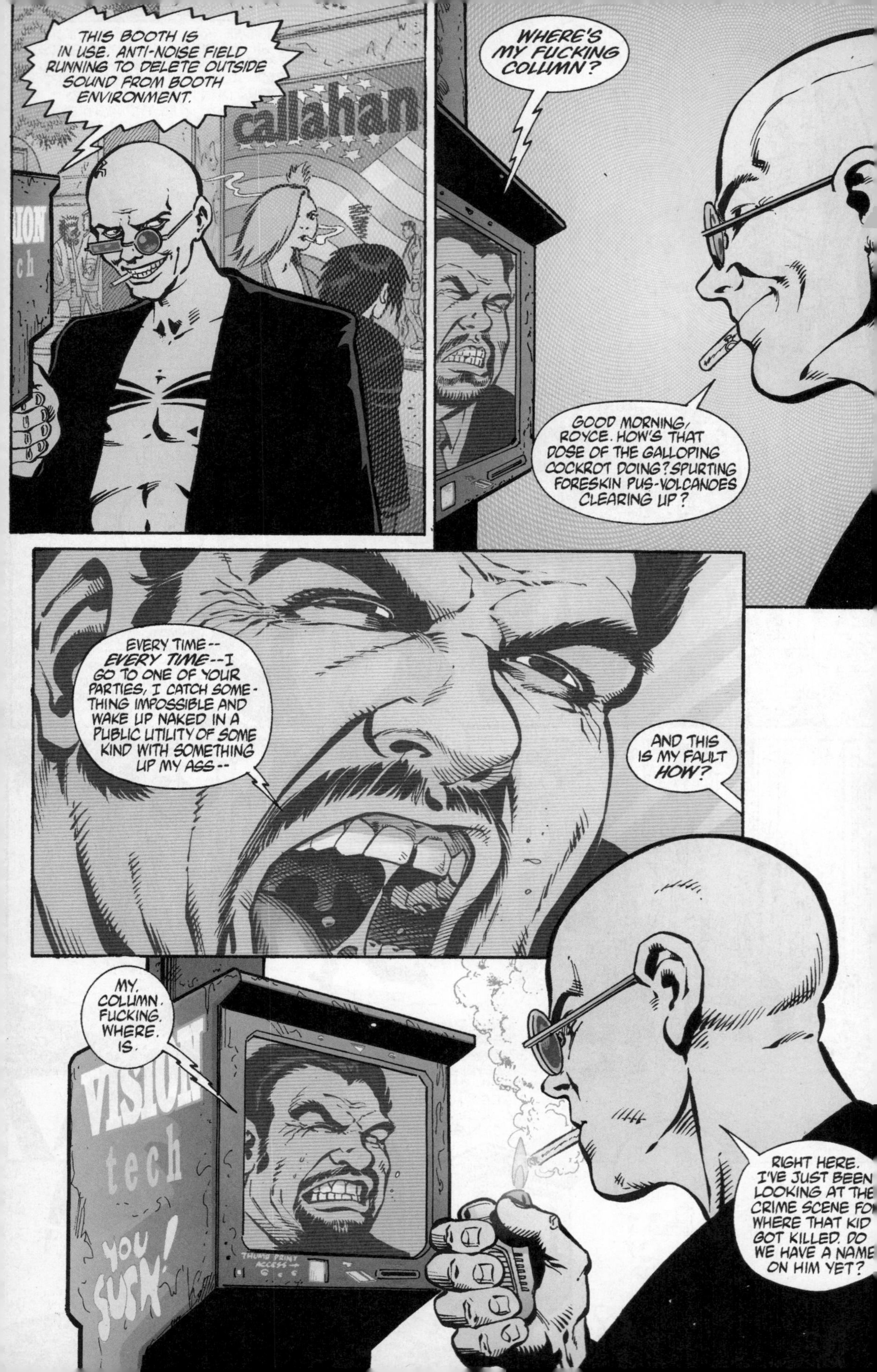
THIS BOOTH IS IN USE. ANTI-NOISE FIELD RUNNING TO DELETE OUTSIDE SOUND FROM BOOTH ENVIRONMENT.
callahan
WHERE'S MY FUCKING COLUMN?
GOOD MORNING, ROYCE. HOW'S THAT DOSE OF THE GALLOPING COCKROT DOING? SPURTING FORESKIN PUS-VOLCANOES CLEARING UP?
EVERY TIME-- EVERY TIME--I GO TO ONE OF YOUR PARTIES, I CATCH SOMETHING IMPOSSIBLE AND WAKE UP NAKED IN A PUBLIC UTILITY OF SOME KIND WITH SOMETHING UP MY ASS--
AND THIS IS MY FAULT HOW?
MY. COLUMN. FUCKING. WHERE. IS.
VISION tech
YOU SUCK!
THUMB PRINT ACCESS
RIGHT HERE. I'VE JUST BEEN LOOKING AT THE CRIME SCENE FO WHERE THAT KID GOT KILLED. DO WE HAVE A NAME ON HIM YET?

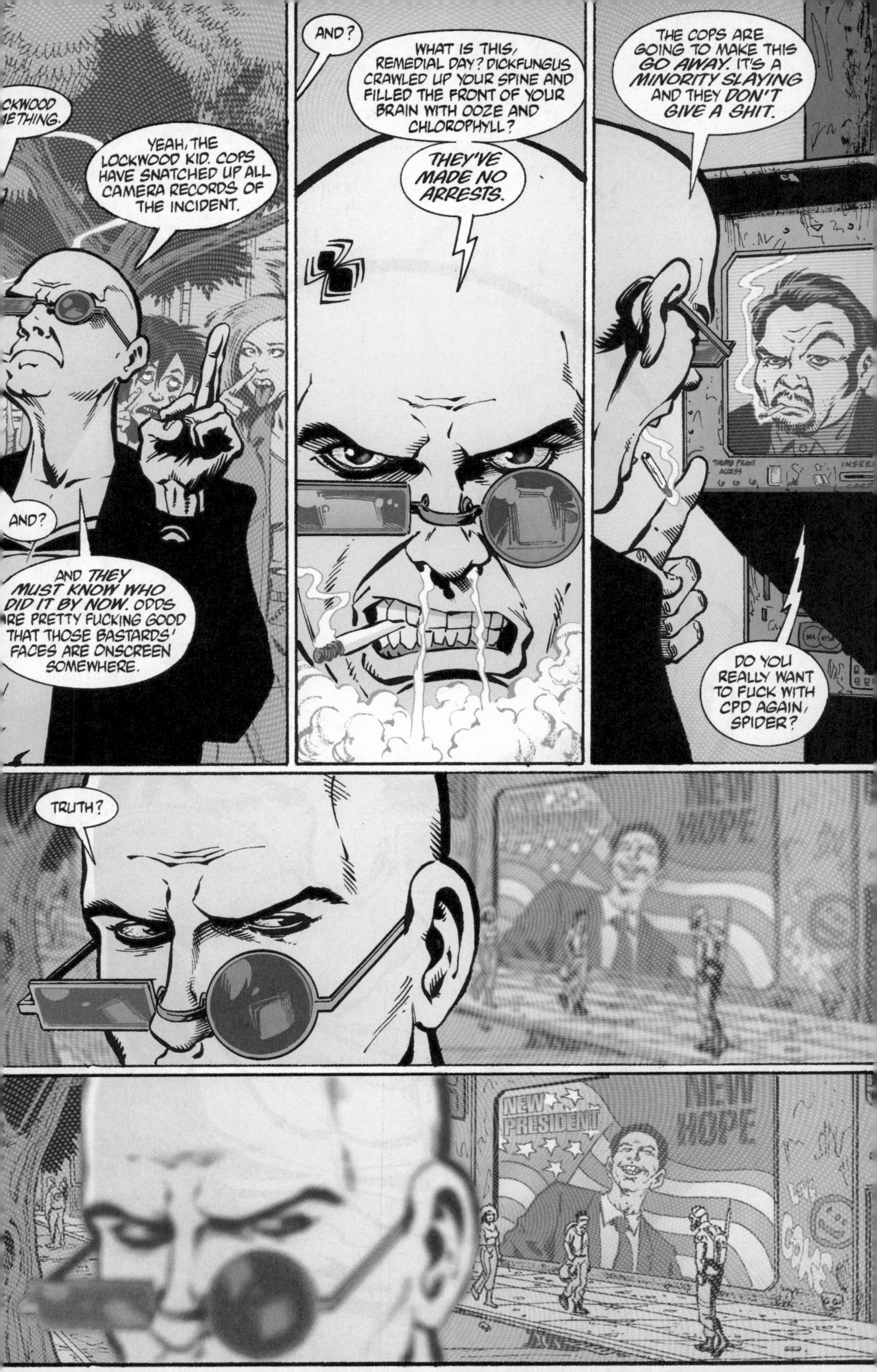

CKWOOD
METHING.
YEAH, THE LOCKWOOD KID. COPS HAVE SNATCHED UP ALL CAMERA RECORDS OF THE INCIDENT.
AND?
AND THEY MUST KNOW WHO DID IT BY NOW. ODDS ARE PRETTY FUCKING GOOD THAT THOSE BASTARDS' FACES ARE ONSCREEN SOMEWHERE.
AND?
WHAT IS THIS, REMEDIAL DAY? DICKFUNGUS CRAWLED UP YOUR SPINE AND FILLED THE FRONT OF YOUR BRAIN WITH OOZE AND CHLOROPHYLL?
THEY'VE MADE NO ARRESTS.
THE COPS ARE GOING TO MAKE THIS GO AWAY. IT'S A MINORITY SLAYING AND THEY DON'T GIVE A SHIT.
DO YOU REALLY WANT TO FUCK WITH CPD AGAIN, SPIDER?
TRUTH?
NEW HOPE
NEW PRESIDENT
NEW HOPE

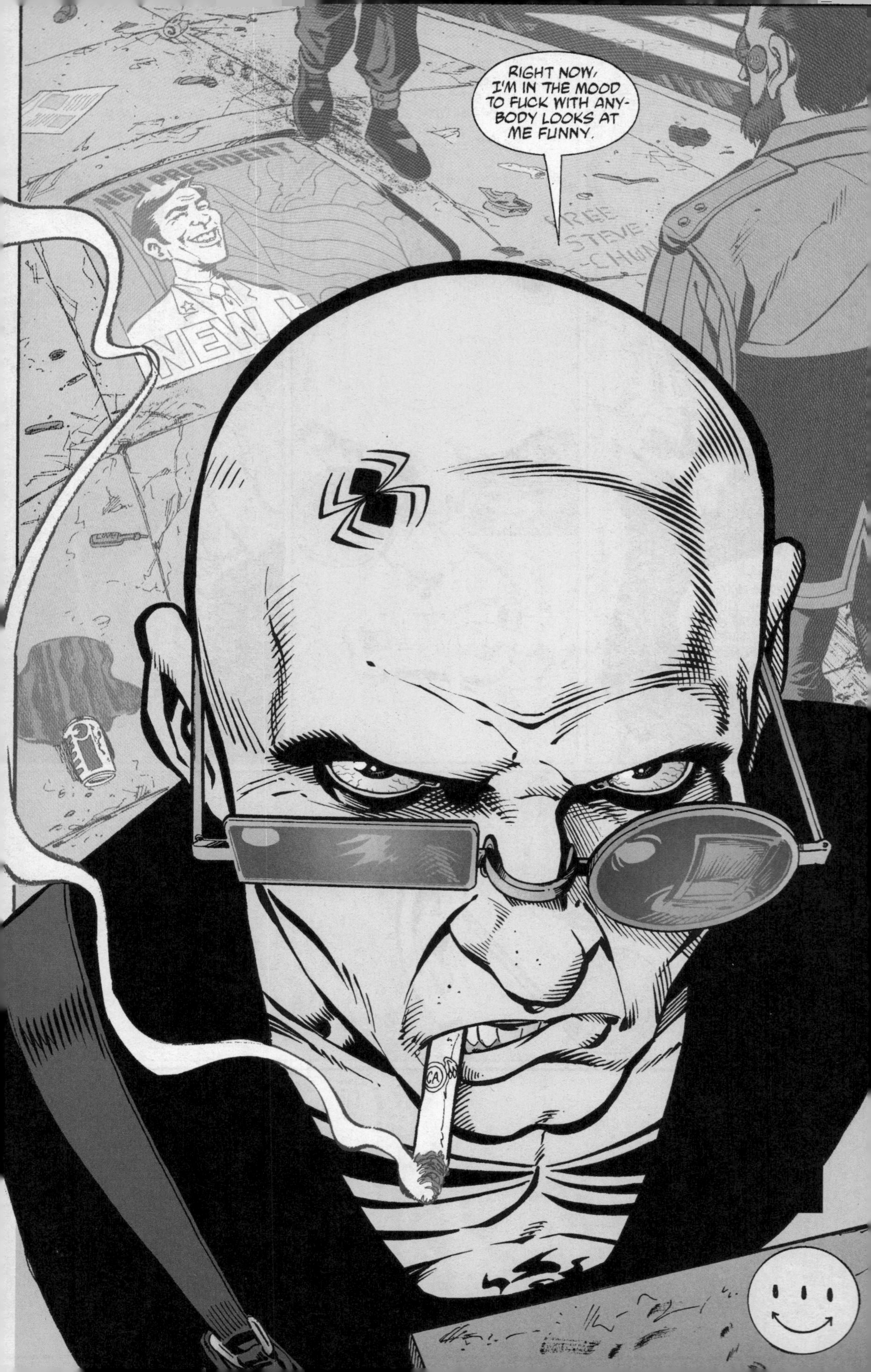

RIGHT NOW, I'M IN THE MOOD TO FUCK WITH ANY-BODY LOOKS AT ME FUNNY.
NEW PRESIDENT
NEW
FREE STEVE CHWA

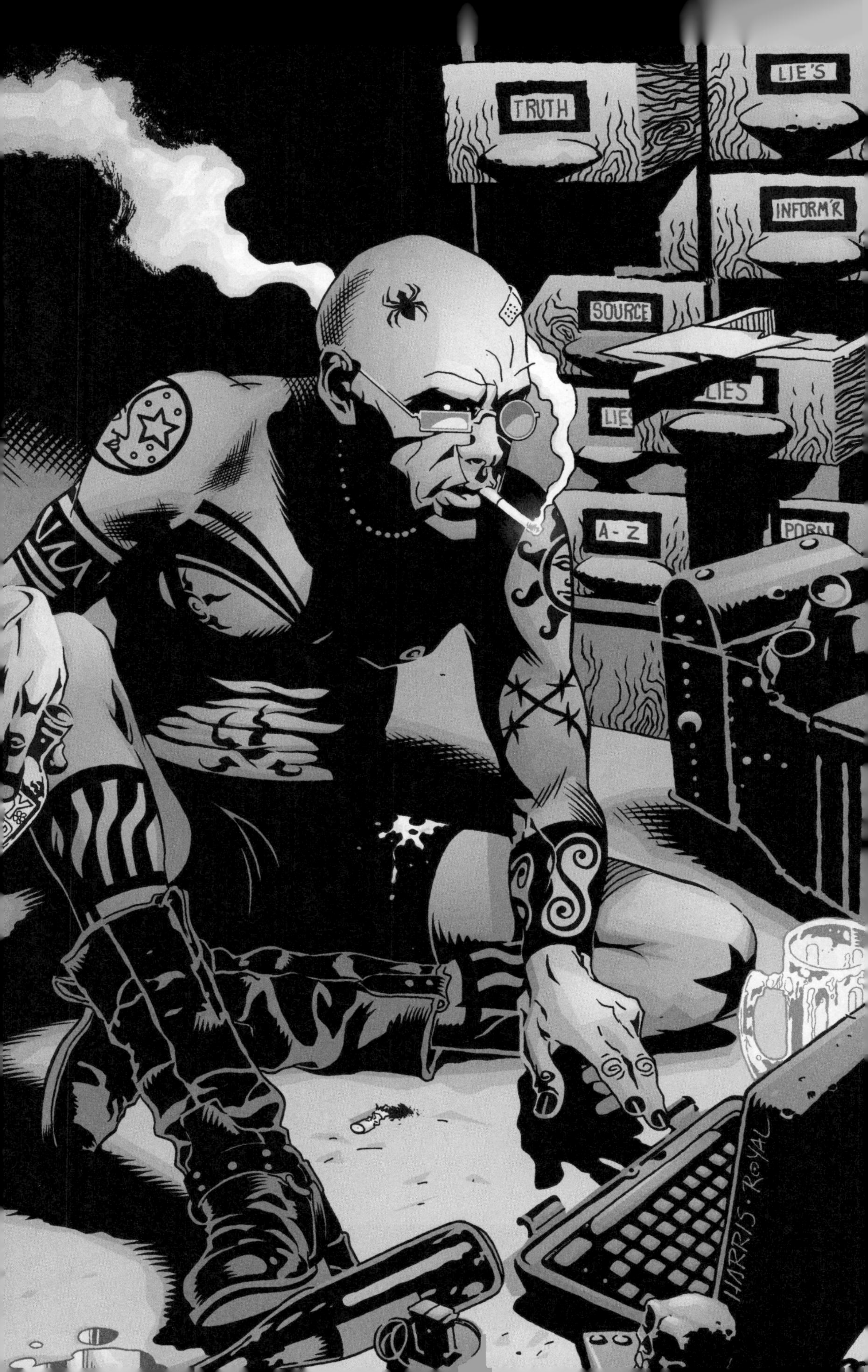

TRUTH
LIE'S
INFORM'R
SOURCE
LIES
LIES
A-Z
PORN
HARRIS · ROYAL

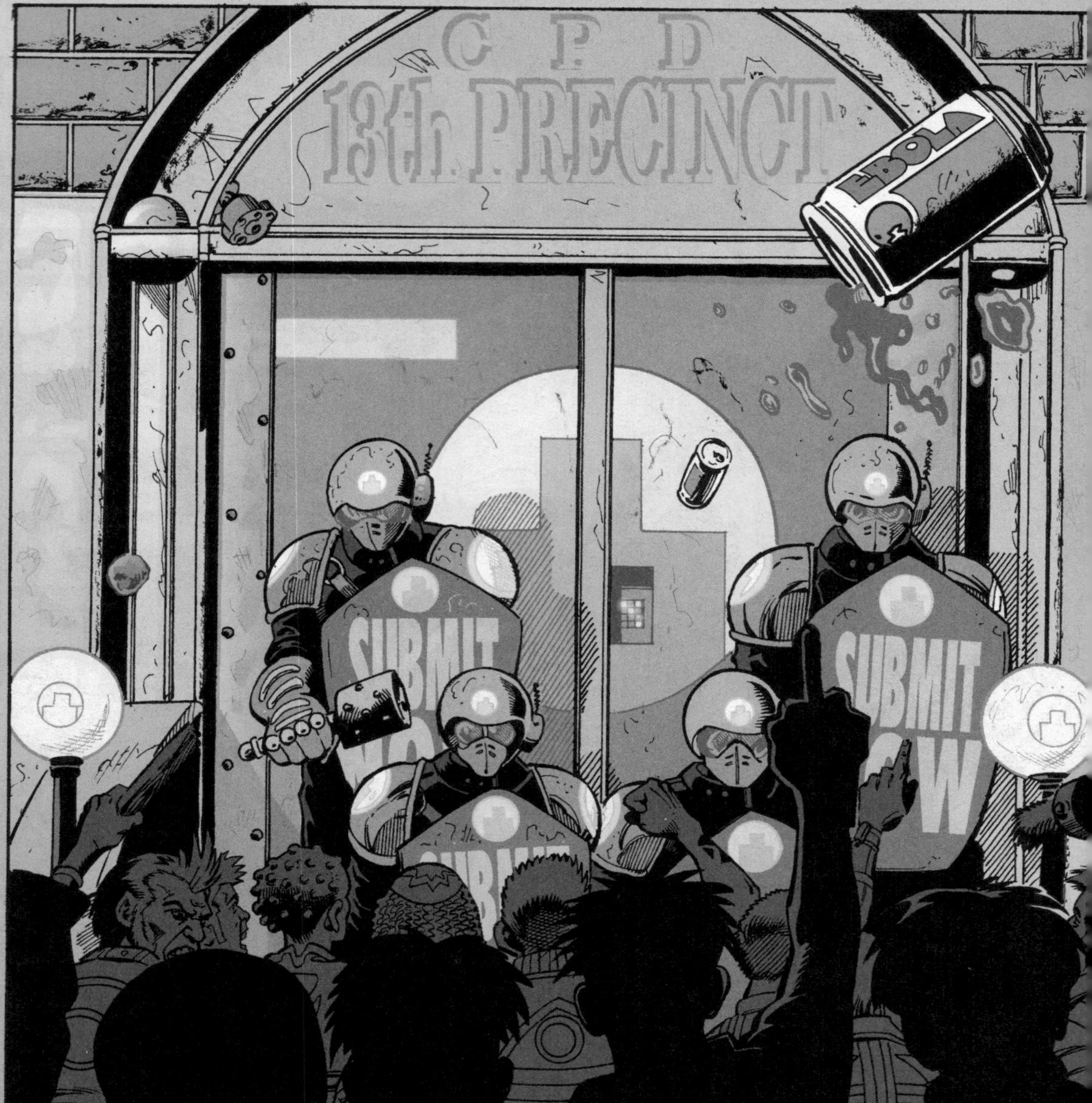
C P D
13th. PRECINCT
EBOLA
SUBMIT
SUBMIT

Warren Ellis writes & Darick Robertson pencils

LONELY CITY

two of three

Rodney Ramos Inker **Clem Robins** Letterer **Nathan Eyring** Color & Seps **Tony Harris** Cover Pencils **Jim Royal** Cover Inks **Cliff Chiang** Editor

TRANSMETROPOLITAN created by Warren Ellis and Darick Robertson

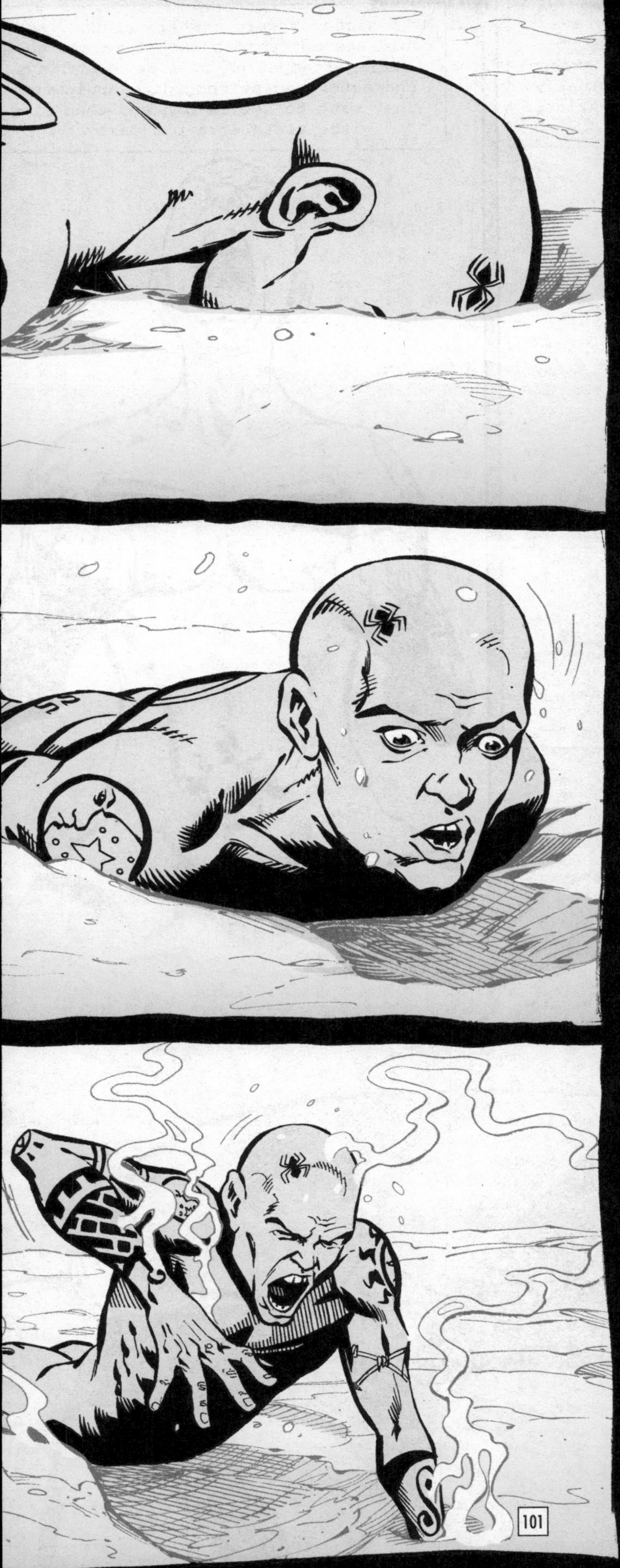

I jabbered and shrieked in the appalling chill of Dante Road, because I was naked and had been shot in the legs by sharpened ballistic popsicles. Strawberry and guava flavor. Fucking disgusting.

Winter apes jeered me from the park, jacking off with manic contempt, their futuristic innovation-packed semen crackling as it froze in the air mid-trajectory.

I found my bowel disruptor and made the noisy bastards shit themselves. They screamed, awful diarrheatic rushes instantly freezing into vile columns that pinned them to the ground by their bare, speckled asses.

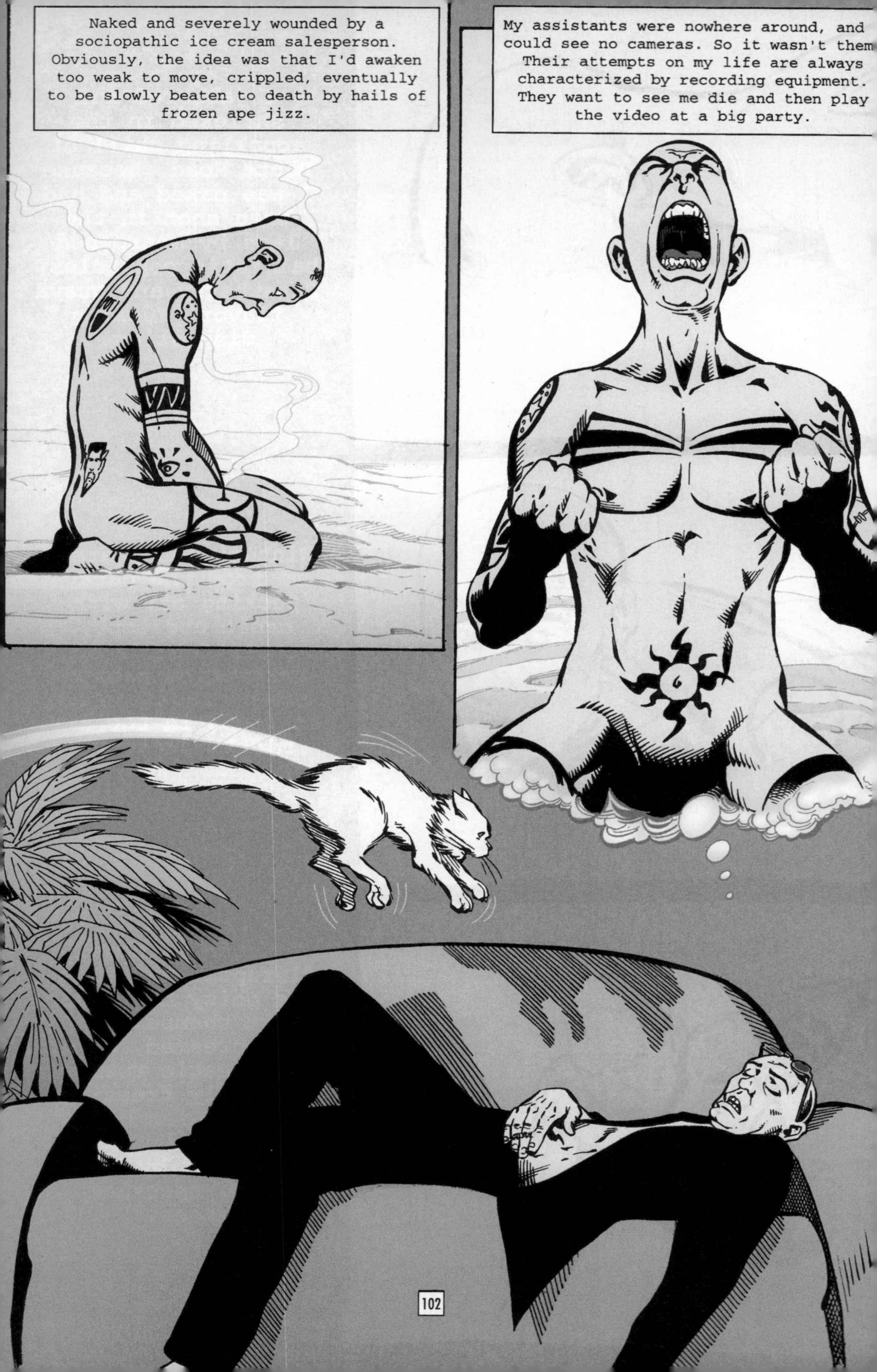
Naked and severely wounded by a sociopathic ice cream salesperson. Obviously, the idea was that I'd awaken too weak to move, crippled, eventually to be slowly beaten to death by hails of frozen ape jizz.
My assistants were nowhere around, and could see no cameras. So it wasn't them Their attempts on my life are always characterized by recording equipment. They want to see me die and then play the video at a big party.

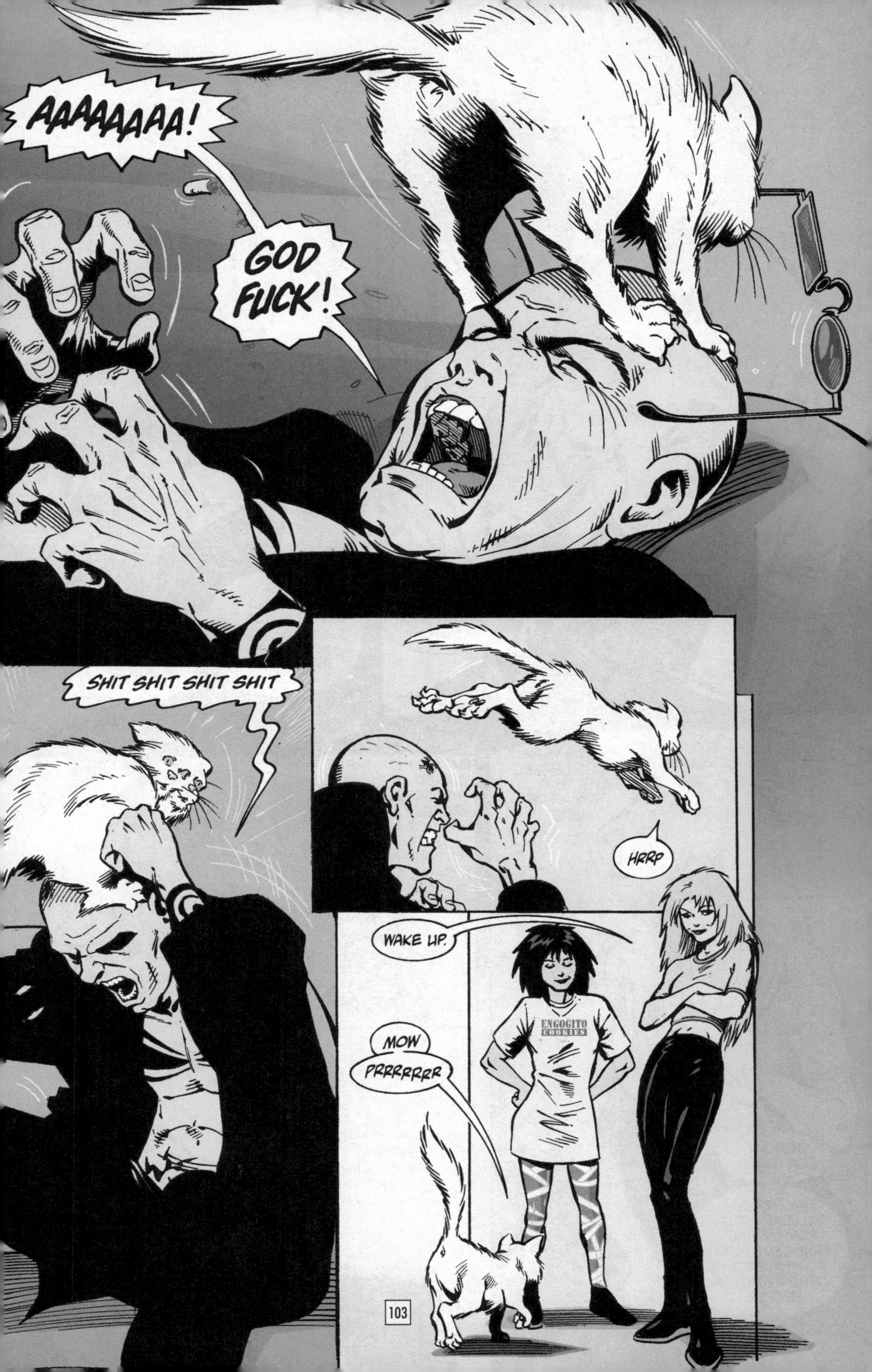
AAAAAAAA!
GOD FUCK!
SHIT SHIT SHIT SHIT
HRRP
WAKE UP.
ENGOGITO COOKIES
MOW
PRRRRRRR

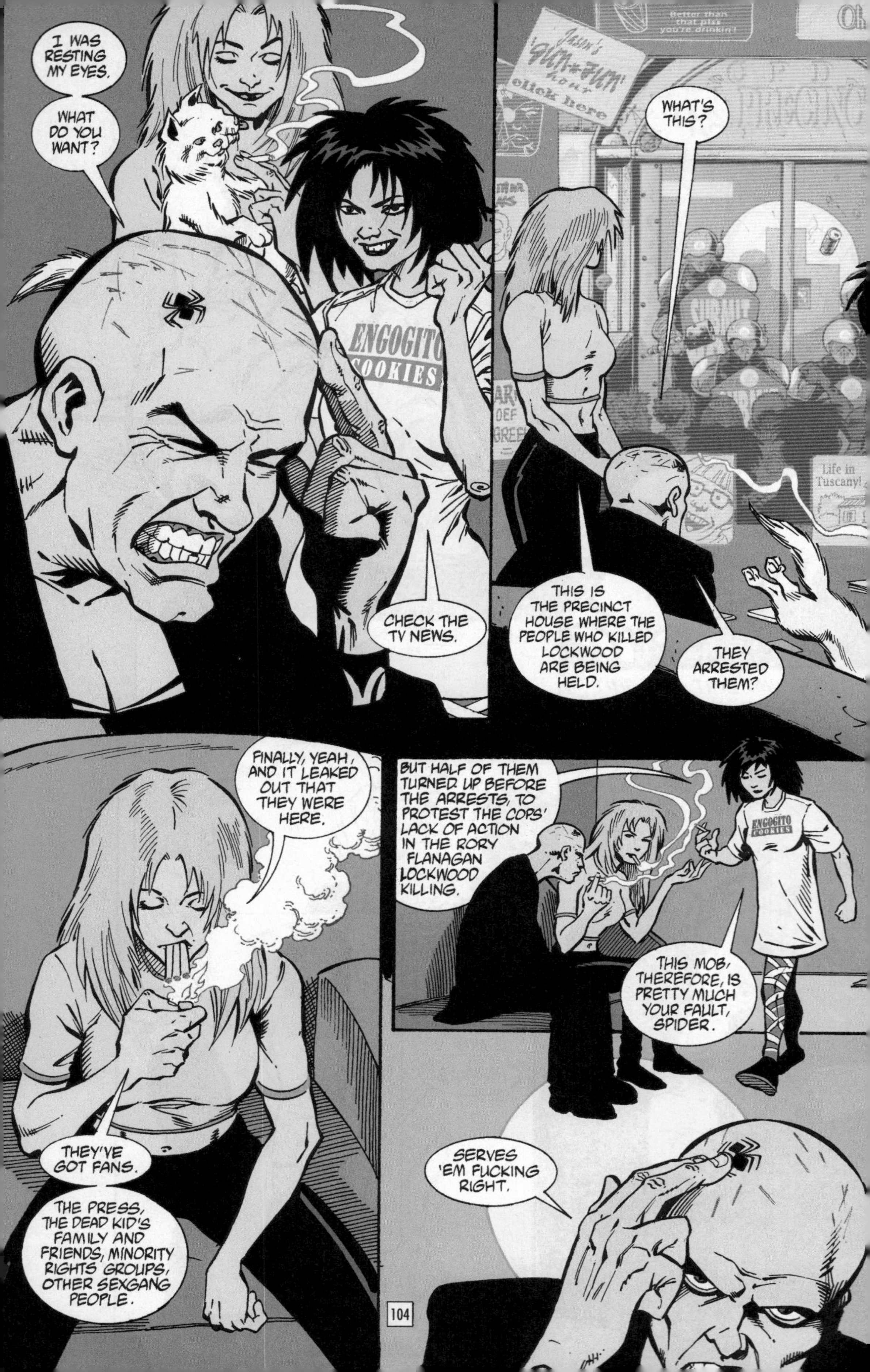
I WAS RESTING MY EYES.
WHAT DO YOU WANT?
ENGOGITO COOKIES
CHECK THE TV NEWS.
Better than that piss you're drinkin'!
Jason's FUN+FUN hour click here
WHAT'S THIS?
THIS IS THE PRECINCT HOUSE WHERE THE PEOPLE WHO KILLED LOCKWOOD ARE BEING HELD.
THEY ARRESTED THEM?
Life in Tuscany!
FINALLY, YEAH, AND IT LEAKED OUT THAT THEY WERE HERE.
THEY'VE GOT FANS.
THE PRESS, THE DEAD KID'S FAMILY AND FRIENDS, MINORITY RIGHTS GROUPS, OTHER SEXGANG PEOPLE.
BUT HALF OF THEM TURNED UP BEFORE THE ARRESTS, TO PROTEST THE COPS' LACK OF ACTION IN THE RORY FLANAGAN LOCKWOOD KILLING.
THIS MOB, THEREFORE, IS PRETTY MUCH YOUR FAULT, SPIDER.
SERVES 'EM FUCKING RIGHT.

LIVE
M DANTE
RECINCT

WANNA
SEE
MOR

WE WANTED THE VISUAL INFORMATION SEQUESTERED WHILE WE STUDIED IT.

LOCKWOO AUTOPS PICS

THE ACCUSED BIOS

HIS APPALLING BEHAVIOR BY THE SS HAS FORCED US BOTH RELEASE THE ED INFORMATION TO PUBLIC AND ARREST E FOUR SUSPECTS IN THE CASE.

CPD

ALAN SINGH
CPD
Spokesperson

THEY NEED A NEW SPOKESPERSON. THEY'VE JUST ADMITTED THAT I FORCED THEM TO DO THEIR FUCKING JOB.

ENCOGITO GROTTES

WHERE IS THIS? WHERE ARE THE BASTARDS BEING KEPT?

DANTE STREET PRECINCT HOUSE.

OKAY, WE'RE GOING DOWN THERE.

TO DO WHAT? BAY WITH THE CROWDS?

TO COVER THE DAMN STORY.

105

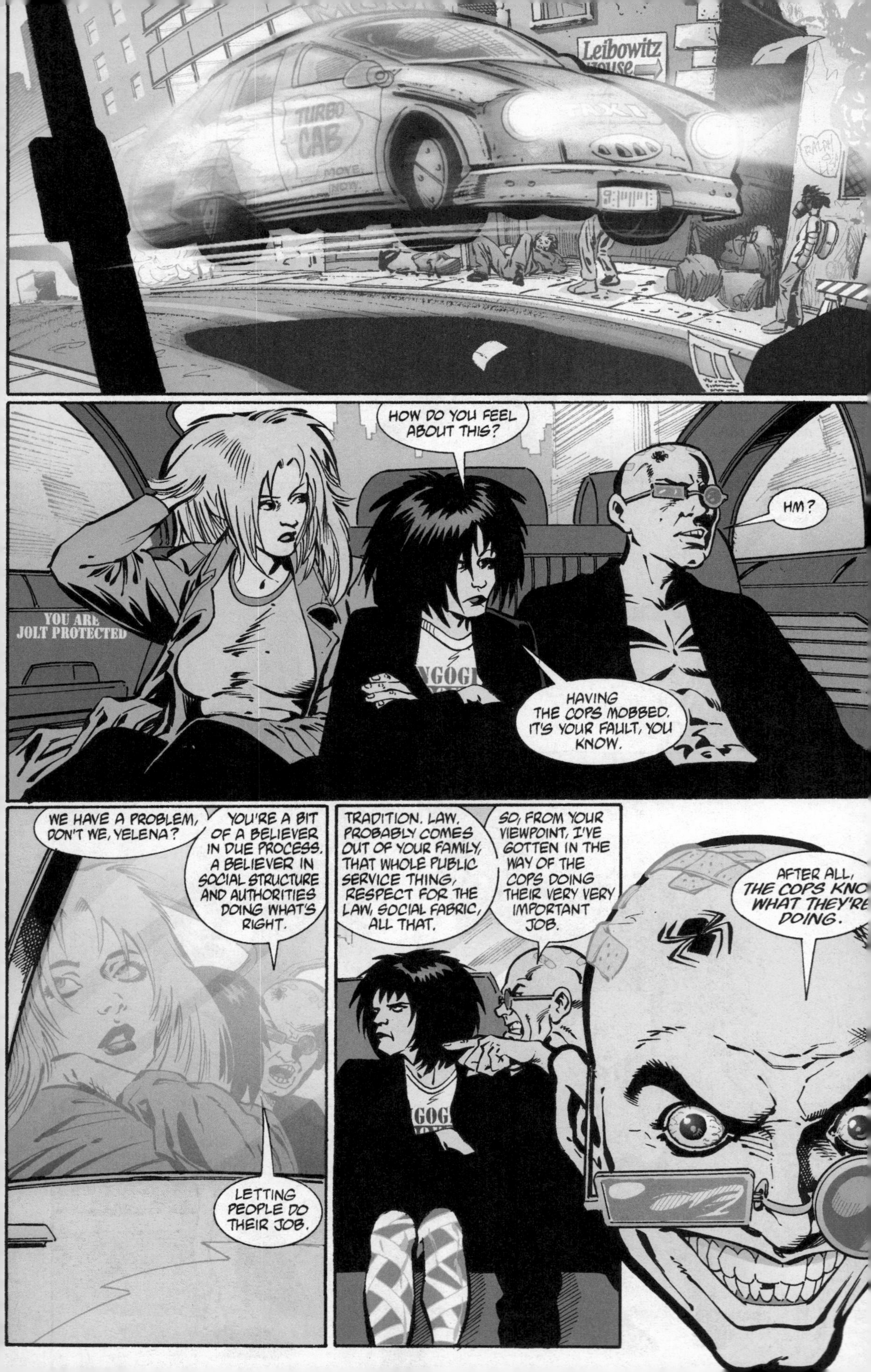
Leibowitz House
TURBO CAB
MOVE NOW
TAXI
HOW DO YOU FEEL ABOUT THIS?
HM?
YOU ARE JOLT PROTECTED
HAVING THE COPS MOBBED. IT'S YOUR FAULT, YOU KNOW.
WE HAVE A PROBLEM, DON'T WE, YELENA?
YOU'RE A BIT OF A BELIEVER IN DUE PROCESS. A BELIEVER IN SOCIAL STRUCTURE AND AUTHORITIES DOING WHAT'S RIGHT.
LETTING PEOPLE DO THEIR JOB.
TRADITION. LAW. PROBABLY COMES OUT OF YOUR FAMILY, THAT WHOLE PUBLIC SERVICE THING, RESPECT FOR THE LAW, SOCIAL FABRIC, ALL THAT.
SO, FROM YOUR VIEWPOINT, I'VE GOTTEN IN THE WAY OF THE COPS DOING THEIR VERY VERY IMPORTANT JOB.
AFTER ALL, THE COPS KNO WHAT THEY'RE DOING.

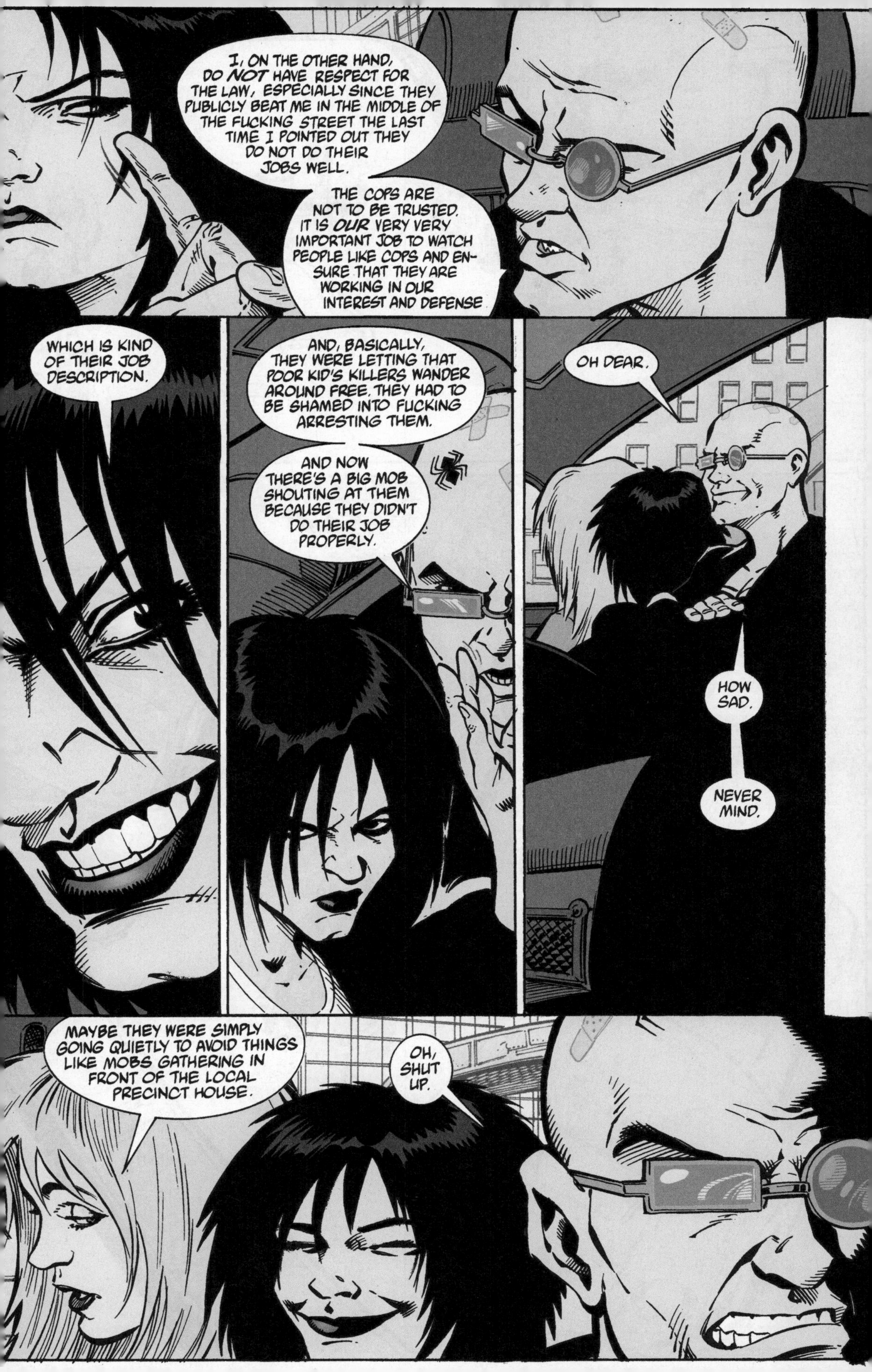

I, ON THE OTHER HAND, DO NOT HAVE RESPECT FOR THE LAW, ESPECIALLY SINCE THEY PUBLICLY BEAT ME IN THE MIDDLE OF THE FUCKING STREET THE LAST TIME I POINTED OUT THEY DO NOT DO THEIR JOBS WELL.
THE COPS ARE NOT TO BE TRUSTED. IT IS OUR VERY VERY IMPORTANT JOB TO WATCH PEOPLE LIKE COPS AND ENSURE THAT THEY ARE WORKING IN OUR INTEREST AND DEFENSE
WHICH IS KIND OF THEIR JOB DESCRIPTION.
AND, BASICALLY, THEY WERE LETTING THAT POOR KID'S KILLERS WANDER AROUND FREE. THEY HAD TO BE SHAMED INTO FUCKING ARRESTING THEM.
AND NOW THERE'S A BIG MOB SHOUTING AT THEM BECAUSE THEY DIDN'T DO THEIR JOB PROPERLY.
OH DEAR.
HOW SAD.
NEVER MIND.
MAYBE THEY WERE SIMPLY GOING QUIETLY TO AVOID THINGS LIKE MOBS GATHERING IN FRONT OF THE LOCAL PRECINCT HOUSE.
OH, SHUT UP.

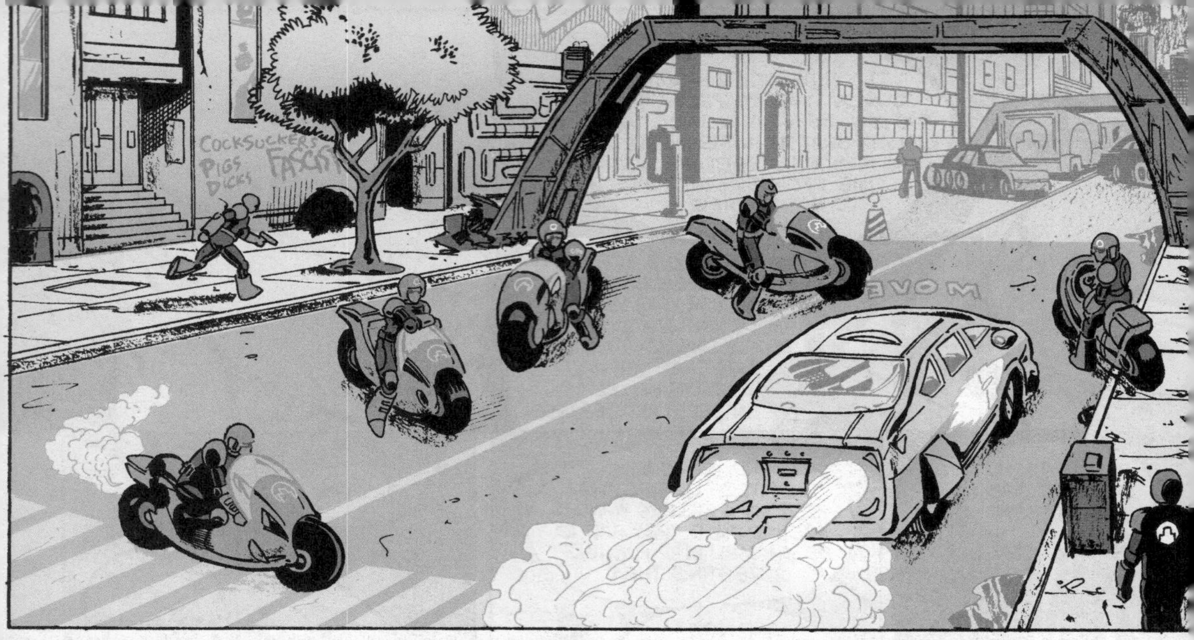
COCKSUCKERS
PIGS
DICKS
MOVE

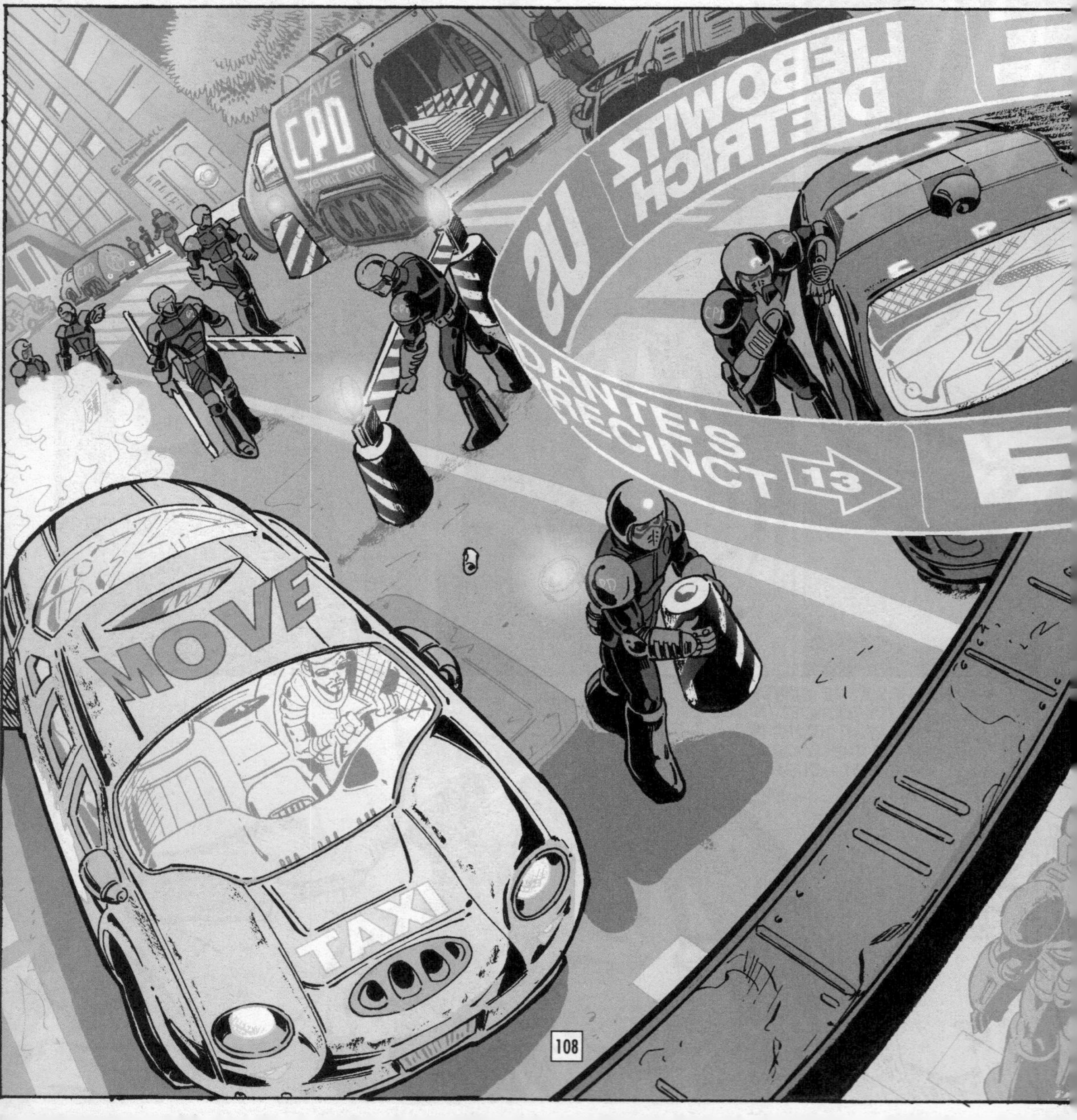
BEHAVE
CPD
SUBMIT NOW
LIEBOWITZ
DIETRICH
US
DANTE'S
RECINCT 13
MOVE
TAXI

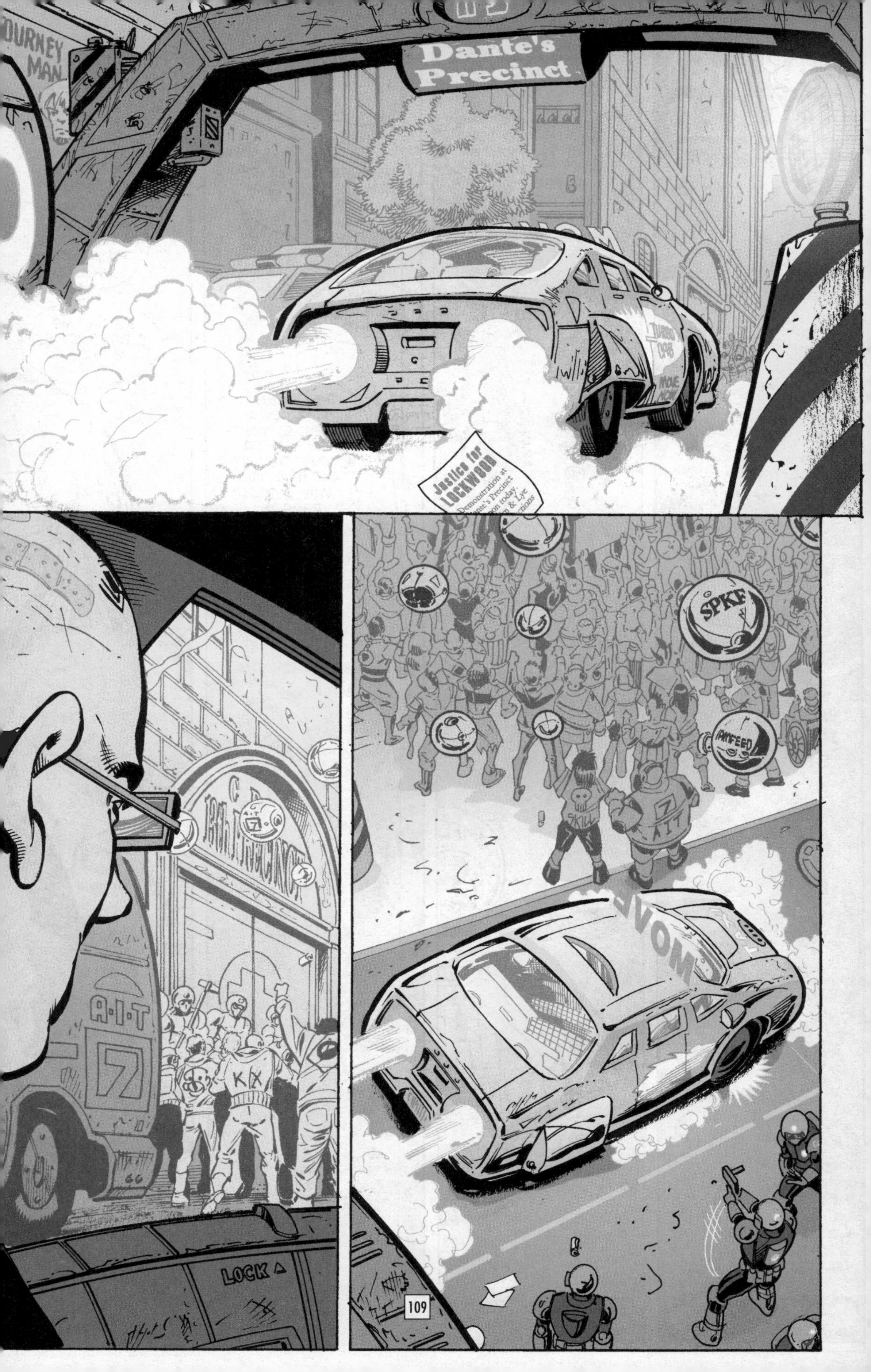
Dante's Precinct
OURNEY MAN
TURBO CAB
MOVE NOW
Justice for LOCKWOOD
Demonstration at
SPKF
AMFEED
A·I·T
KX
LOCK

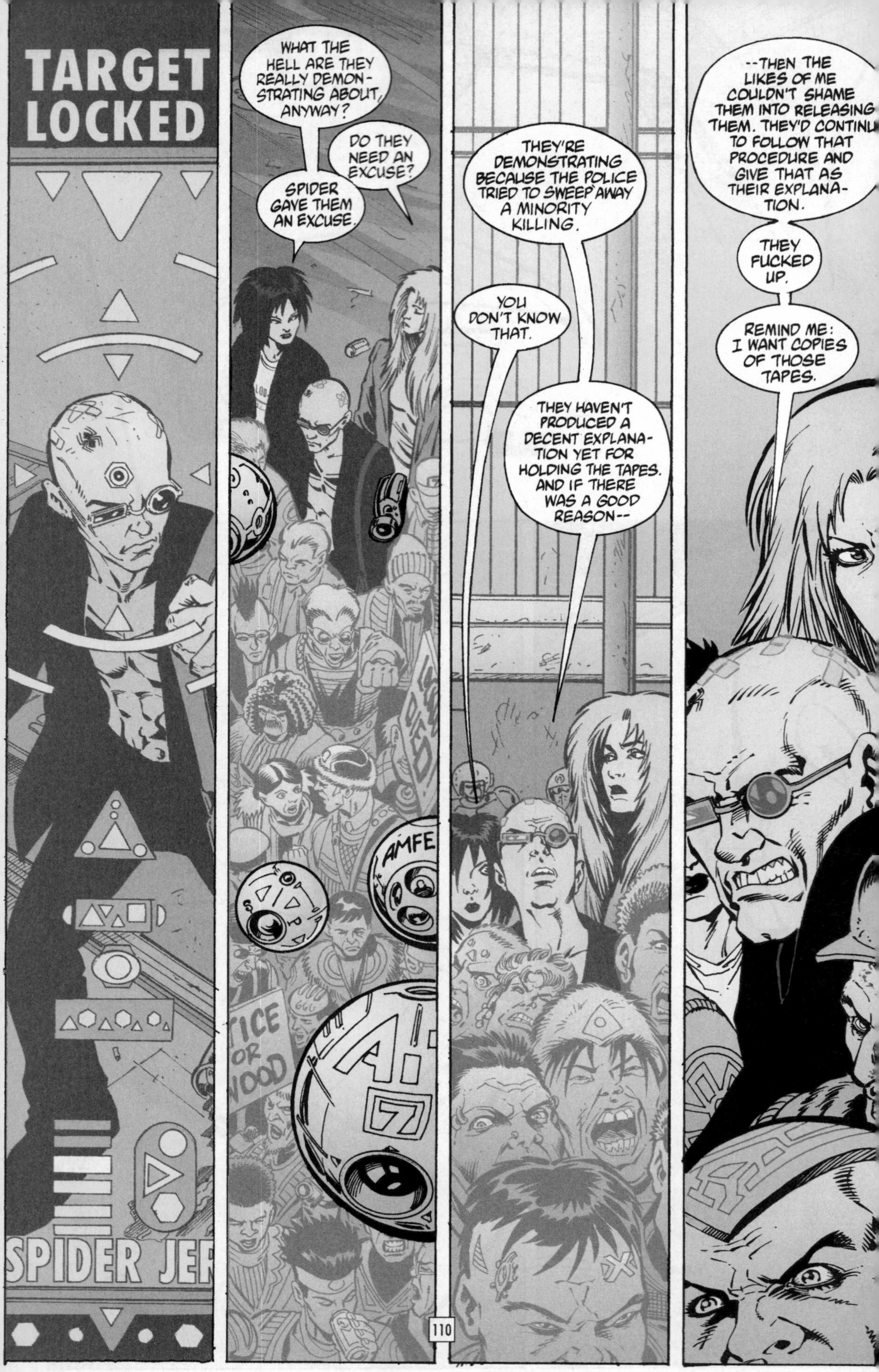
TARGET LOCKED
SPIDER JER
WHAT THE HELL ARE THEY REALLY DEMON-STRATING ABOUT, ANYWAY?
DO THEY NEED AN EXCUSE?
SPIDER GAVE THEM AN EXCUSE.
AMFE
TICE OR WOOD
THEY'RE DEMONSTRATING BECAUSE THE POLICE TRIED TO SWEEP AWAY A MINORITY KILLING.
YOU DON'T KNOW THAT.
THEY HAVEN'T PRODUCED A DECENT EXPLANA-TION YET FOR HOLDING THE TAPES. AND IF THERE WAS A GOOD REASON--
--THEN THE LIKES OF ME COULDN'T SHAME THEM INTO RELEASING THEM. THEY'D CONTINU TO FOLLOW THAT PROCEDURE AND GIVE THAT AS THEIR EXPLANA-TION.
THEY FUCKED UP.
REMIND ME: I WANT COPIES OF THOSE TAPES.

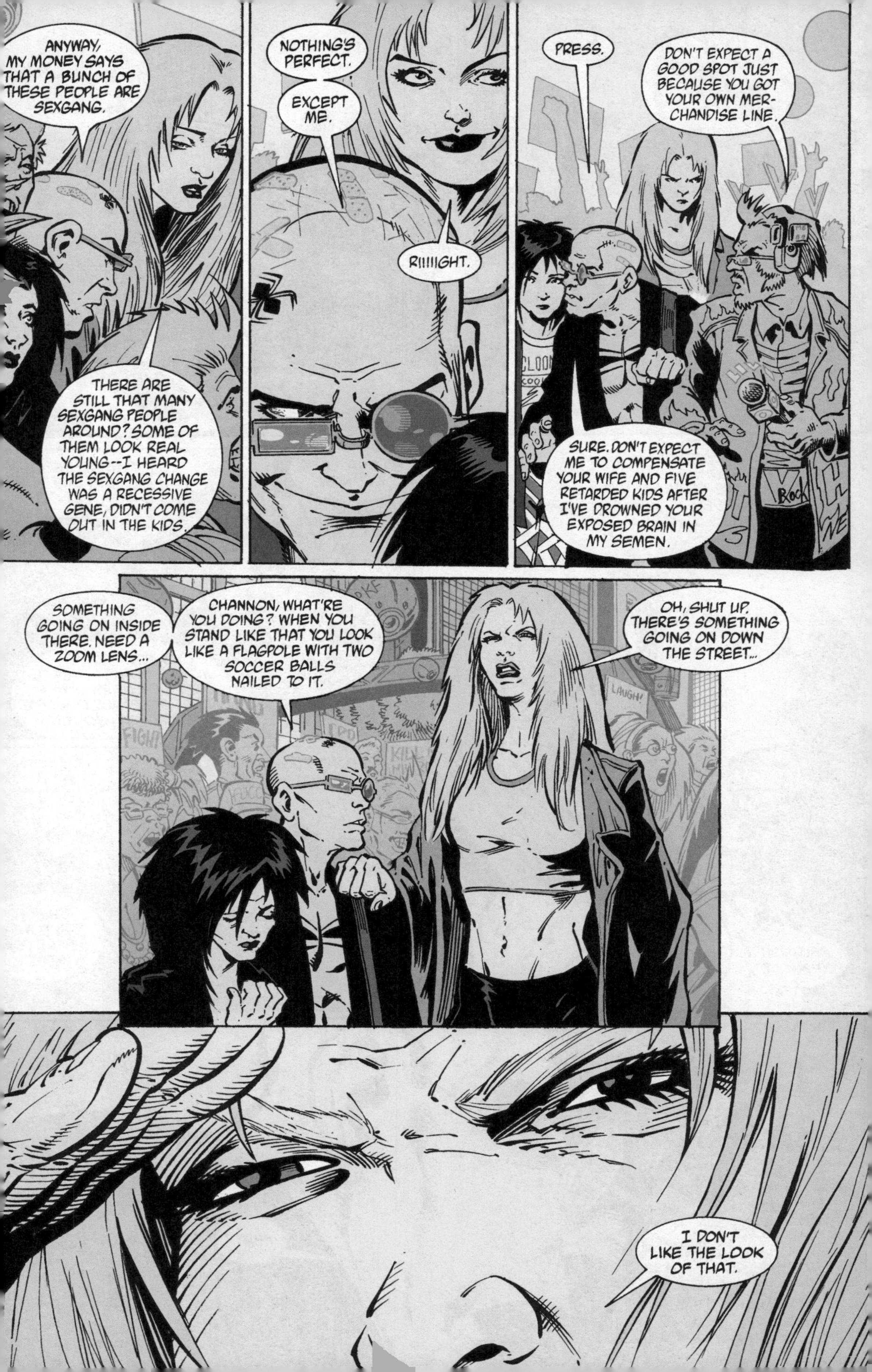
ANYWAY, MY MONEY SAYS THAT A BUNCH OF THESE PEOPLE ARE SEXGANG.
THERE ARE STILL THAT MANY SEXGANG PEOPLE AROUND? SOME OF THEM LOOK REAL YOUNG--I HEARD THE SEXGANG CHANGE WAS A RECESSIVE GENE, DIDN'T COME OUT IN THE KIDS.
NOTHING'S PERFECT.
EXCEPT ME.
RIIIIIGHT.
PRESS.
DON'T EXPECT A GOOD SPOT JUST BECAUSE YOU GOT YOUR OWN MER-CHANDISE LINE.
SURE. DON'T EXPECT ME TO COMPENSATE YOUR WIFE AND FIVE RETARDED KIDS AFTER I'VE DROWNED YOUR EXPOSED BRAIN IN MY SEMEN.
SOMETHING GOING ON INSIDE THERE. NEED A ZOOM LENS...
CHANNON, WHAT'RE YOU DOING? WHEN YOU STAND LIKE THAT YOU LOOK LIKE A FLAGPOLE WITH TWO SOCCER BALLS NAILED TO IT.
OH, SHUT UP. THERE'S SOMETHING GOING ON DOWN THE STREET...
I DON'T LIKE THE LOOK OF THAT.

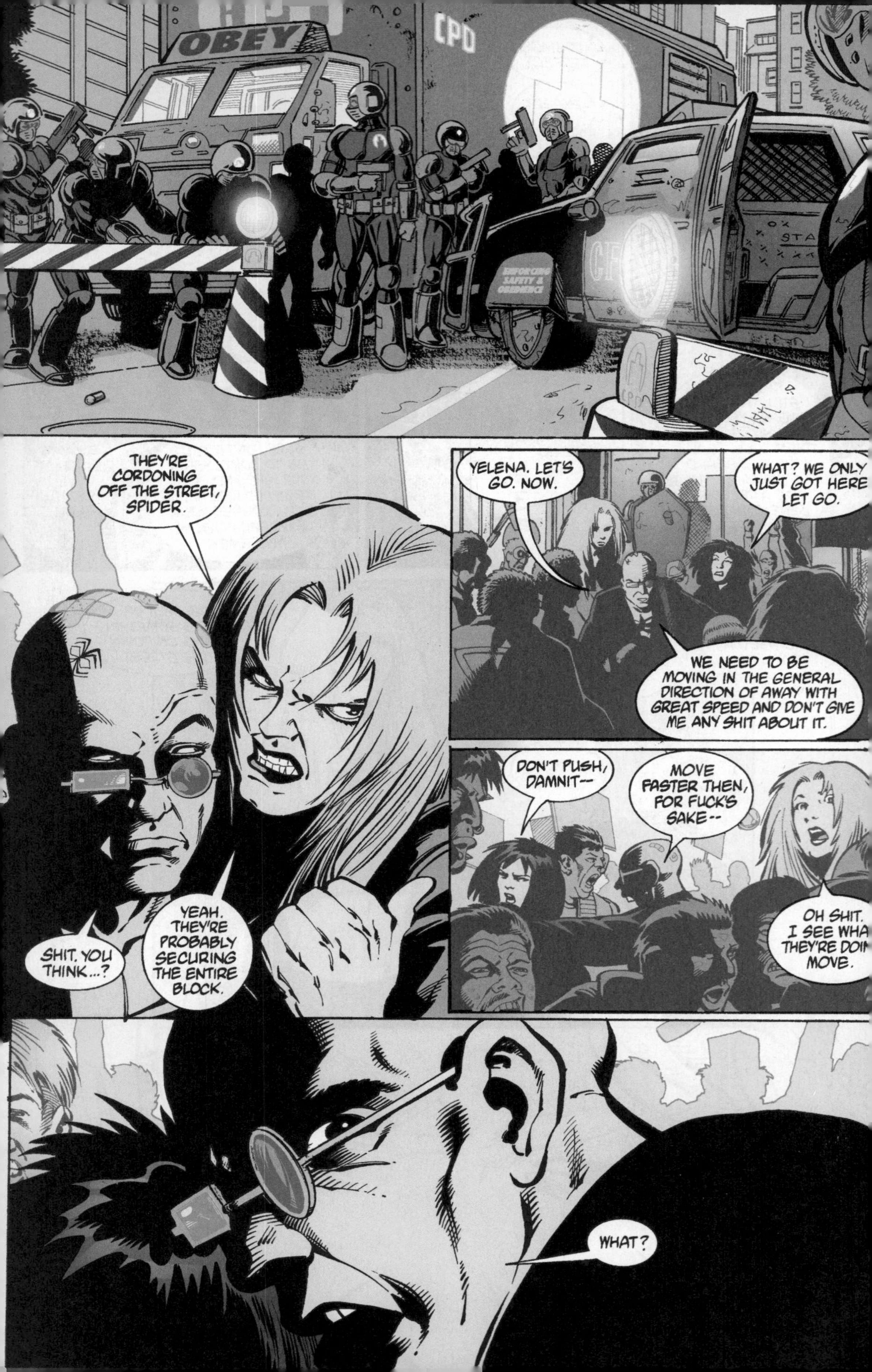
OBEY
CPD
ENFORCING SAFETY & OBEDIENCE
THEY'RE CORDONING OFF THE STREET, SPIDER.
SHIT. YOU THINK...?
YEAH. THEY'RE PROBABLY SECURING THE ENTIRE BLOCK.
YELENA. LET'S GO. NOW.
WHAT? WE ONLY JUST GOT HERE LET GO.
WE NEED TO BE MOVING IN THE GENERAL DIRECTION OF AWAY WITH GREAT SPEED AND DON'T GIVE ME ANY SHIT ABOUT IT.
DON'T PUSH, DAMNIT--
MOVE FASTER THEN, FOR FUCK'S SAKE--
OH SHIT. I SEE WHA THEY'RE DOIN MOVE.
WHAT?

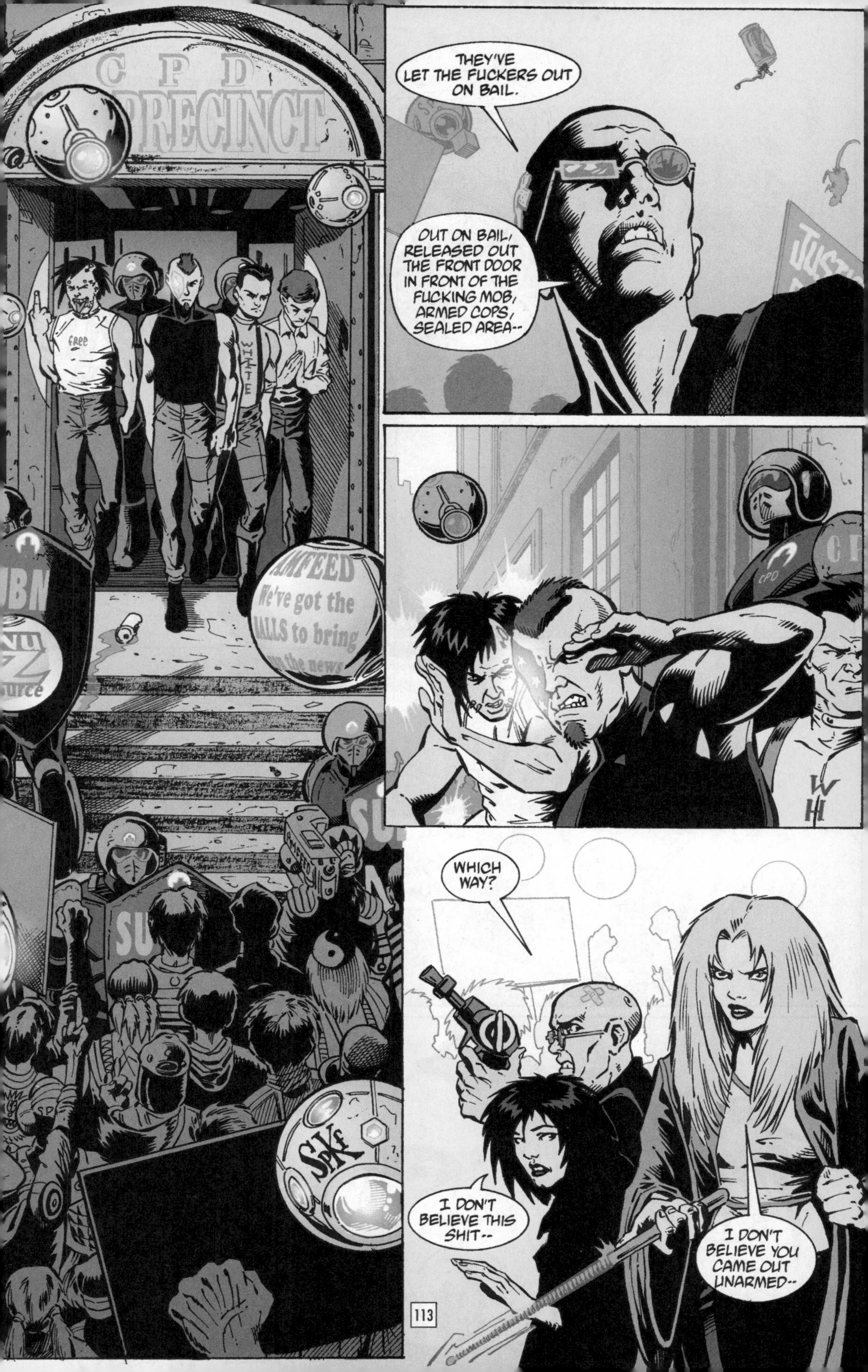
CPD
PRECINCT
We've got the
ALLS to bring
THEY'VE LET THE FUCKERS OUT ON BAIL.
OUT ON BAIL, RELEASED OUT THE FRONT DOOR IN FRONT OF THE FUCKING MOB, ARMED COPS, SEALED AREA--
WHICH WAY?
I DON'T BELIEVE THIS SHIT--
I DON'T BELIEVE YOU CAME OUT UNARMED--

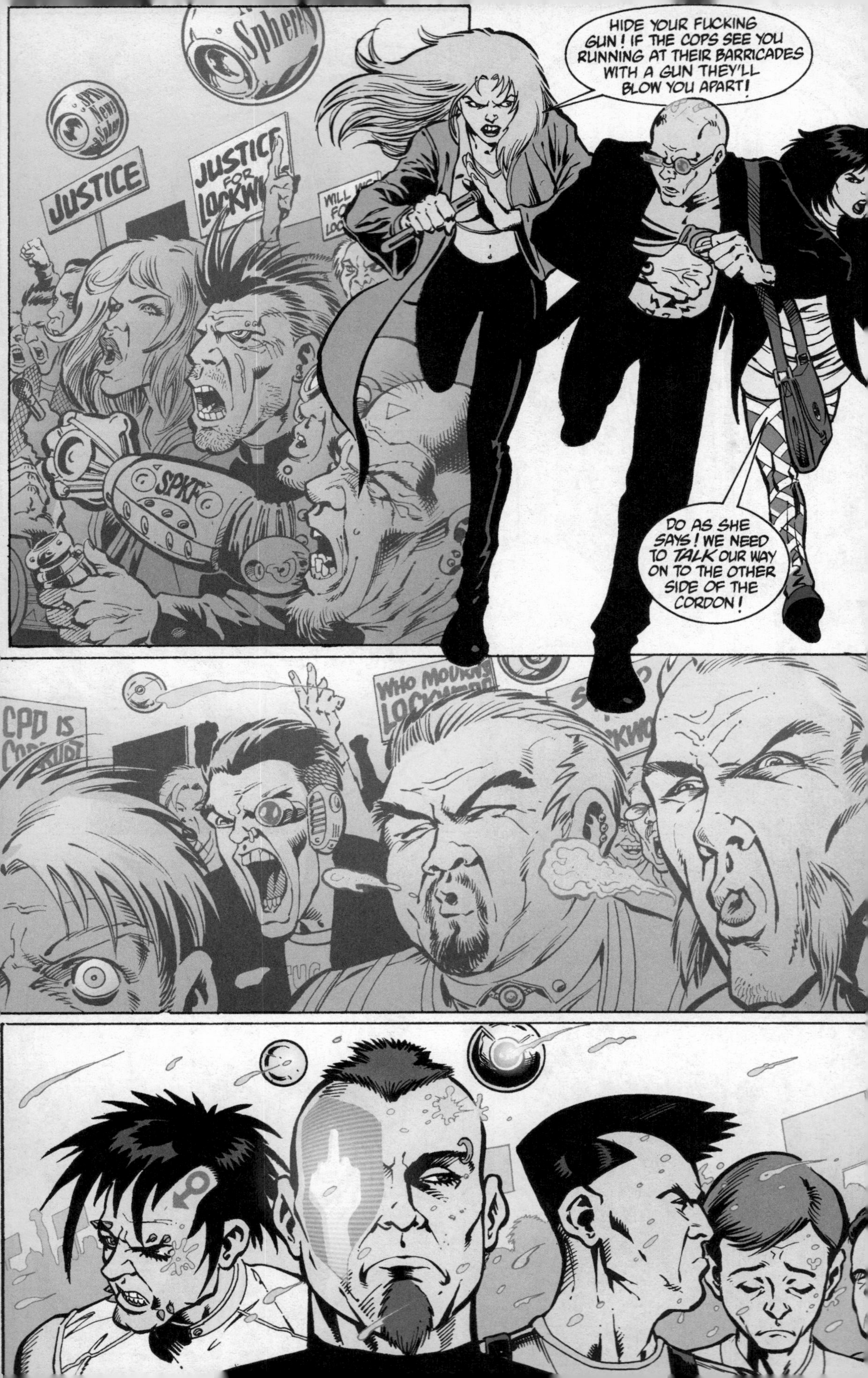
JUSTICE
JUSTICE FOR LOCKW
HIDE YOUR FUCKING GUN! IF THE COPS SEE YOU RUNNING AT THEIR BARRICADES WITH A GUN THEY'LL BLOW YOU APART!
SPKF
DO AS SHE SAYS! WE NEED TO TALK OUR WAY ON TO THE OTHER SIDE OF THE CORDON!
WHO MOURNS
CPD IS

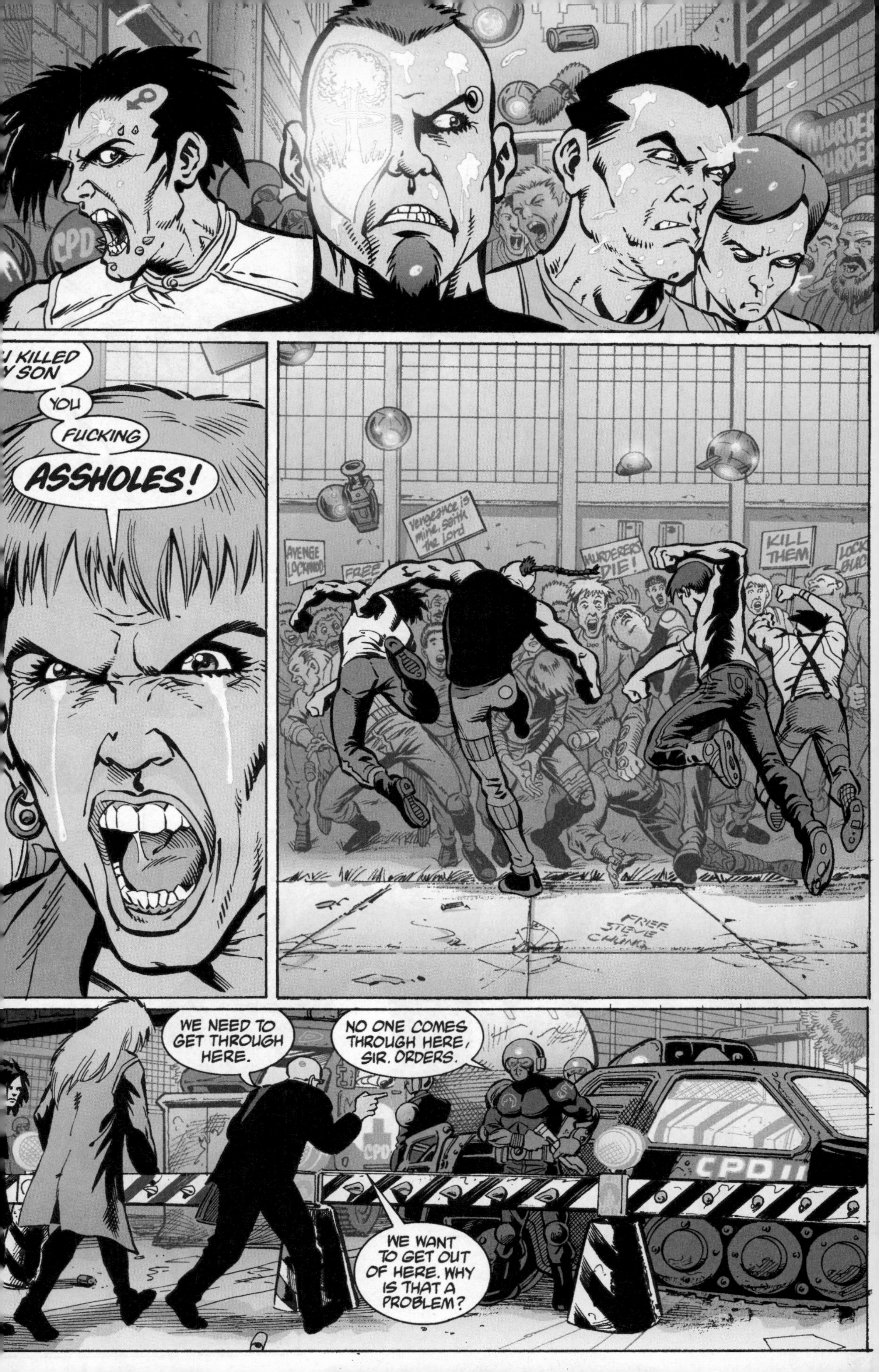
CPD
MURDER
MURDER
...U KILLED
...Y SON
YOU
FUCKING
ASSHOLES!
Vengeance is mine, saith the Lord
AVENGE LOCKWOOD
FREE
MURDERERS DIE!
KILL THEM
FREE STEVE CHUNG
WE NEED TO GET THROUGH HERE.
NO ONE COMES THROUGH HERE, SIR. ORDERS.
CPD
CPD 11
WE WANT TO GET OUT OF HERE. WHY IS THAT A PROBLEM?

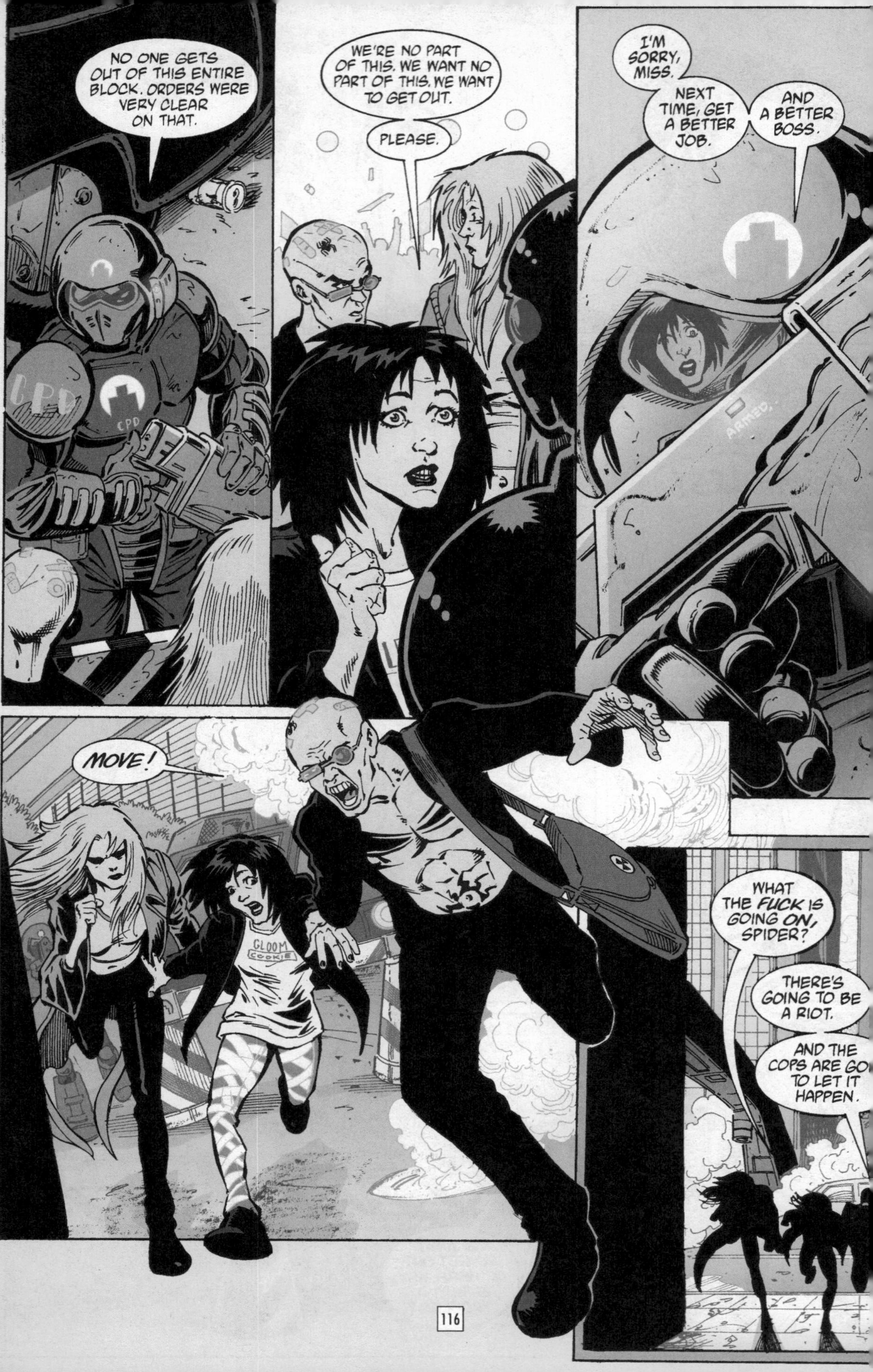
NO ONE GETS OUT OF THIS ENTIRE BLOCK. ORDERS WERE VERY CLEAR ON THAT.
CPD
CPD
WE'RE NO PART OF THIS. WE WANT NO PART OF THIS. WE WANT TO GET OUT.
PLEASE.
I'M SORRY, MISS.
NEXT TIME, GET A BETTER JOB.
AND A BETTER BOSS.
ARMED
MOVE!
GLOOM COOKIE
WHAT THE FUCK IS GOING ON, SPIDER?
THERE'S GOING TO BE A RIOT.
AND THE COPS ARE GO TO LET IT HAPPEN.

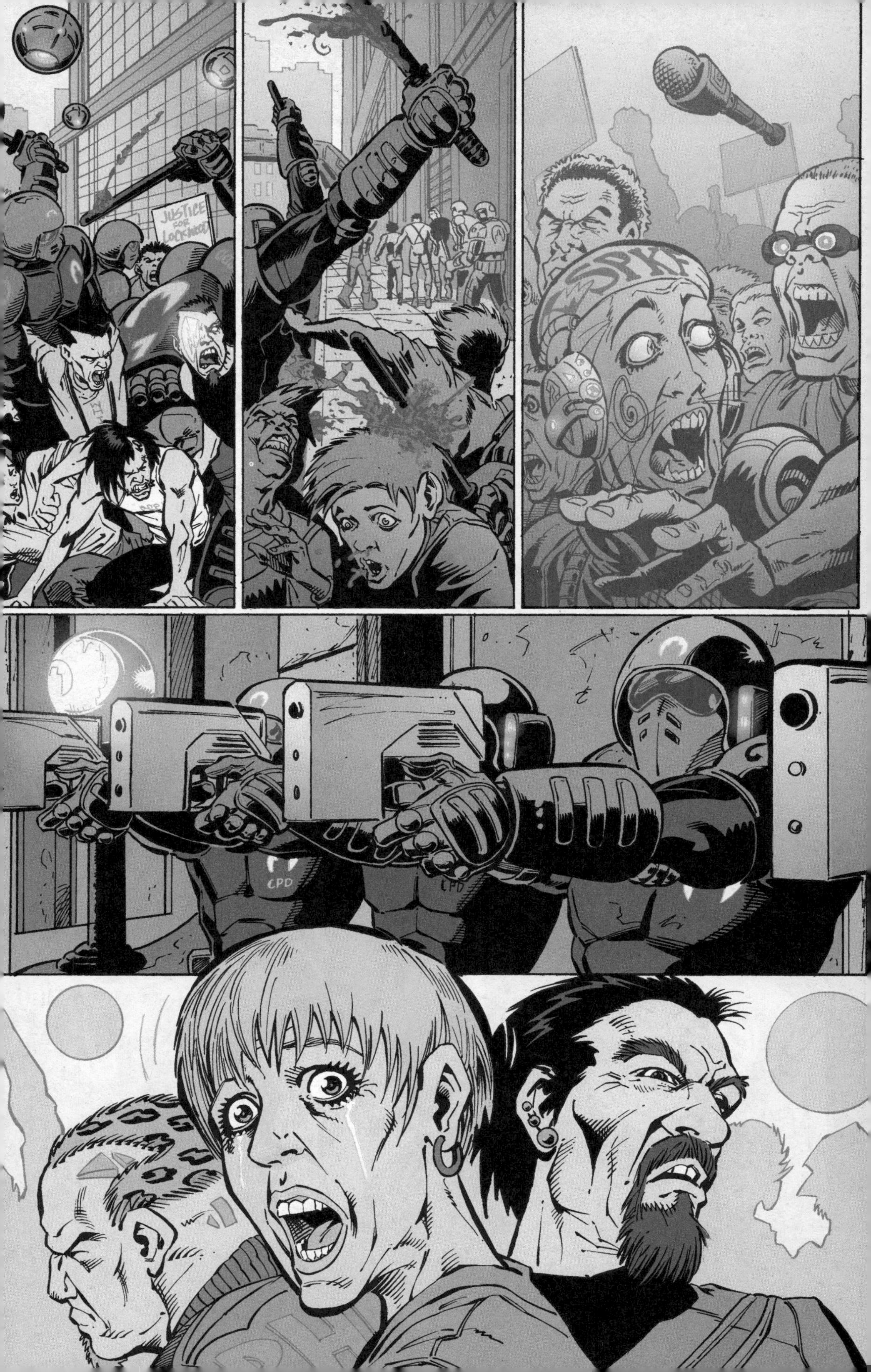
JUSTICE FOR LOCKWOOD
CPD
CPD

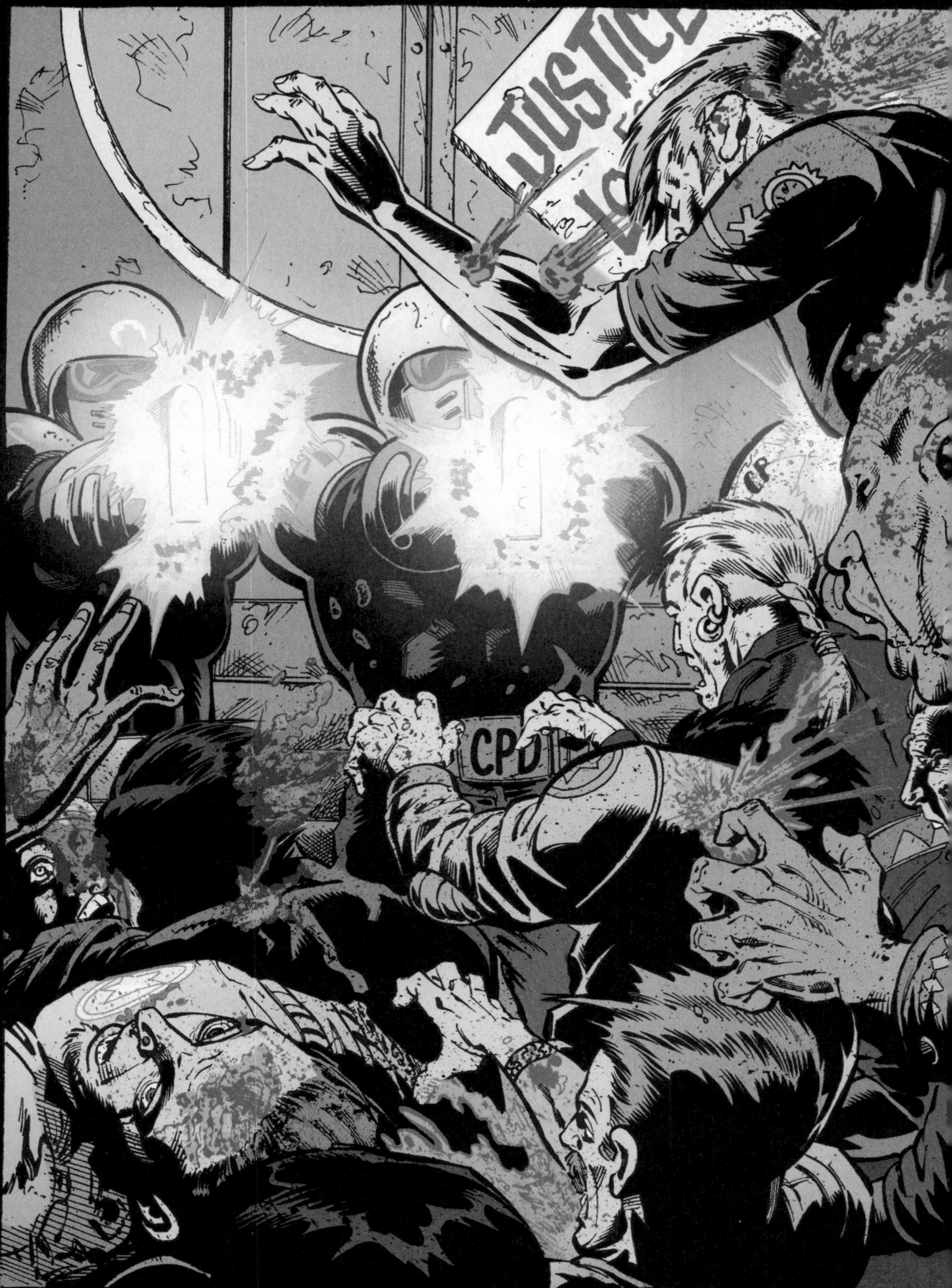
JUSTICE
CPD

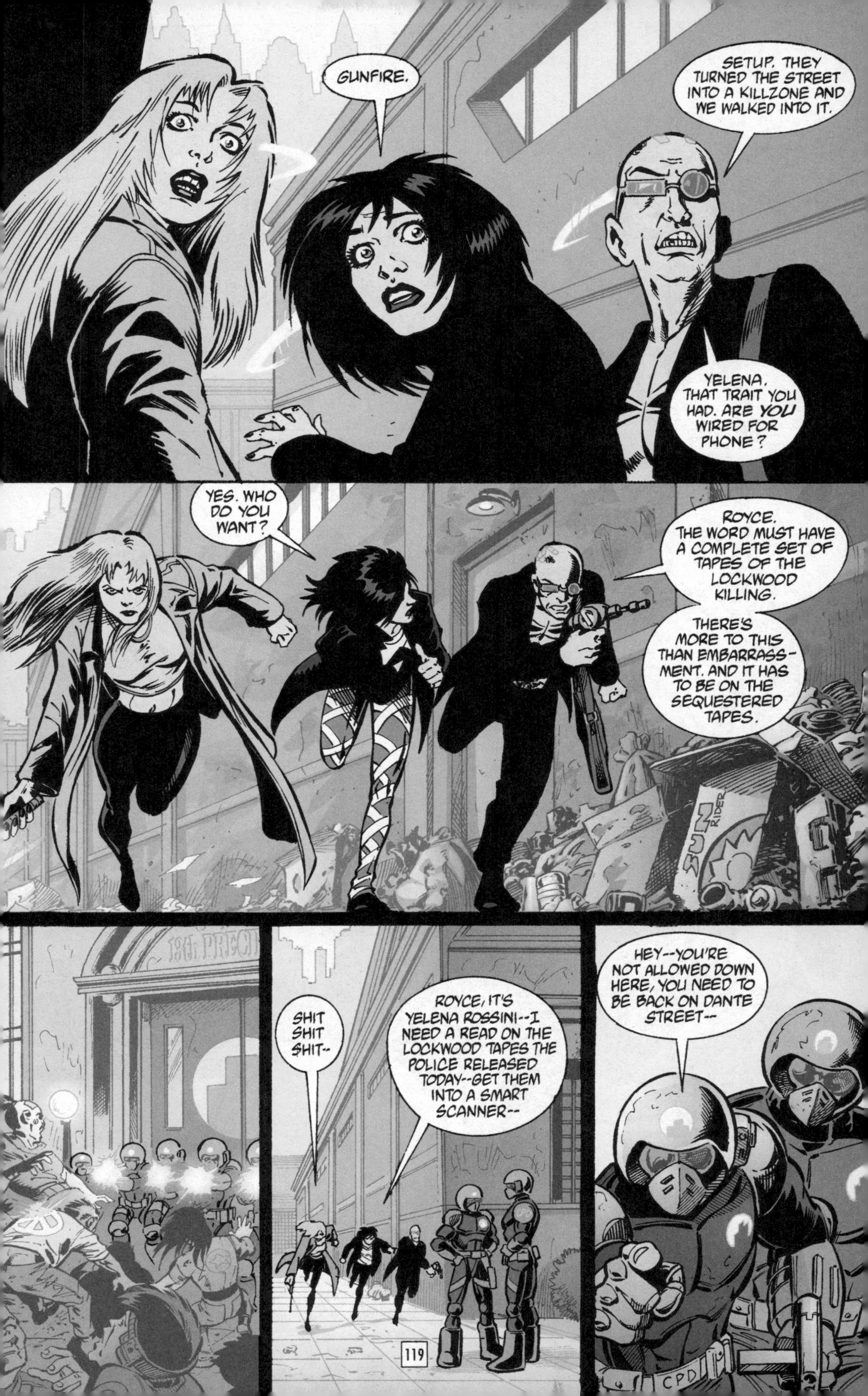
GUNFIRE.
SETUP. THEY TURNED THE STREET INTO A KILLZONE AND WE WALKED INTO IT.
YELENA, THAT TRAIT YOU HAD. ARE YOU WIRED FOR PHONE?
YES. WHO DO YOU WANT?
ROYCE. THE WORD MUST HAVE A COMPLETE SET OF TAPES OF THE LOCKWOOD KILLING.
THERE'S MORE TO THIS THAN EMBARRASS-MENT. AND IT HAS TO BE ON THE SEQUESTERED TAPES.
SUN RIDER
18th PRECI
SHIT SHIT SHIT--
ROYCE, IT'S YELENA ROSSINI--I NEED A READ ON THE LOCKWOOD TAPES THE POLICE RELEASED TODAY--GET THEM INTO A SMART SCANNER--
HEY--YOU'RE NOT ALLOWED DOWN HERE, YOU NEED TO BE BACK ON DANTE STREET--
CPD

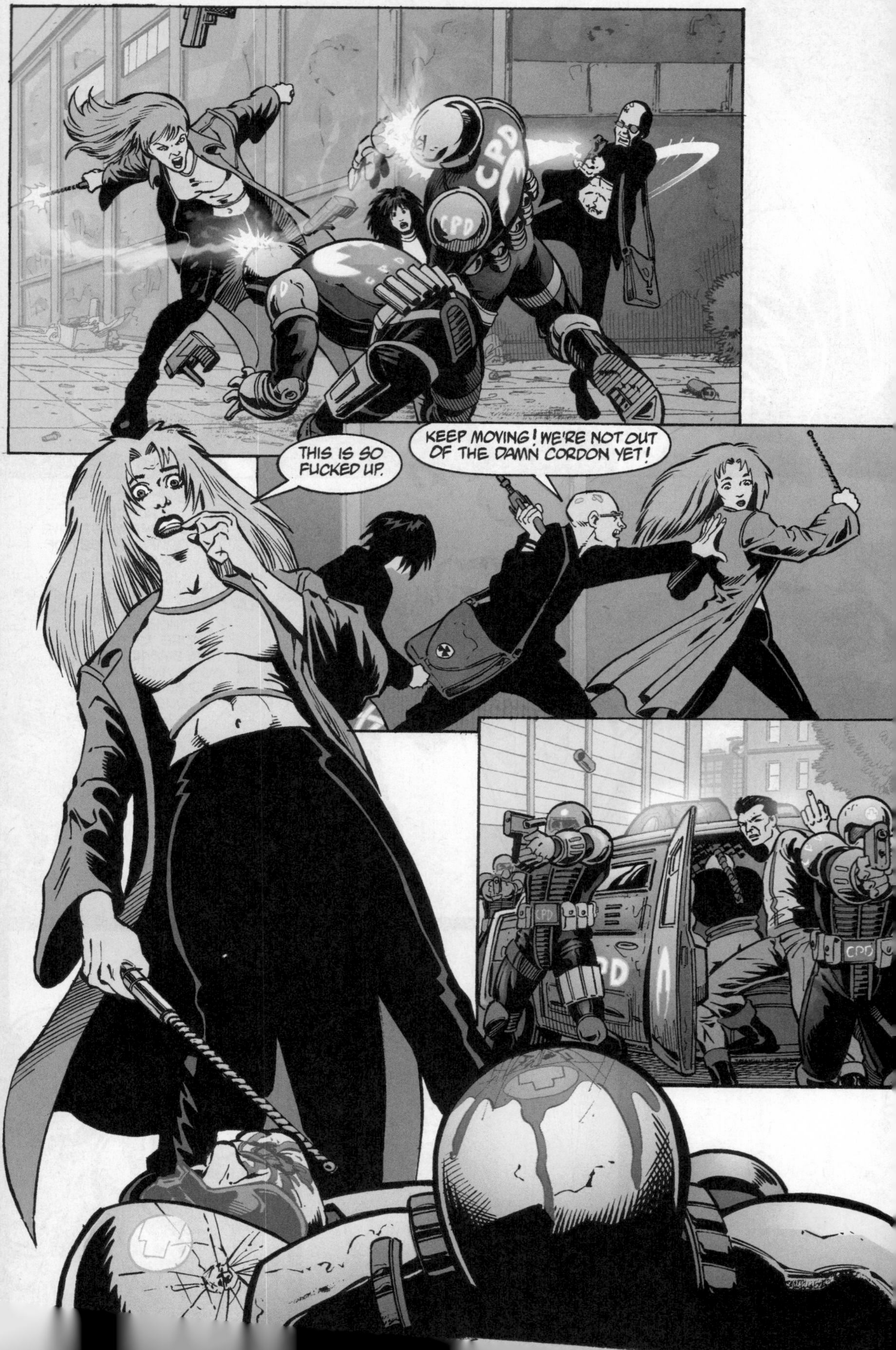
THIS IS SO FUCKED UP.
KEEP MOVING! WE'RE NOT OUT OF THE DAMN CORDON YET!
CPD

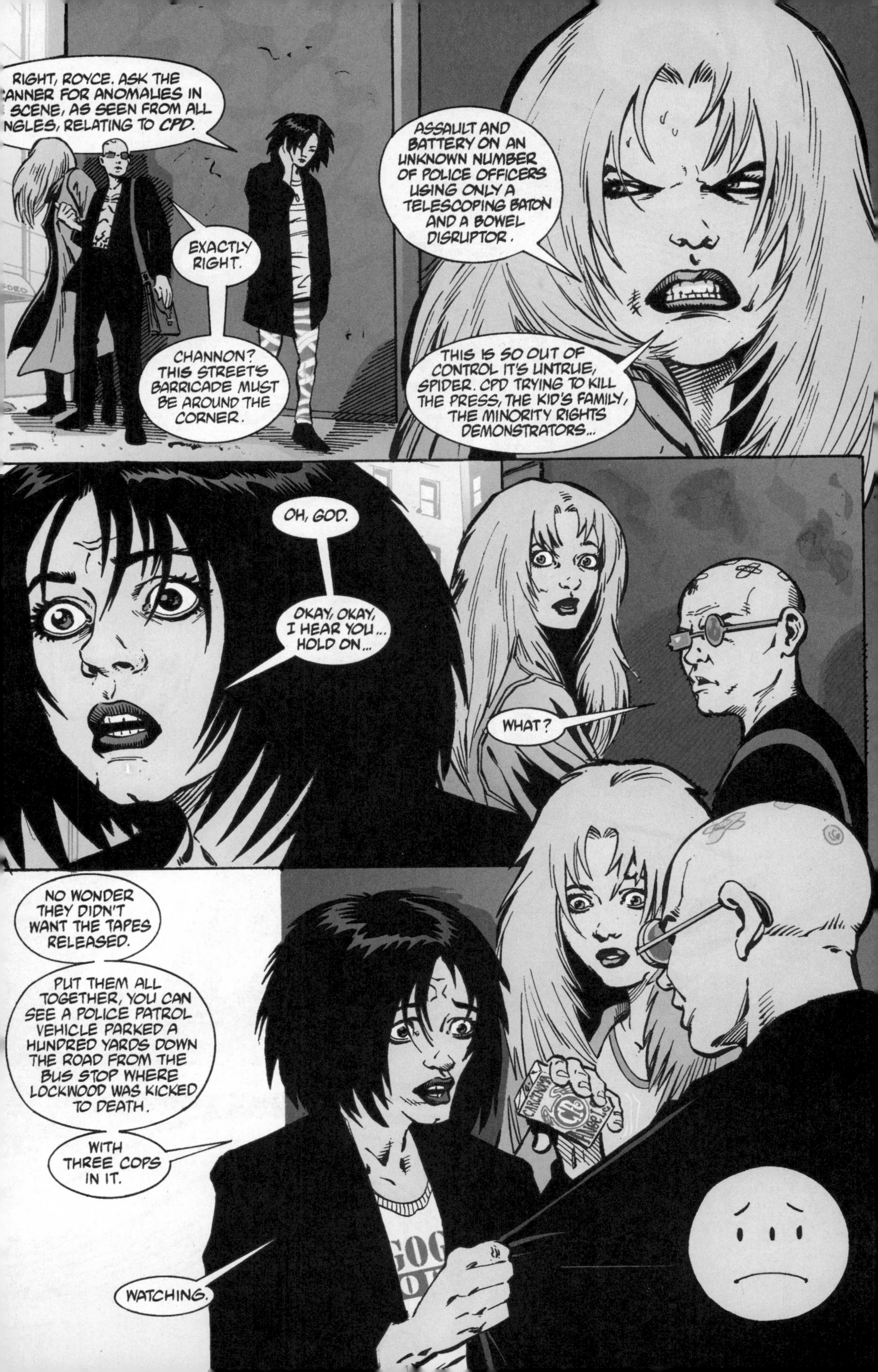
RIGHT, ROYCE. ASK THE SCANNER FOR ANOMALIES IN SCENE, AS SEEN FROM ALL ANGLES, RELATING TO CPD.
EXACTLY RIGHT.
CHANNON? THIS STREET'S BARRICADE MUST BE AROUND THE CORNER.
ASSAULT AND BATTERY ON AN UNKNOWN NUMBER OF POLICE OFFICERS USING ONLY A TELESCOPING BATON AND A BOWEL DISRUPTOR.
THIS IS SO OUT OF CONTROL IT'S UNTRUE, SPIDER. CPD TRYING TO KILL THE PRESS, THE KID'S FAMILY, THE MINORITY RIGHTS DEMONSTRATORS...
OH, GOD.
OKAY, OKAY, I HEAR YOU... HOLD ON...
WHAT?
NO WONDER THEY DIDN'T WANT THE TAPES RELEASED.
PUT THEM ALL TOGETHER, YOU CAN SEE A POLICE PATROL VEHICLE PARKED A HUNDRED YARDS DOWN THE ROAD FROM THE BUS STOP WHERE LOCKWOOD WAS KICKED TO DEATH.
WITH THREE COPS IN IT.
WATCHING.

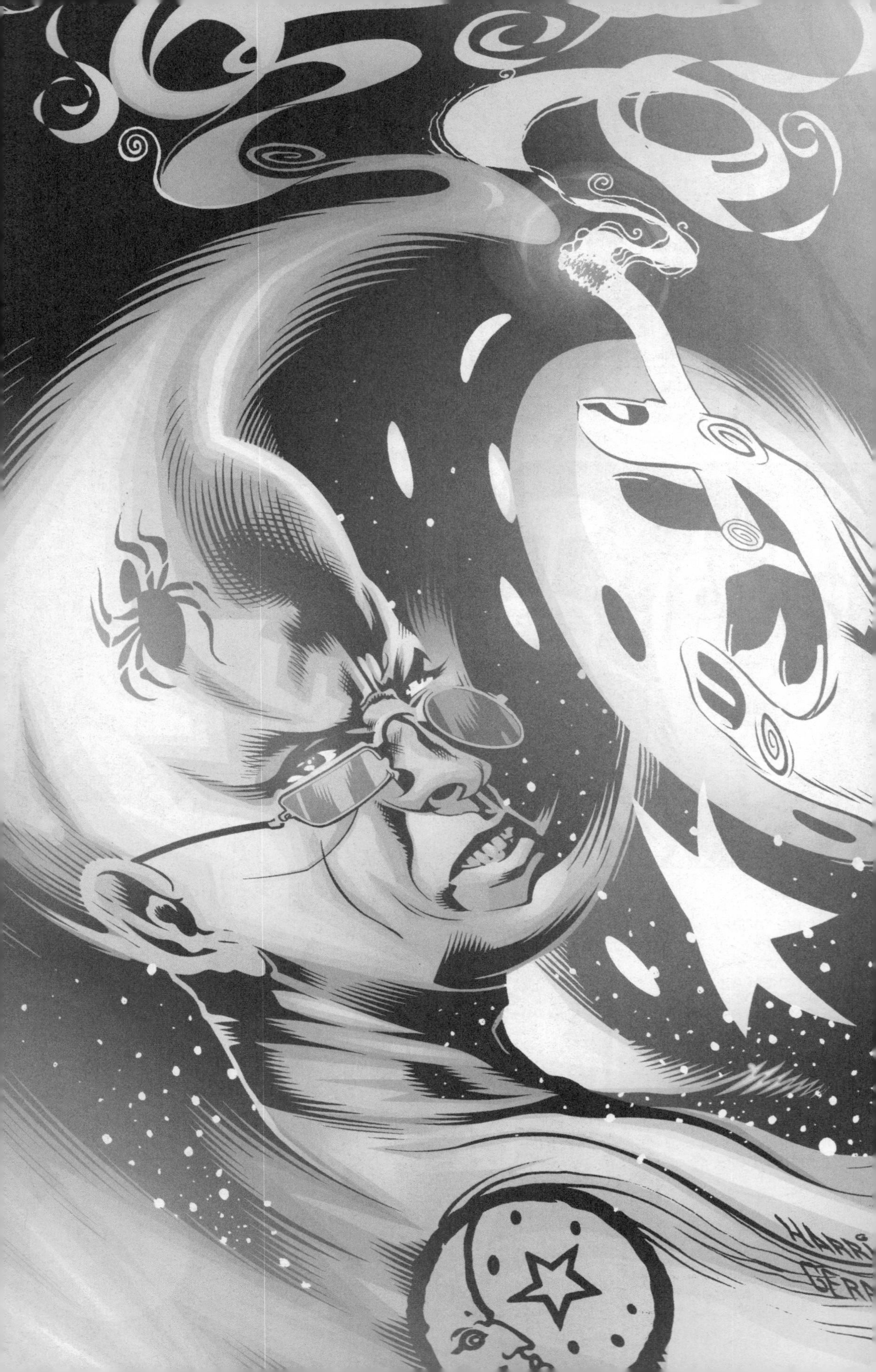

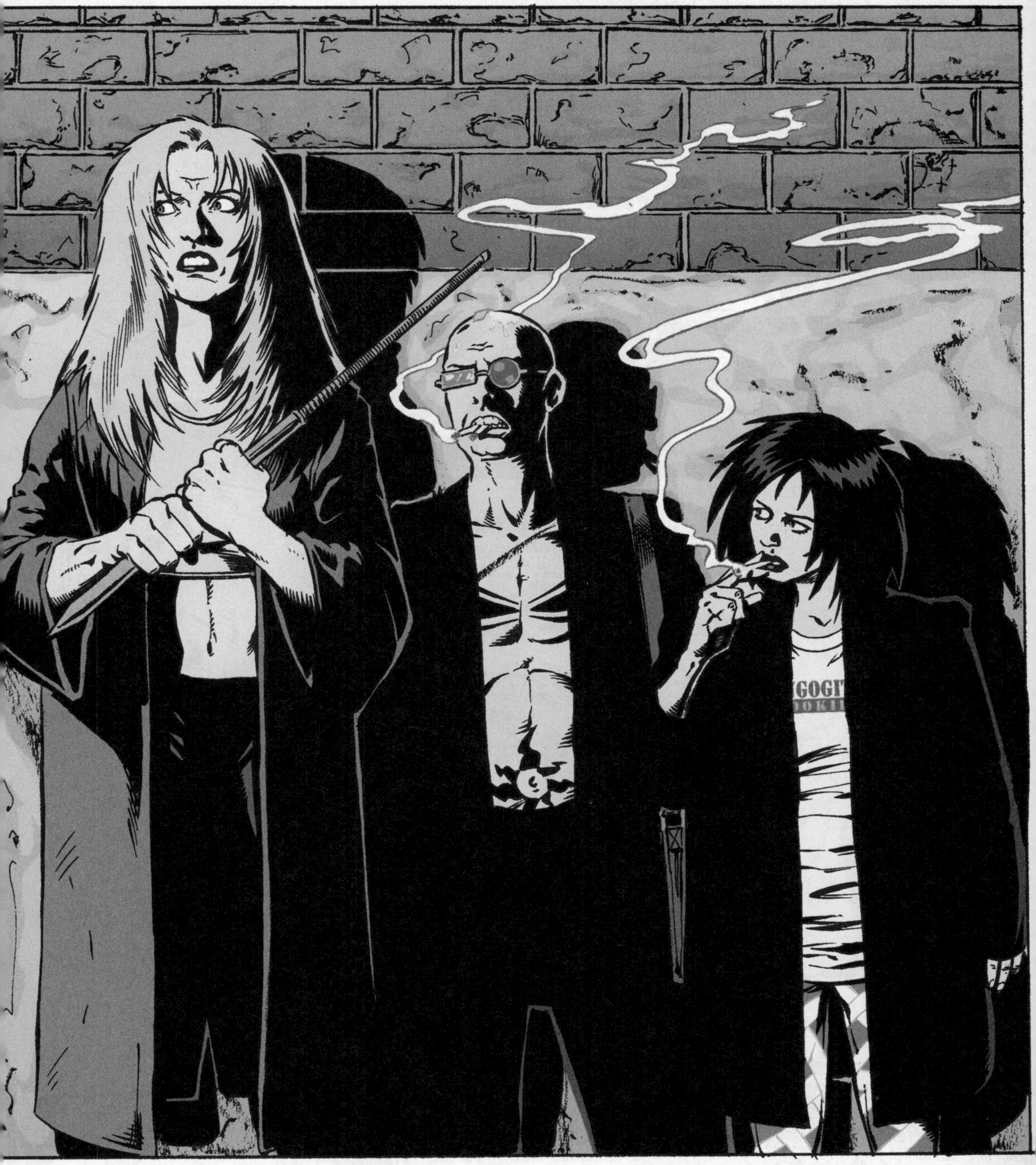

Warren Ellis writes & Darick Robertson pencils

LONELY CITY

three of three

Rodney Ramos Inker **Clem Robins** Letterer **Nathan Eyring** Color & Seps **Tony Harris** Cover Pencils **Drew Geraci** Cover Inks **Cliff Chiang** Editor

TRANSMETROPOLITAN created by Warren Ellis and Darick Robertson

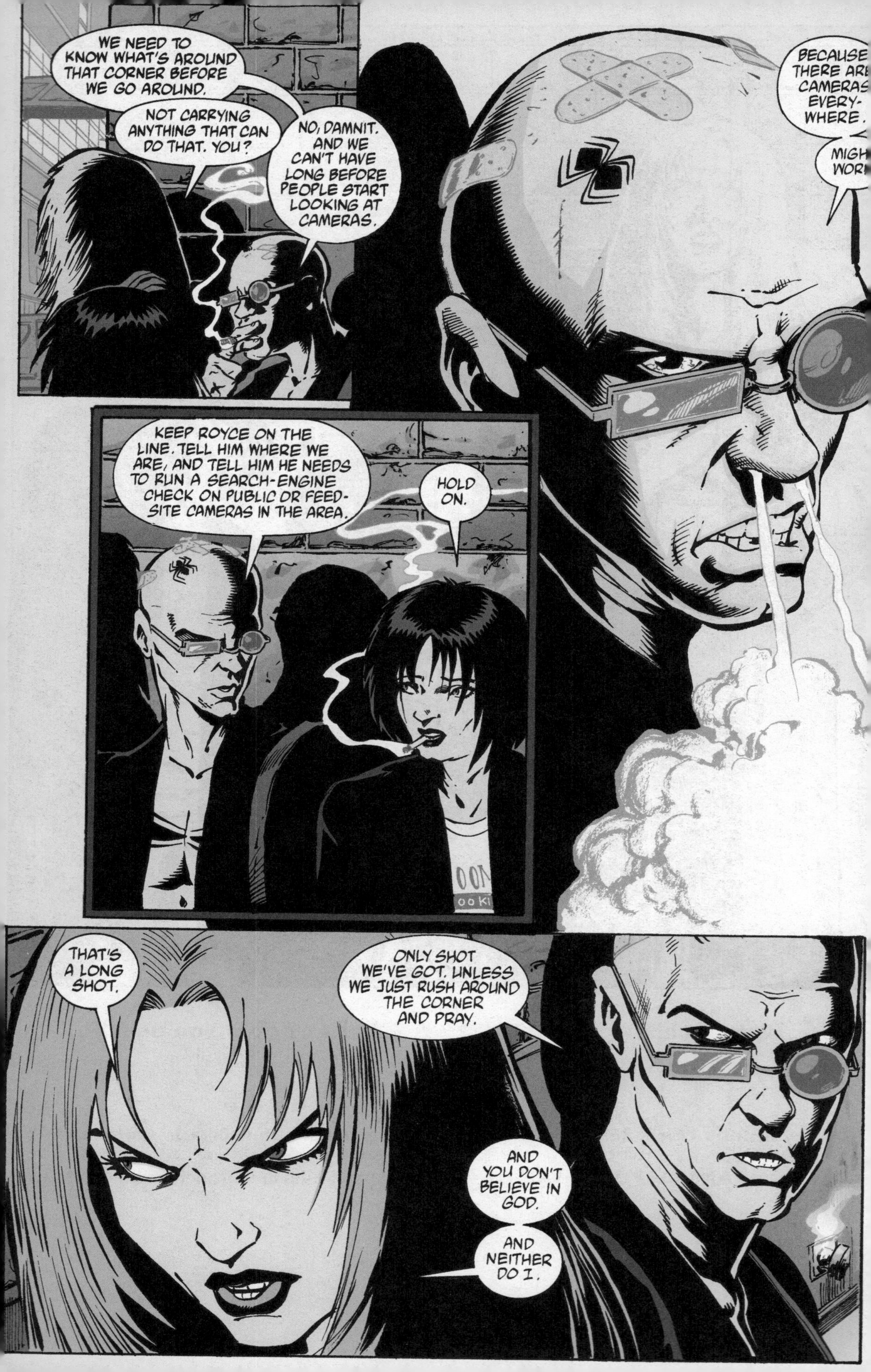
WE NEED TO KNOW WHAT'S AROUND THAT CORNER BEFORE WE GO AROUND.
NOT CARRYING ANYTHING THAT CAN DO THAT. YOU?
NO, DAMNIT. AND WE CAN'T HAVE LONG BEFORE PEOPLE START LOOKING AT CAMERAS.
BECAUSE THERE ARE CAMERAS EVERY-WHERE.
MIGH WOR
KEEP ROYCE ON THE LINE. TELL HIM WHERE WE ARE, AND TELL HIM HE NEEDS TO RUN A SEARCH-ENGINE CHECK ON PUBLIC OR FEED-SITE CAMERAS IN THE AREA.
HOLD ON.
THAT'S A LONG SHOT.
ONLY SHOT WE'VE GOT. UNLESS WE JUST RUSH AROUND THE CORNER AND PRAY.
AND YOU DON'T BELIEVE IN GOD.
AND NEITHER DO I.

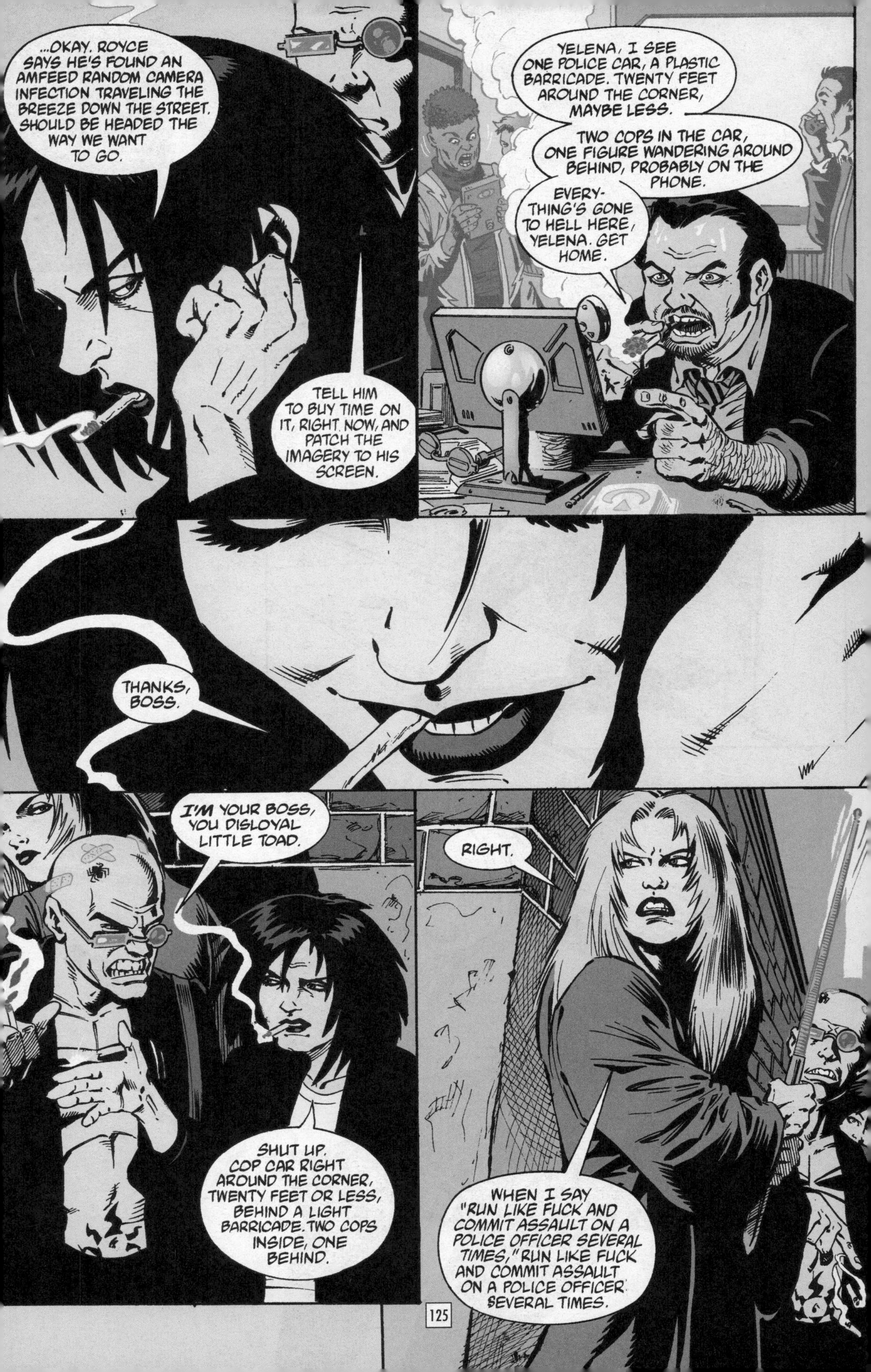

...OKAY. ROYCE SAYS HE'S FOUND AN AMFEED RANDOM CAMERA INFECTION TRAVELING THE BREEZE DOWN THE STREET. SHOULD BE HEADED THE WAY WE WANT TO GO.
TELL HIM TO BUY TIME ON IT, RIGHT NOW, AND PATCH THE IMAGERY TO HIS SCREEN.
YELENA, I SEE ONE POLICE CAR, A PLASTIC BARRICADE. TWENTY FEET AROUND THE CORNER, MAYBE LESS.
TWO COPS IN THE CAR, ONE FIGURE WANDERING AROUND BEHIND, PROBABLY ON THE PHONE.
EVERY-THING'S GONE TO HELL HERE, YELENA. GET HOME.
THANKS, BOSS.
I'M YOUR BOSS, YOU DISLOYAL LITTLE TOAD.
SHUT UP. COP CAR RIGHT AROUND THE CORNER, TWENTY FEET OR LESS, BEHIND A LIGHT BARRICADE. TWO COPS INSIDE, ONE BEHIND.
RIGHT.
WHEN I SAY "RUN LIKE FUCK AND COMMIT ASSAULT ON A POLICE OFFICER SEVERAL TIMES," RUN LIKE FUCK AND COMMIT ASSAULT ON A POLICE OFFICER SEVERAL TIMES.

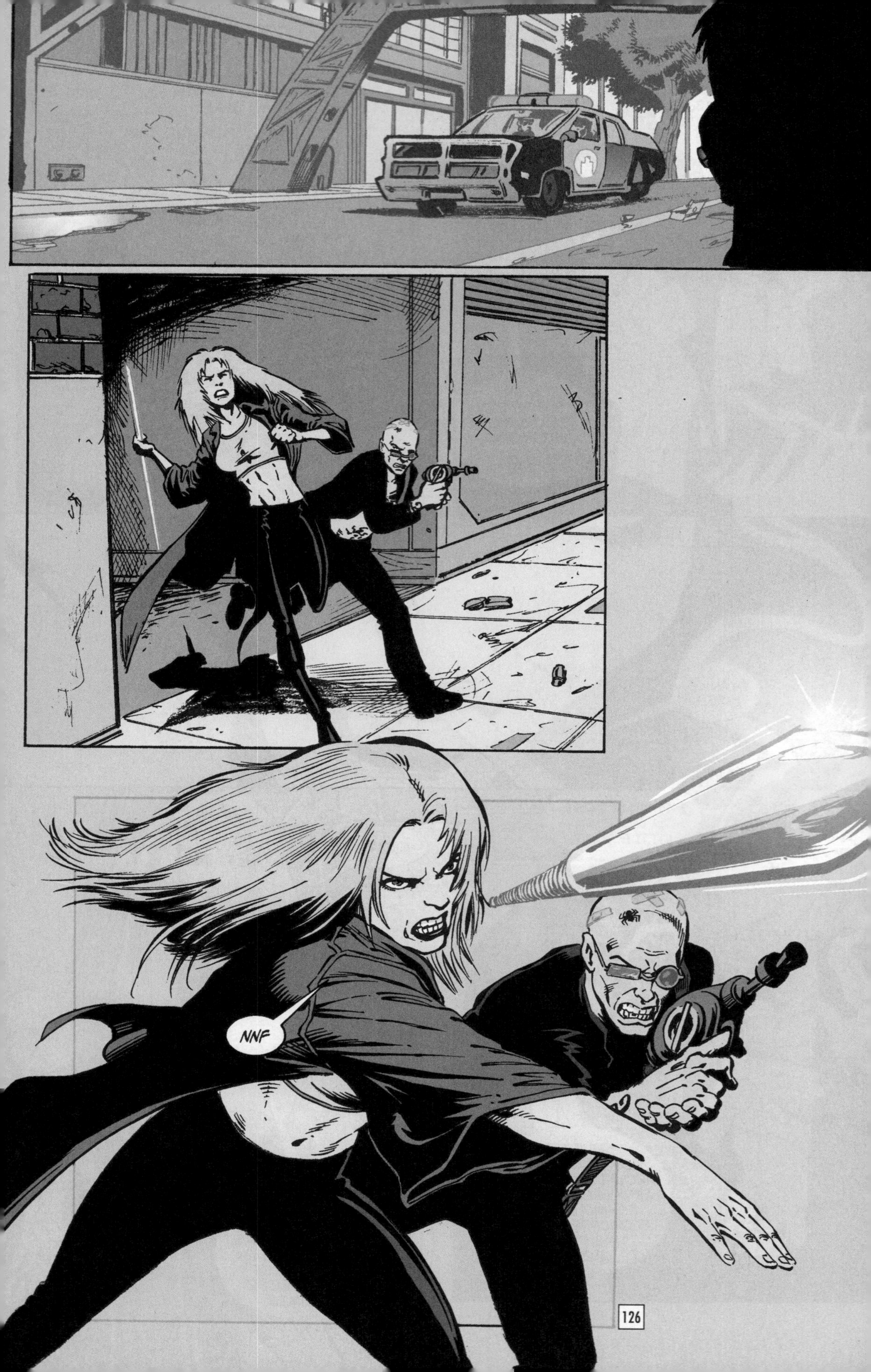
NNF

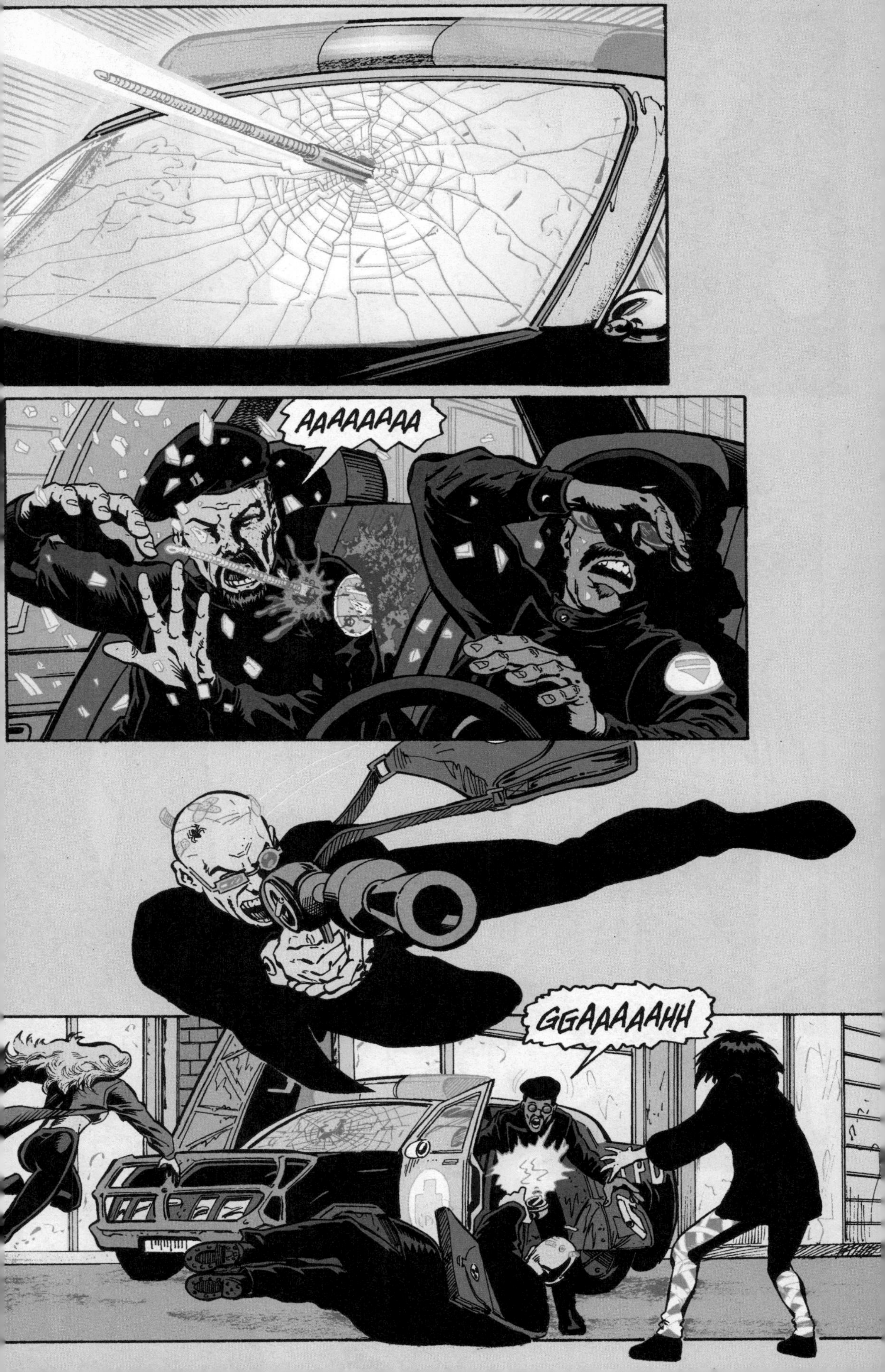
AAAAAAAA
GGAAAAAHH

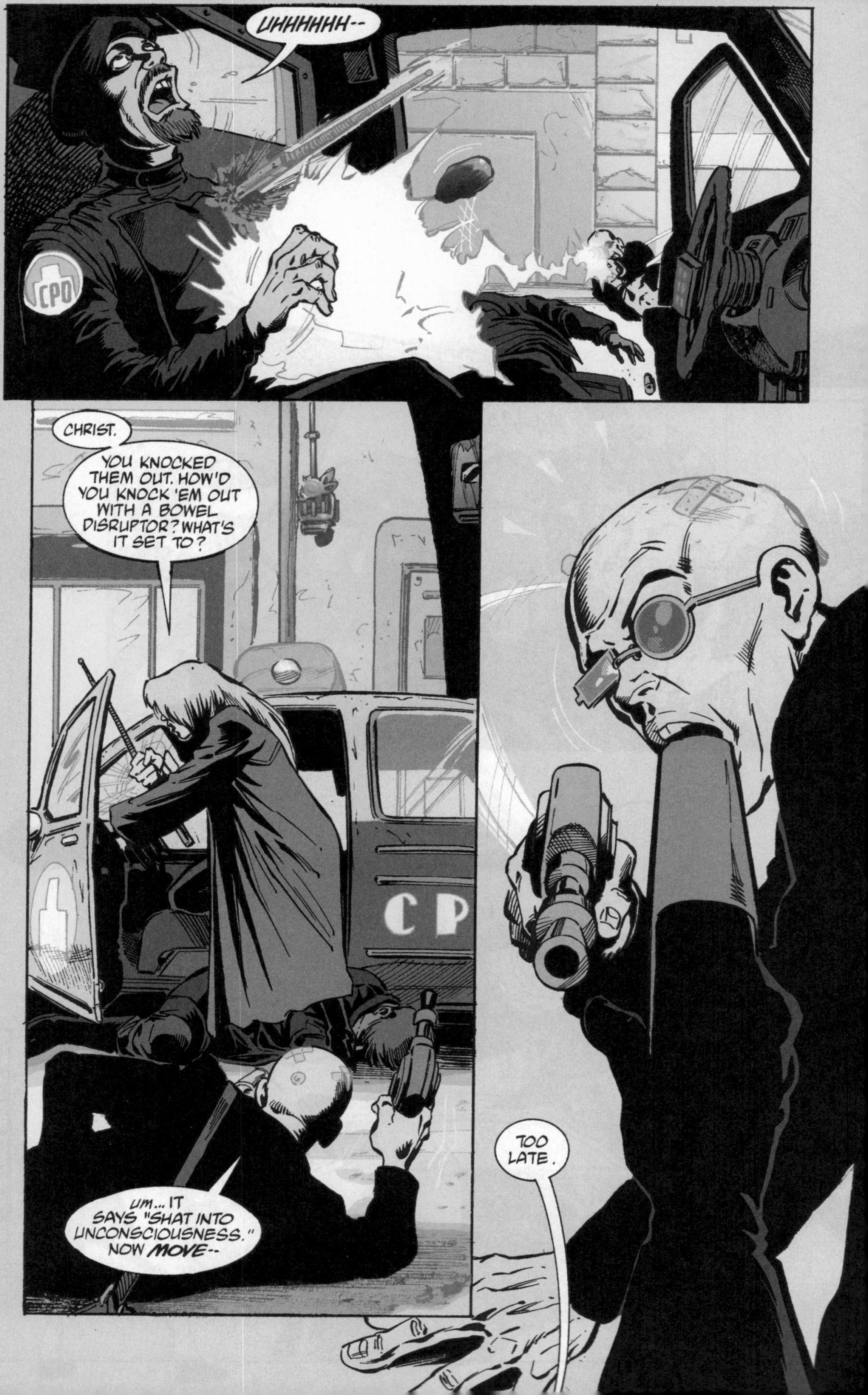
UHHHHHH--
CHRIST.
YOU KNOCKED THEM OUT. HOW'D YOU KNOCK 'EM OUT WITH A BOWEL DISRUPTOR? WHAT'S IT SET TO?
UM... IT SAYS "SHAT INTO UNCONSCIOUSNESS." NOW MOVE--
TOO LATE.
CPO
CP

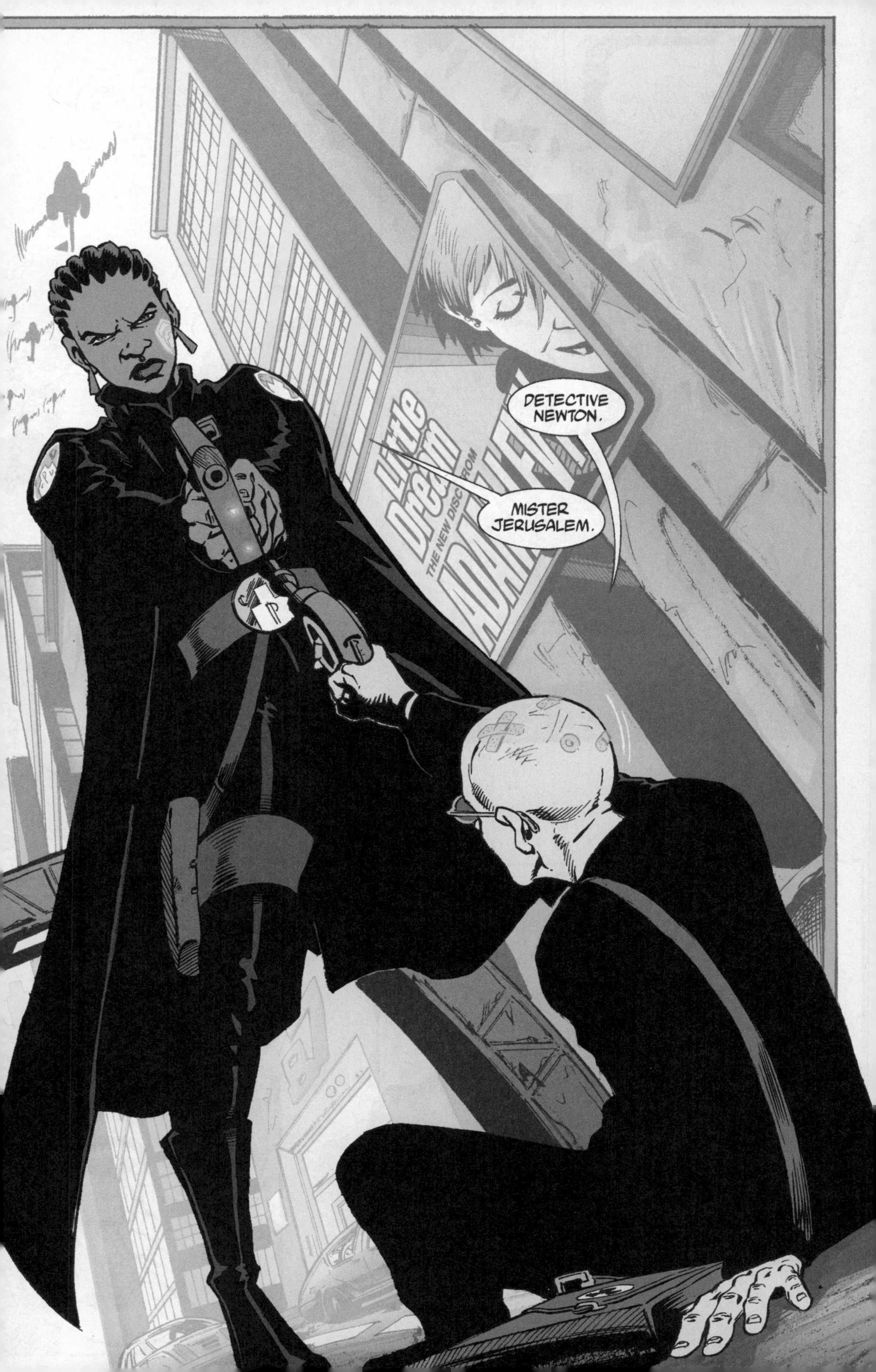

DETECTIVE NEWTON.
MISTER JERUSALEM.
Little Dream
THE NEW DISC FROM

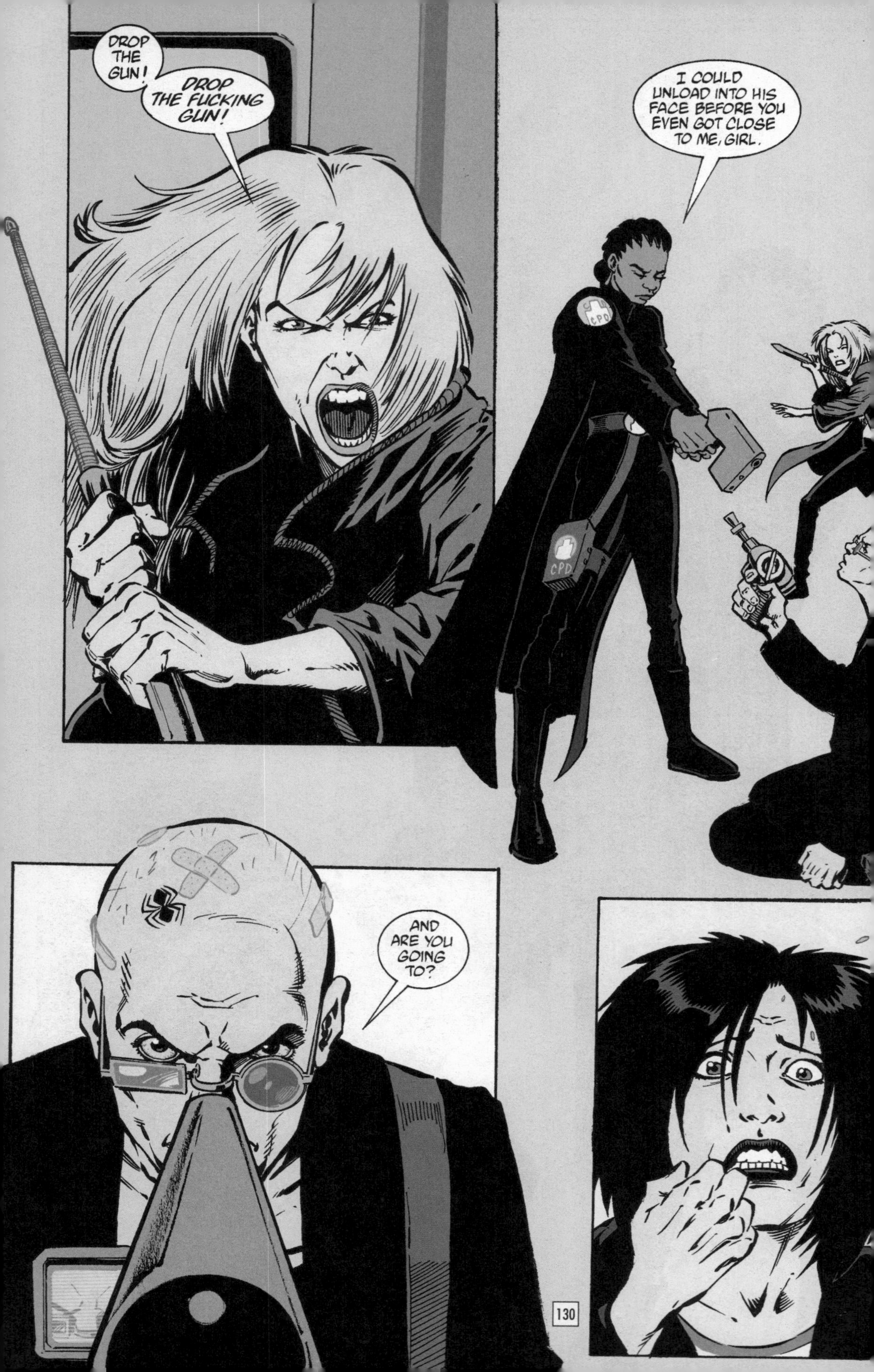
DROP THE GUN!
DROP THE FUCKING GUN!
I COULD UNLOAD INTO HIS FACE BEFORE YOU EVEN GOT CLOSE TO ME, GIRL.
CPD
CPD
AND ARE YOU GOING TO?

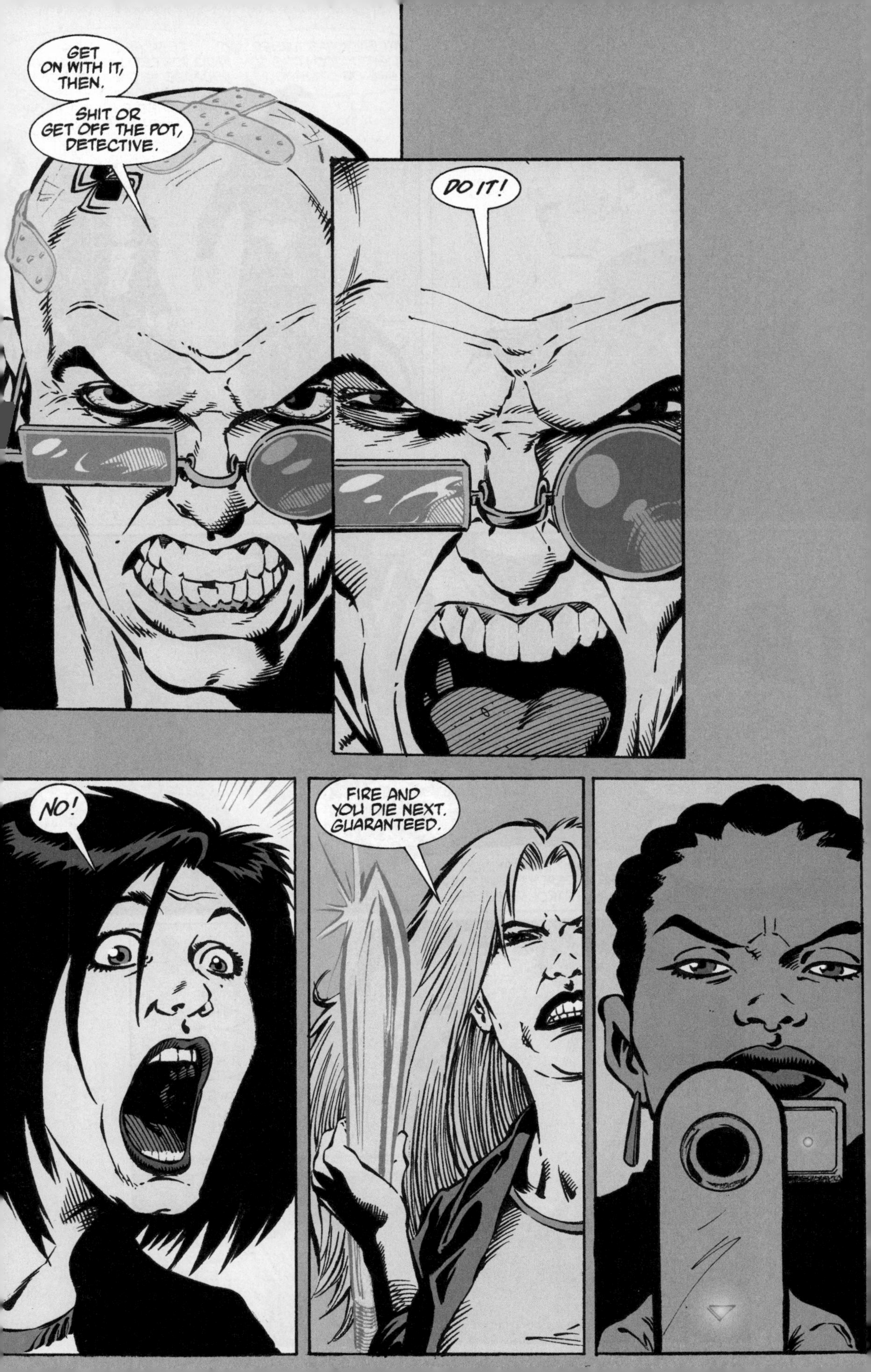
GET ON WITH IT, THEN.
SHIT OR GET OFF THE POT, DETECTIVE.
DO IT!
NO!
FIRE AND YOU DIE NEXT. GUARANTEED.

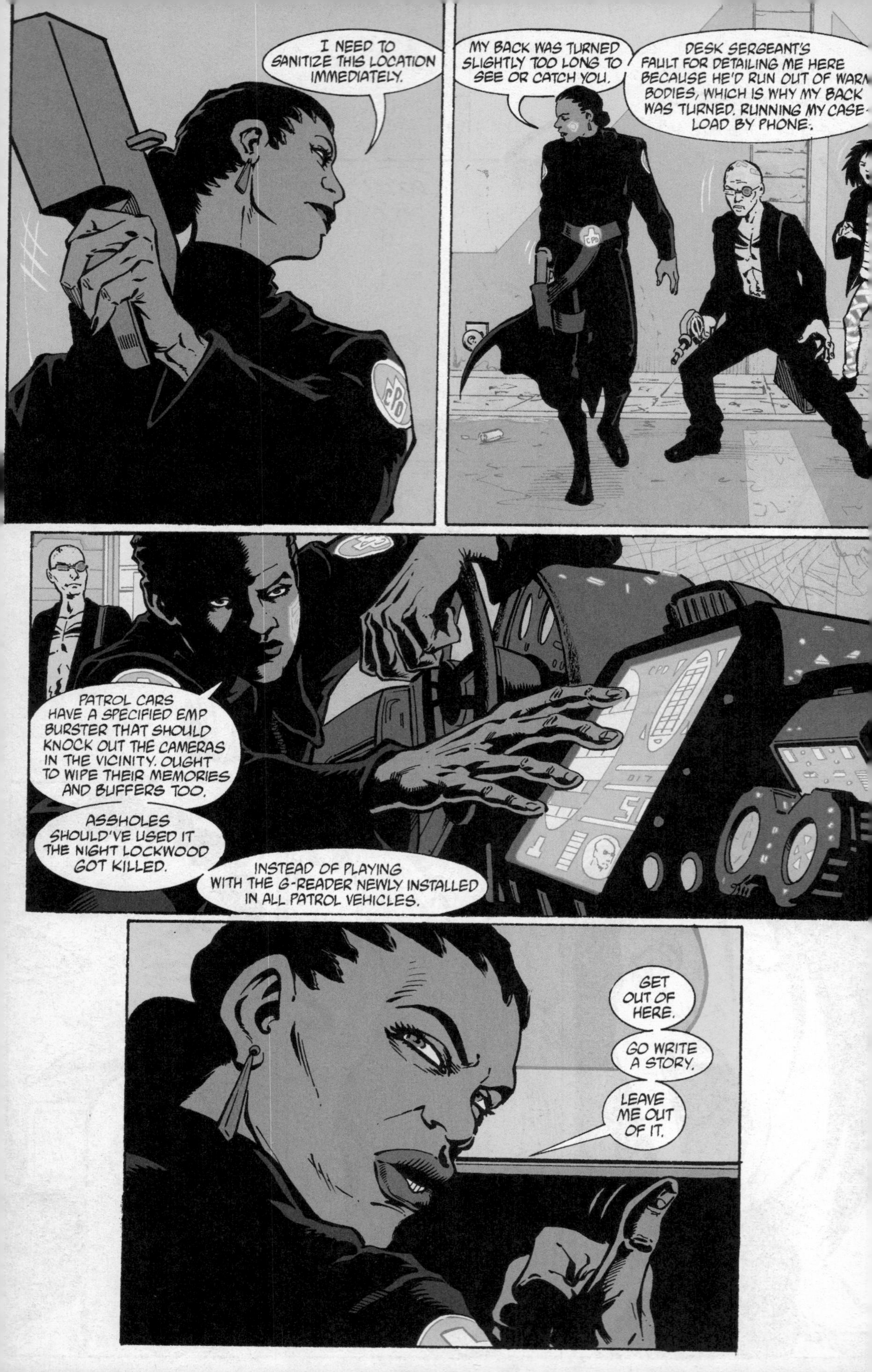
I NEED TO SANITIZE THIS LOCATION IMMEDIATELY.
MY BACK WAS TURNED SLIGHTLY TOO LONG TO SEE OR CATCH YOU.
DESK SERGEANT'S FAULT FOR DETAILING ME HERE BECAUSE HE'D RUN OUT OF WARM BODIES, WHICH IS WHY MY BACK WAS TURNED. RUNNING MY CASE-LOAD BY PHONE.
PATROL CARS HAVE A SPECIFIED EMP BURSTER THAT SHOULD KNOCK OUT THE CAMERAS IN THE VICINITY. OUGHT TO WIPE THEIR MEMORIES AND BUFFERS TOO.
ASSHOLES SHOULD'VE USED IT THE NIGHT LOCKWOOD GOT KILLED.
INSTEAD OF PLAYING WITH THE G-READER NEWLY INSTALLED IN ALL PATROL VEHICLES.
GET OUT OF HERE.
GO WRITE A STORY.
LEAVE ME OUT OF IT.

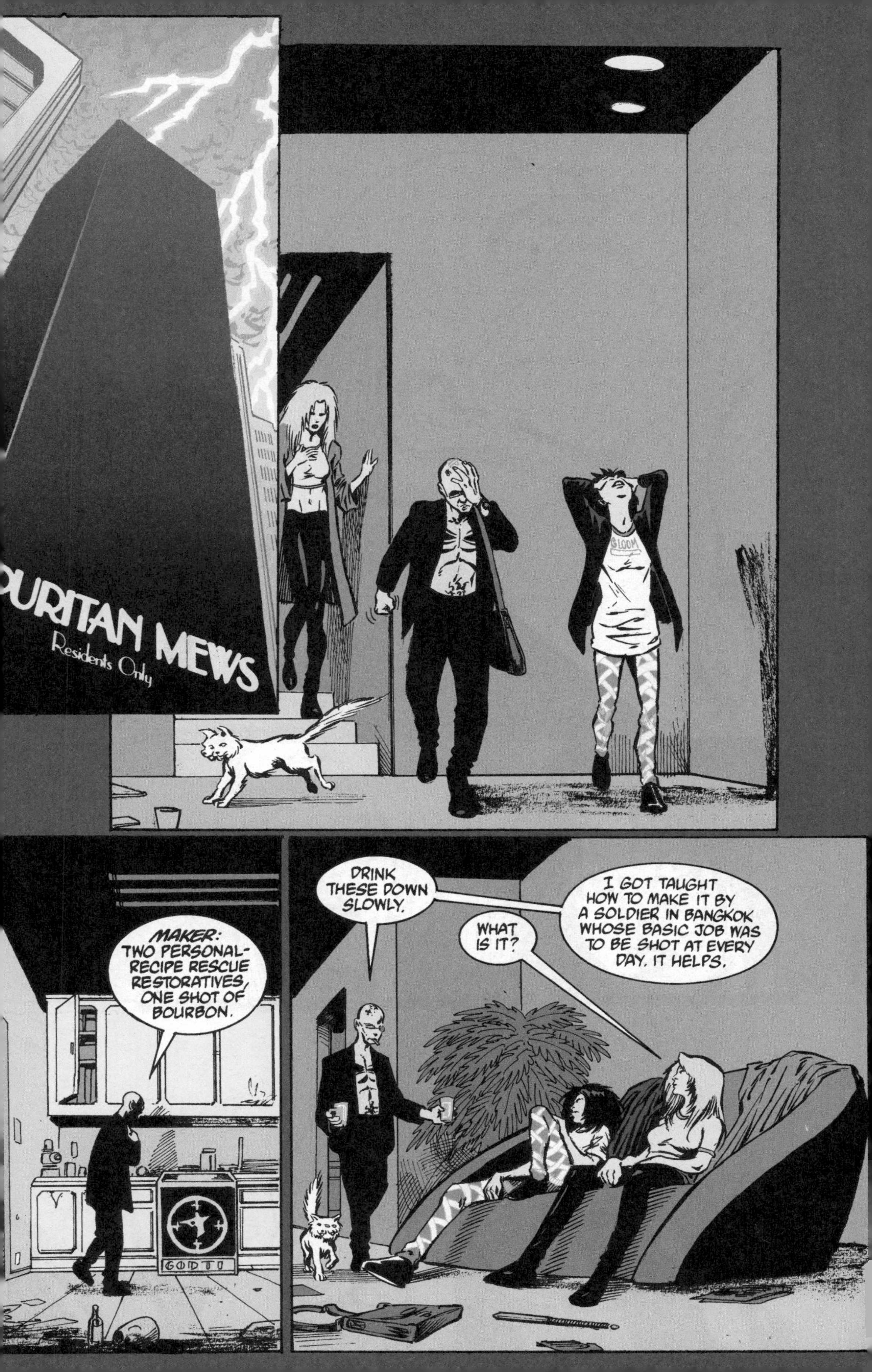
PURITAN MEWS
Residents Only
GLOOM
MAKER: TWO PERSONAL-RECIPE RESCUE RESTORATIVES, ONE SHOT OF BOURBON.
DRINK THESE DOWN SLOWLY.
WHAT IS IT?
I GOT TAUGHT HOW TO MAKE IT BY A SOLDIER IN BANGKOK WHOSE BASIC JOB WAS TO BE SHOT AT EVERY DAY. IT HELPS.

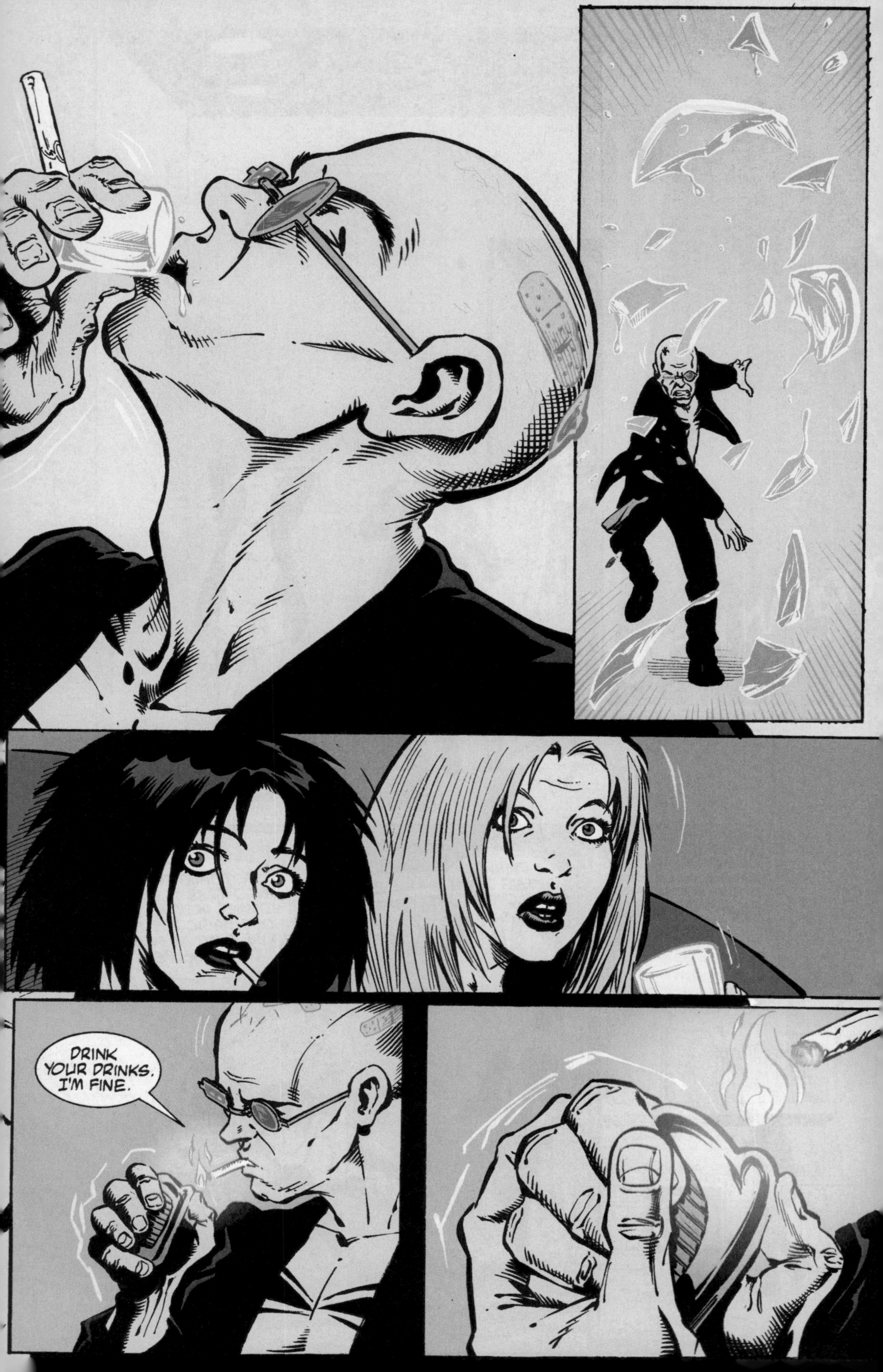
DRINK YOUR DRINKS. I'M FINE.

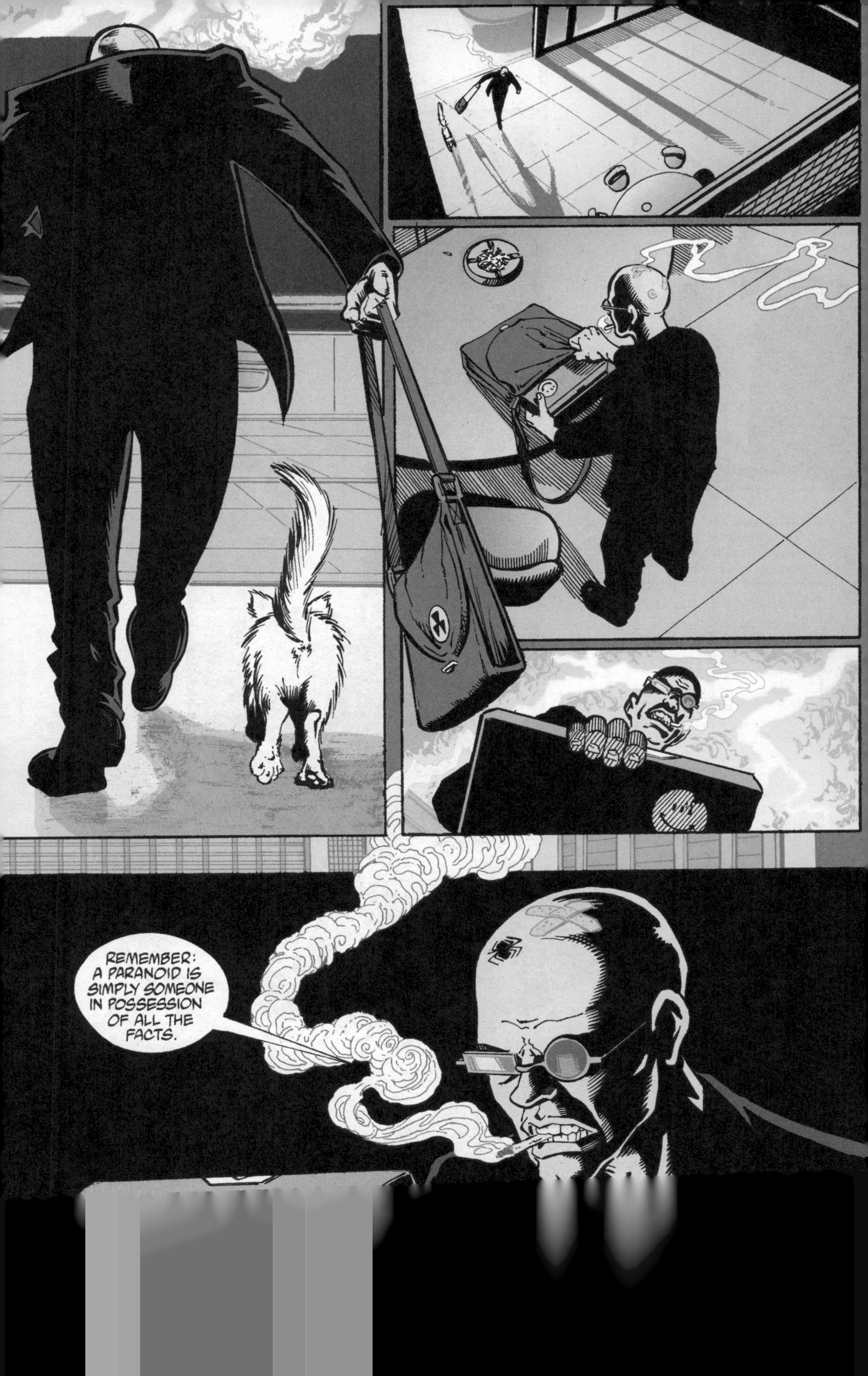
REMEMBER: A PARANOID IS SIMPLY SOMEONE IN POSSESSION OF ALL THE FACTS.

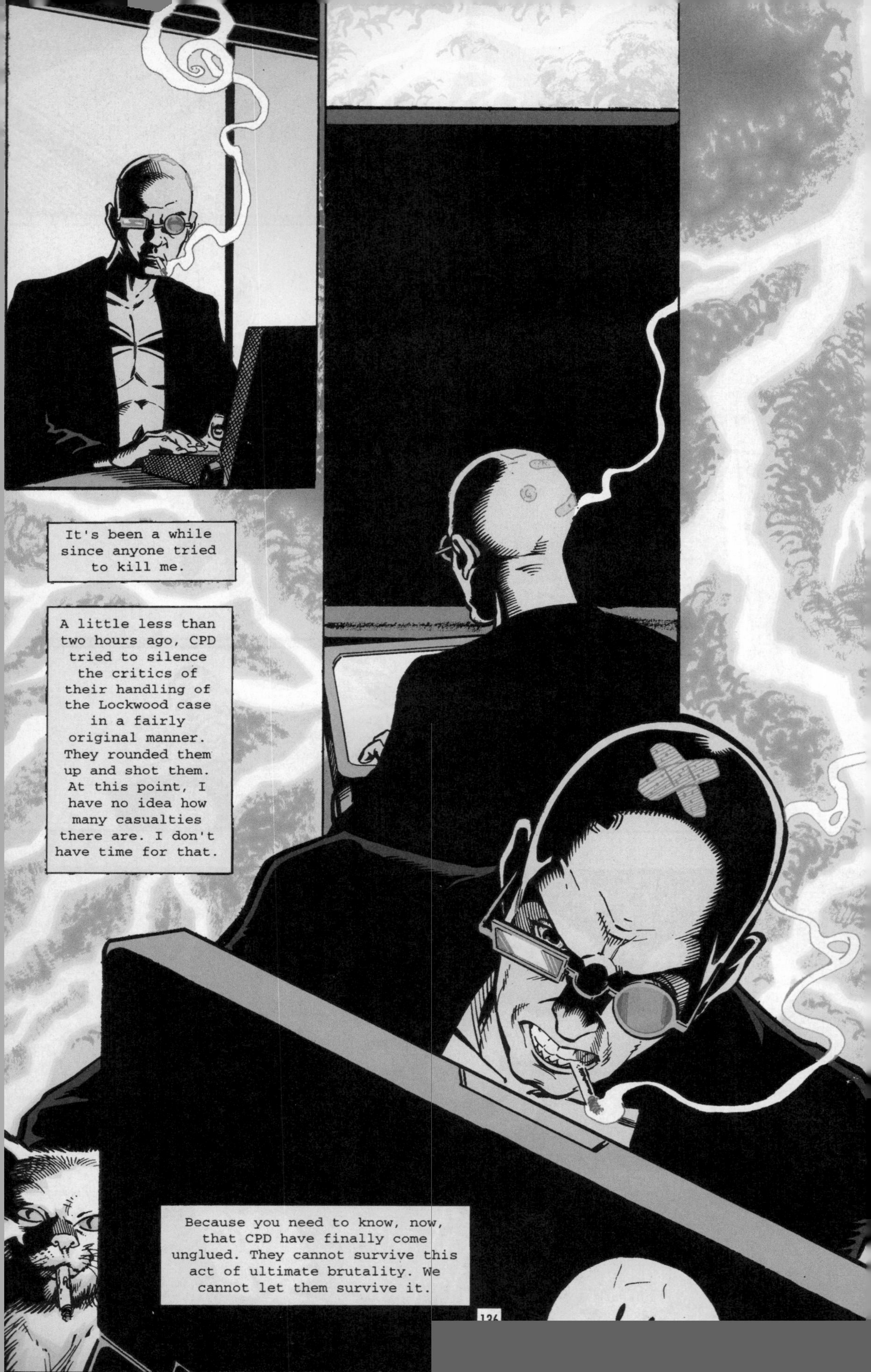
It's been a while since anyone tried to kill me.
A little less than two hours ago, CPD tried to silence the critics of their handling of the Lockwood case in a fairly original manner. They rounded them up and shot them. At this point, I have no idea how many casualties there are. I don't have time for that.
Because you need to know, now, that CPD have finally come unglued. They cannot survive this act of ultimate brutality. We cannot let them survive it.

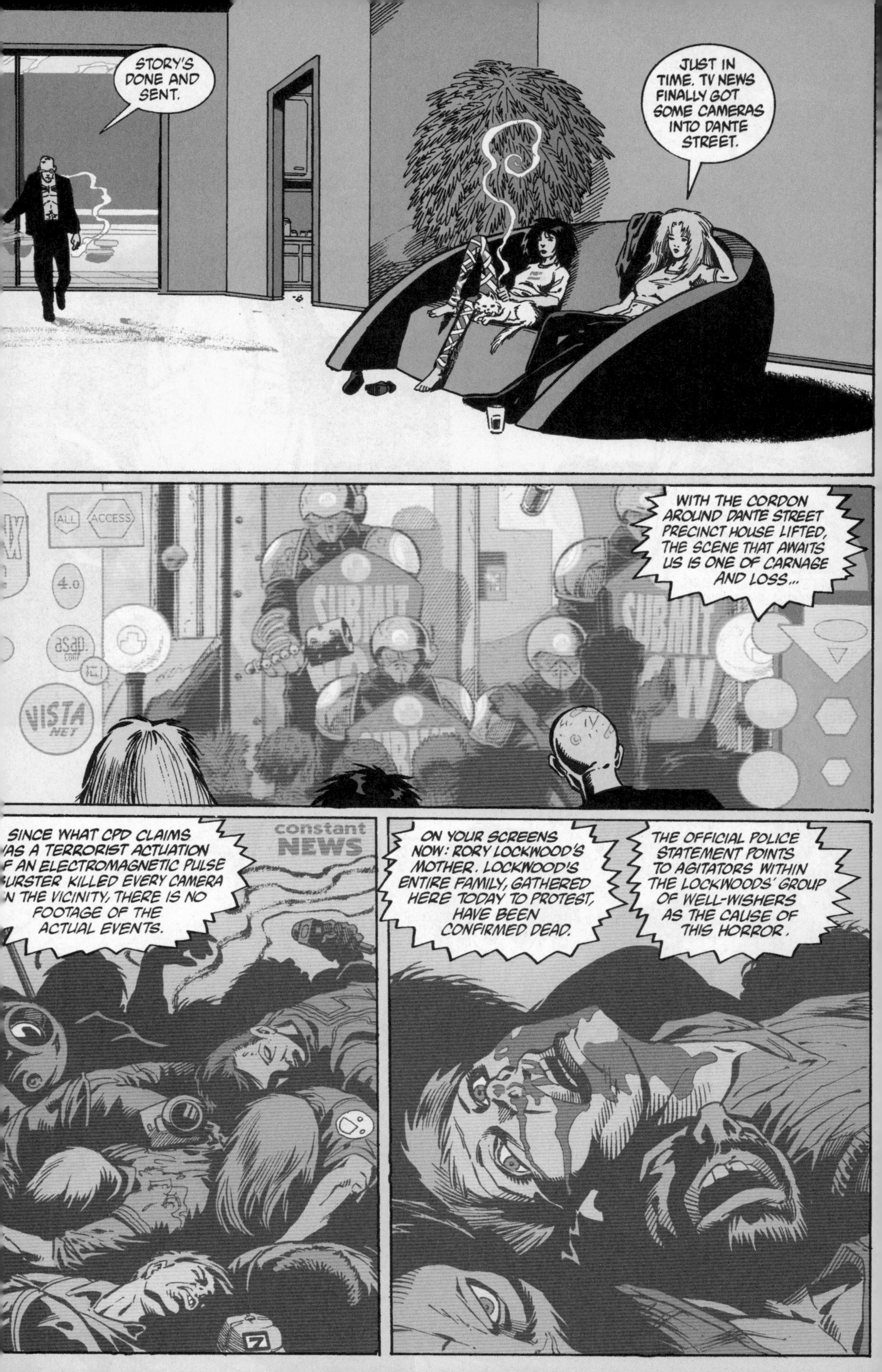
STORY'S DONE AND SENT.
JUST IN TIME. TV NEWS FINALLY GOT SOME CAMERAS INTO DANTE STREET.
WITH THE CORDON AROUND DANTE STREET PRECINCT HOUSE LIFTED, THE SCENE THAT AWAITS US IS ONE OF CARNAGE AND LOSS...
ALL ACCESS
4.0
VISTA NET
SINCE WHAT CPD CLAIMS WAS A TERRORIST ACTUATION OF AN ELECTROMAGNETIC PULSE BURSTER KILLED EVERY CAMERA IN THE VICINITY, THERE IS NO FOOTAGE OF THE ACTUAL EVENTS.
constant NEWS
ON YOUR SCREENS NOW: RORY LOCKWOOD'S MOTHER. LOCKWOOD'S ENTIRE FAMILY, GATHERED HERE TODAY TO PROTEST, HAVE BEEN CONFIRMED DEAD.
THE OFFICIAL POLICE STATEMENT POINTS TO AGITATORS WITHIN THE LOCKWOODS' GROUP OF WELL-WISHERS AS THE CAUSE OF THIS HORROR.

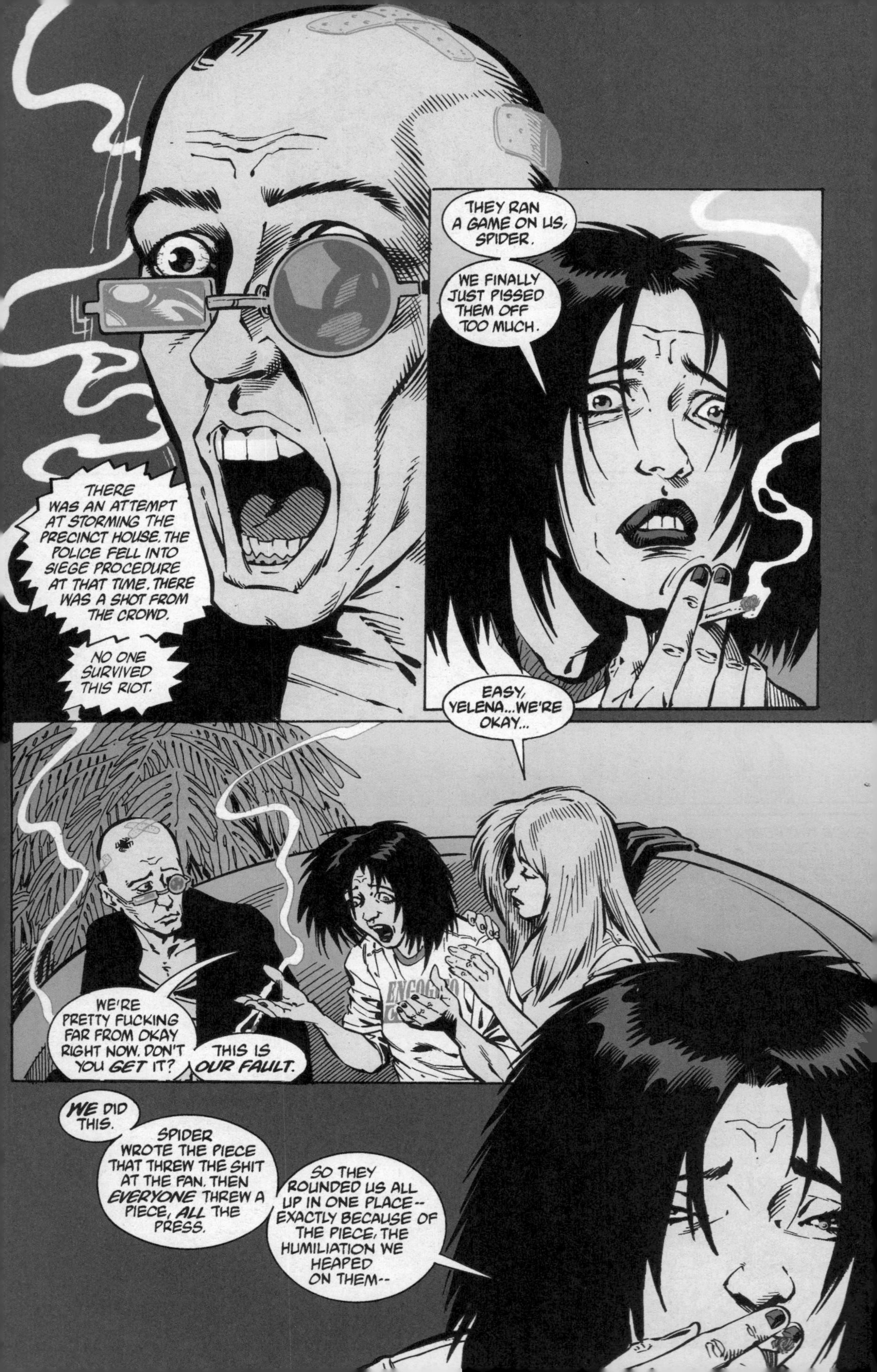
THEY RAN A GAME ON US, SPIDER.
WE FINALLY JUST PISSED THEM OFF TOO MUCH.
THERE WAS AN ATTEMPT AT STORMING THE PRECINCT HOUSE. THE POLICE FELL INTO SIEGE PROCEDURE AT THAT TIME. THERE WAS A SHOT FROM THE CROWD.
NO ONE SURVIVED THIS RIOT.
EASY, YELENA...WE'RE OKAY...
WE'RE PRETTY FUCKING FAR FROM OKAY RIGHT NOW. DON'T YOU GET IT?
THIS IS OUR FAULT.
WE DID THIS.
SPIDER WROTE THE PIECE THAT THREW THE SHIT AT THE FAN. THEN EVERYONE THREW A PIECE, ALL THE PRESS.
SO THEY ROUNDED US ALL UP IN ONE PLACE-- EXACTLY BECAUSE OF THE PIECE, THE HUMILIATION WE HEAPED ON THEM--

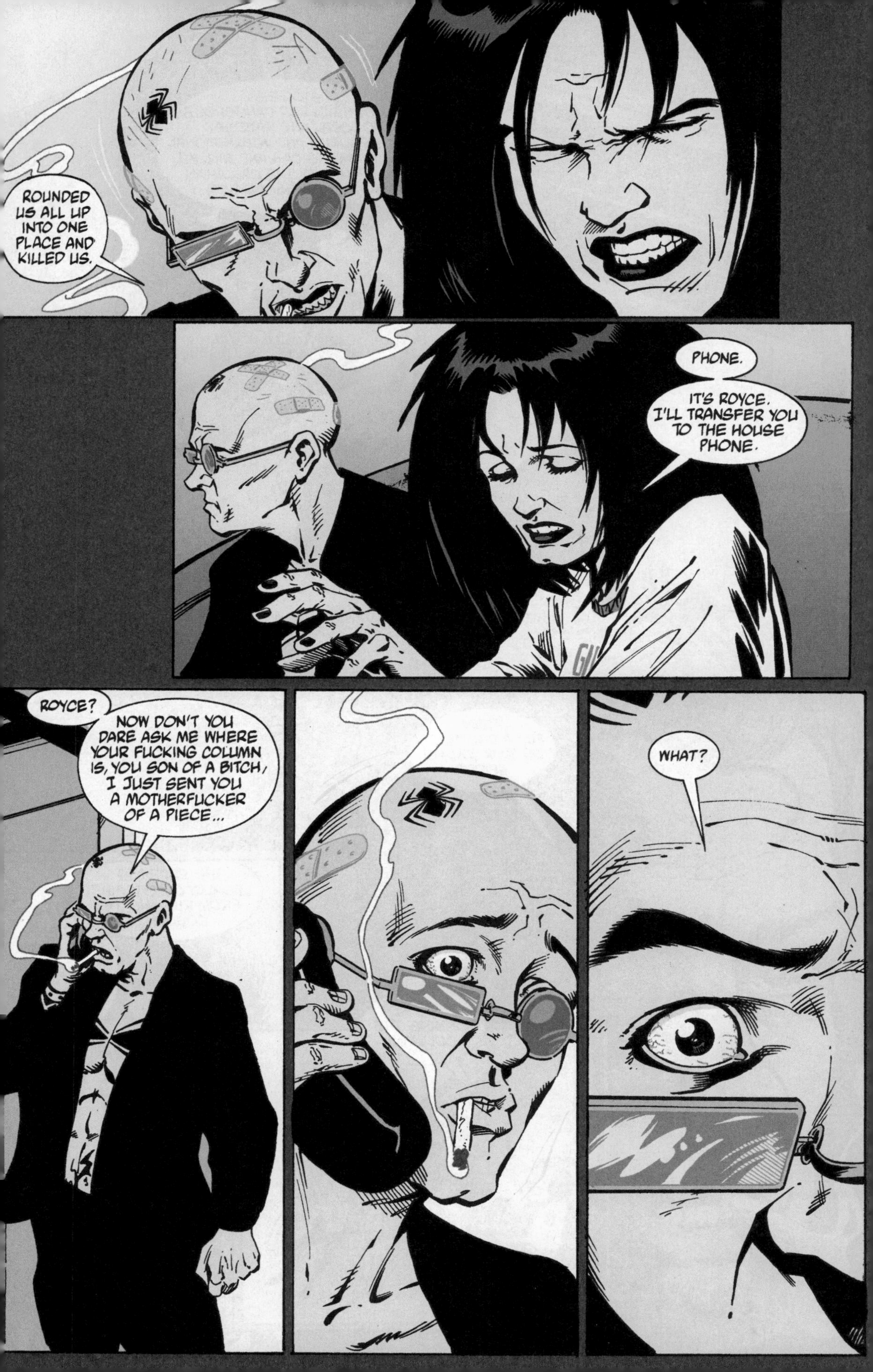
ROUNDED US ALL UP INTO ONE PLACE AND KILLED US.
PHONE.
IT'S ROYCE. I'LL TRANSFER YOU TO THE HOUSE PHONE.
ROYCE?
NOW DON'T YOU DARE ASK ME WHERE YOUR FUCKING COLUMN IS, YOU SON OF A BITCH, I JUST SENT YOU A MOTHERFUCKER OF A PIECE...
WHAT?

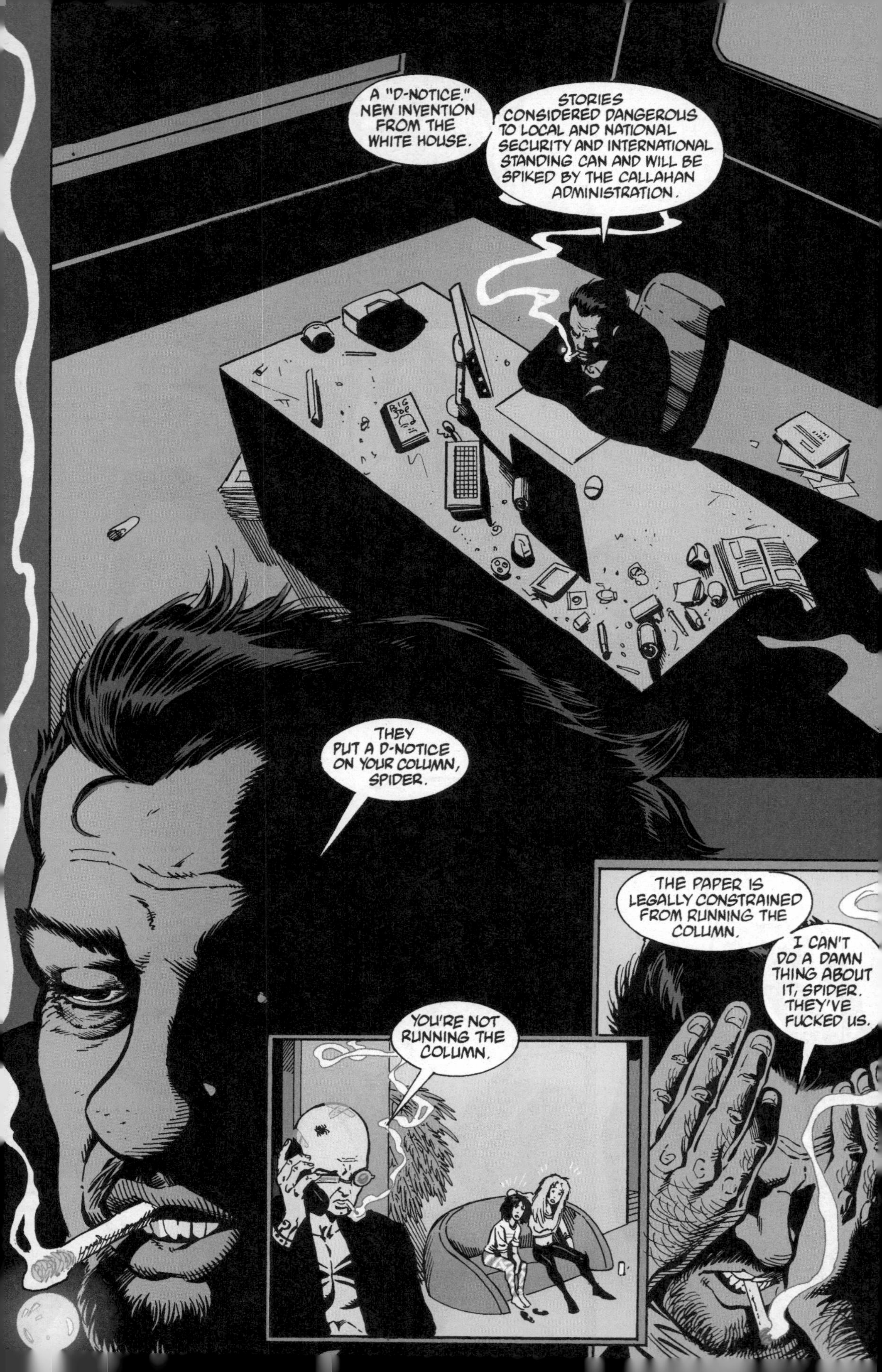
A "D-NOTICE." NEW INVENTION FROM THE WHITE HOUSE.
STORIES CONSIDERED DANGEROUS TO LOCAL AND NATIONAL SECURITY AND INTERNATIONAL STANDING CAN AND WILL BE SPIKED BY THE CALLAHAN ADMINISTRATION.
THEY PUT A D-NOTICE ON YOUR COLUMN, SPIDER.
THE PAPER IS LEGALLY CONSTRAINED FROM RUNNING THE COLUMN.
I CAN'T DO A DAMN THING ABOUT IT, SPIDER. THEY'VE FUCKED US.
YOU'RE NOT RUNNING THE COLUMN.

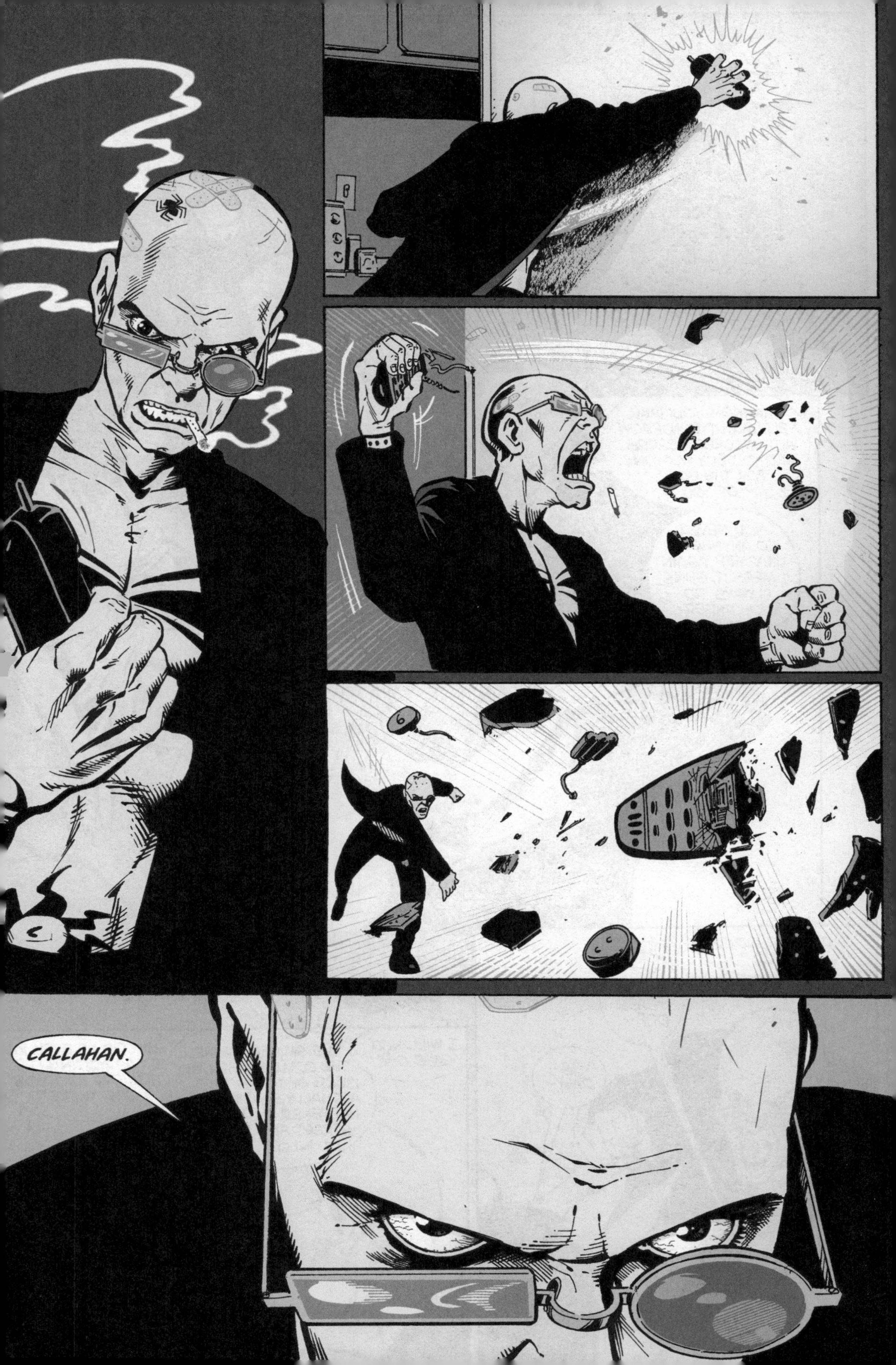
CALLAHAN.

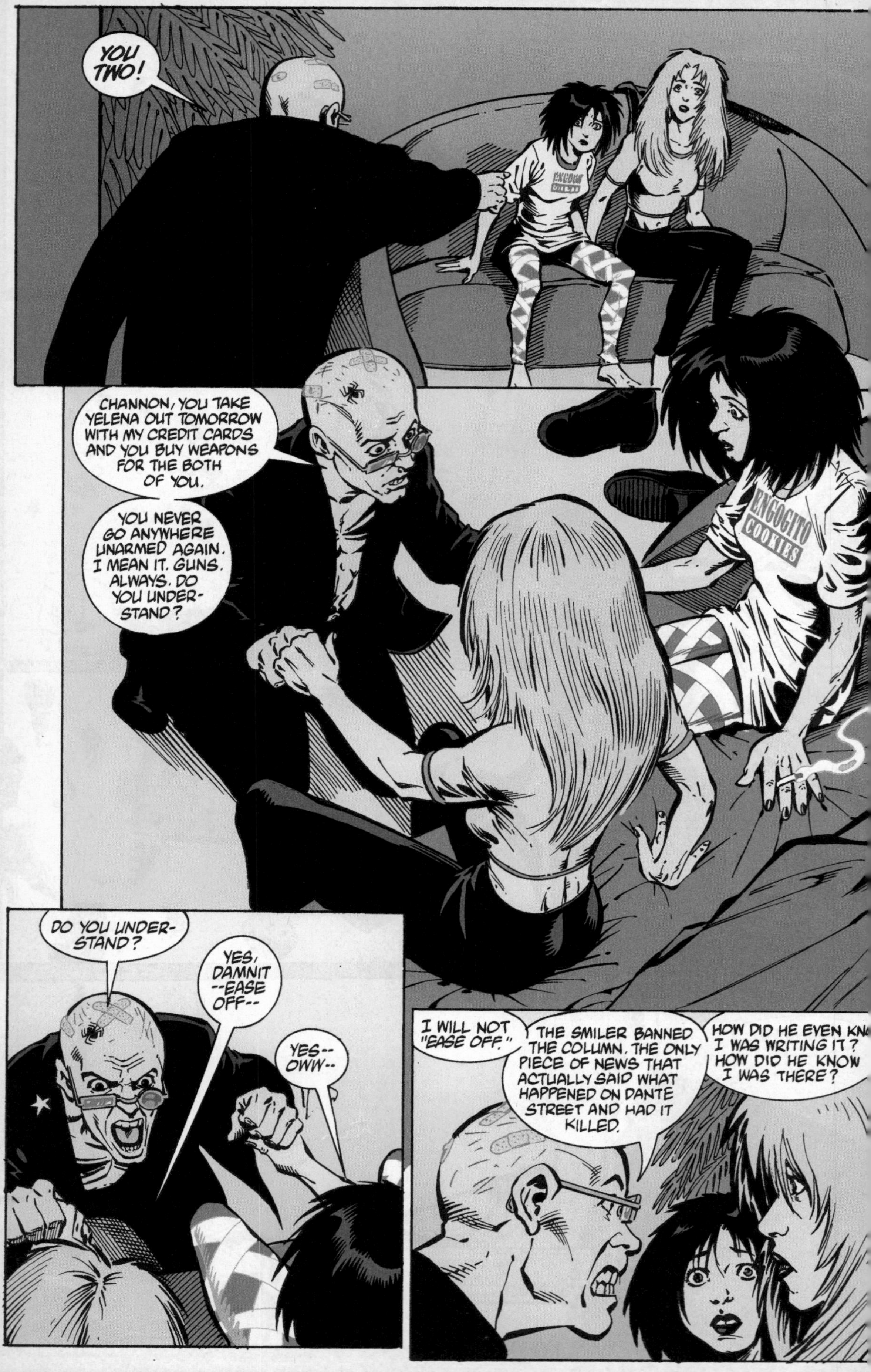
YOU TWO!
CHANNON, YOU TAKE YELENA OUT TOMORROW WITH MY CREDIT CARDS AND YOU BUY WEAPONS FOR THE BOTH OF YOU.
YOU NEVER GO ANYWHERE UNARMED AGAIN. I MEAN IT. GUNS. ALWAYS. DO YOU UNDER-STAND?
ENGOGITO COOKIES
DO YOU UNDER-STAND?
YES, DAMNIT --EASE OFF--
YES-- OWW--
I WILL NOT "EASE OFF."
THE SMILER BANNED THE COLUMN. THE ONLY PIECE OF NEWS THAT ACTUALLY SAID WHAT HAPPENED ON DANTE STREET AND HAD IT KILLED.
HOW DID HE EVEN KNO I WAS WRITING IT? HOW DID HE KNOW I WAS THERE?

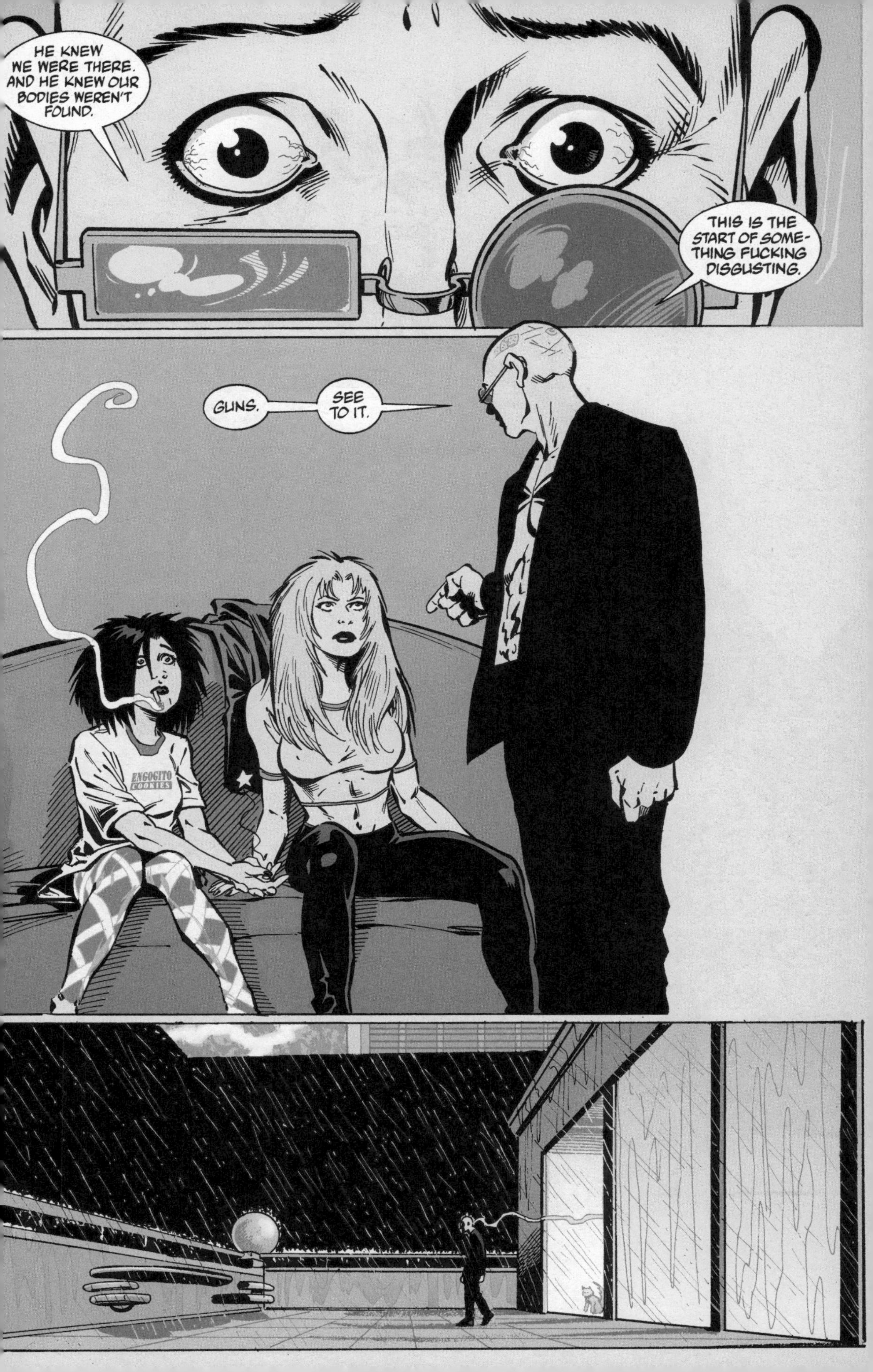
HE KNEW WE WERE THERE. AND HE KNEW OUR BODIES WEREN'T FOUND.
THIS IS THE START OF SOME-THING FUCKING DISGUSTING.
GUNS.
SEE TO IT.
ENGOGITO COOKIES

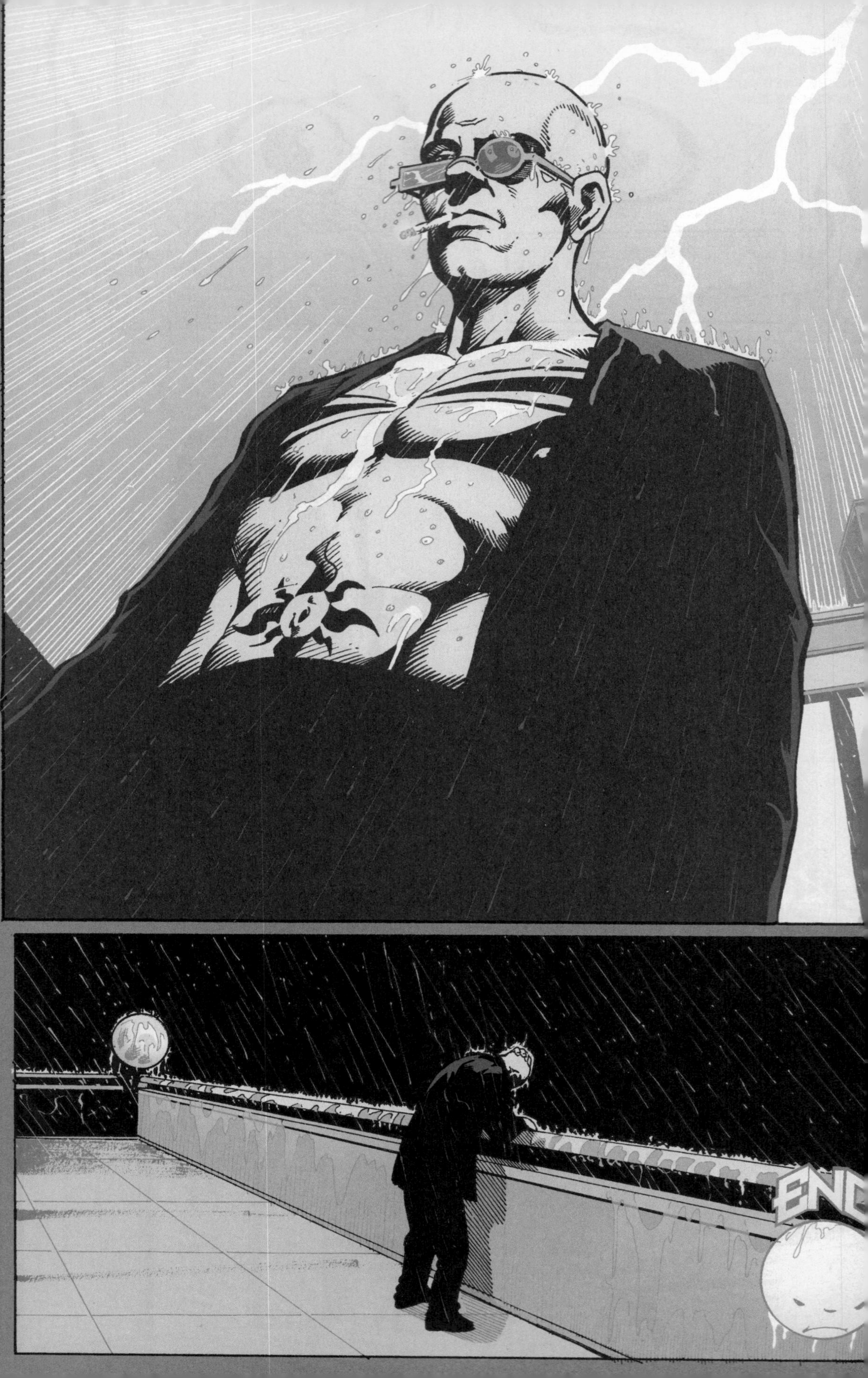